SYSTEMATIC COUNSELING

A GUIDE FOR THE PRACTITIONER

JOSEPH H. BROWN / CAROLYN S. BROWN

RESEARCH PRESS COMPANY
2612 NORTH MATTIS AVENUE
CHAMPAIGN ILLINOIS 61820

Contents

Preface

Three important points provided the motivation for our writing this book. The first was our felt need for explicating the competencies a successful counselor should be able to demonstrate upon completion of a counselor training program. In addition to explicating the competencies, we felt the need for objective evaluation techniques and for specifying each competency in measurable terms, which would indicate the skill to be taught and the degree to which it should be developed.

The second reason for the book is related to the current trends toward accountability and the reduction of school counseling services. Because of such trends, counselors may well have to defend their very existence in the future. This can best be done through demonstrating skill in selected areas and being able to show through various measures that positive behaviors do in fact take place as a result of counseling.

Still a third reason for the book is to outline a systematic approach to counseling which would enable the counselor to select techniques leading to the most effective and efficient realization of her goals. The model outlined in the book provides a sequential approach to counseling, guides the trainee to gather necessary information, and then directs him toward selecting an appropriate intervention strategy. Obviously, there currently is not enough evidence to show conclusively that one strategy is *the* best to use in a given situation, but given the general goal of either increasing or decreasing a behavior, there are some approaches which are more likely than others to result in favorable outcomes.

This book is intended to be a practical guide for trainees in the helping professions including school counselors, school psychologists, and community mental health workers. Chapter 1 describes the general model, and additional chapters focus on various subsystems of the model. Each chapter, except the introductory one, contains a criterion test of information covered, instructions for implementing various sub-skills within the larger skills, programmed examples of appropriate counselor behavior or verbalizations for each task, and a checklist to monitor the trainee's performance. The trainee's performance can be evaluated at a cognitive level, then, but more importantly, can further be evaluated by his ability to implement these skills with clients.

Clearly, this book can serve only as a guide and not as a complete training program; the counselor educators who use it are obligated to use their own ideas in fitting the techniques to the needs of their trainees. It is our purpose and hope that readers will find the basic set of skills and methods of evaluating these helpful in meeting the needs of their clientele.

1 The Counseling Model

There appears to be a growing confusion regarding the concept of counseling and its meaning since counseling, like other changing professions, reflects the times. Many diverse theories and procedures have evolved over the past few years (Hosford and de Visser, 1974). While one can be encouraged by the technological advances which have occurred, one cannot always be sure of their proper use or efficacy.

Unfortunately, professional organizations have been of little assistance in clarifying counseling and its role and function. Policy statements and standards for counselor preparation and the professional role often lack clarity (Froehle and Lauver, 1971). Existing standards indicate some general values, but they do not identify skills a trainee should learn, nor do they give specific guidelines for the counseling process itself. Unfortunately, this is probably because counselor educators and trainees are still uncertain about minimum competencies the counselor should possess at the end of training.

SPECIFYING MINIMAL COMPETENCIES

Only recently have counselor educators begun to specify minimal competencies for counselor training and consequently to encourage a more systematic approach (Hendricks, Ferguson, and Thoresen, 1973). One example of this is the current state certification plan in Washington based on behaviorally stated objectives related to client outcomes. Similar programs have recently been established at North Texas State, Stanford, and Michigan State universities.

A feature common to all of these programs is the measurement of counselor effectiveness through the trainees' demonstrated abilities to effect desirable changes in client behavior. It seems logical, then, to adopt for training programs counseling techniques which have proven effective in producing client change. To determine when client change

1

has occurred, however, objectives must be stated in terms of the specific desired behavior of the client, i.e., what he will be doing following counseling, under what conditions, and to what extent (Thoresen and Hosford, 1973).

THE NEED FOR A BROAD-BASED MODEL

While questioning the operation and effects of techniques is necessary, there is also a strong need for conceptualizing counseling strategies into a broad-based model suitable for the practitioner. That is, a stepwise model is needed to guide the practitioner's use of specific counseling techniques. Although counselors may have knowledge of specific techniques, they do not always know under what conditions and/or in what sequence these techniques should be utilized.

The following variables are important in determining the most effective counseling techniques to use:

1. type of behavior and the conditions under which it is emitted
2. degree to which the client can accept responsibility for his own change program
3. techniques appropriate for the particular stage of the counseling process the client is in
4. forces or constraints which are preventing the problem from being solved

The basic technology for designing training models which take into account these variables is available, but models have not been widely designed and/or disseminated. The need in this area is evident, and counselor training programs seem to be the logical medium by which competencies can be established and then examined in terms of the trainee's ability to effect behavior change. The particular training model described in this book is currently in use at the University of Louisville. The model specifies a set of minimal counselor competencies and provides criterion measures to determine the trainee's ability to attain these. Each of the subsystems of the model is described briefly in the remaining pages of this chapter.

FEATURES OF THE MODEL IN THIS BOOK

The counseling model described here indicates various counseling techniques to use and specifies conditions under which they should be selected. The model provides the counselor a guide for systematically

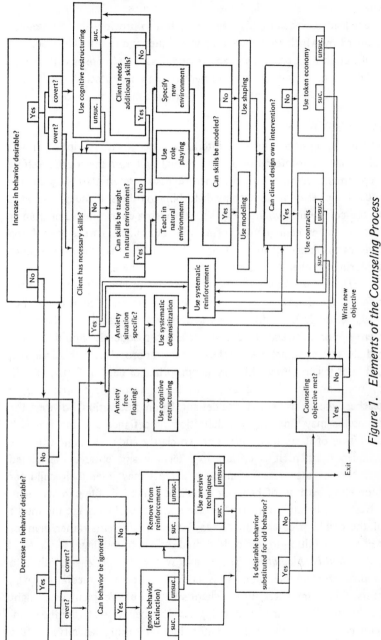

Figure 1. Elements of the Counseling Process

selecting counseling techniques which will most efficiently and effectively lead to reaching his objectives. It also provides the counselor a standard by which to compare his techniques and results. The elements of the counseling process are labeled and described in boxes with arrows indicating the preferred order for performing various techniques (Figure 1). More detailed descriptions of the various subsystems follow.

Process Referral

The initiation of a counseling interaction occurs with receipt of a referral, either a self-referral or a more formal one from the courts, Welfare Department, or other agency. When clients are referred, it is usually because their behavior has become disturbing to others. If the client comes to the counselor involuntarily (e.g., through a court referral or from an institution for delinquents), often the counselor must use special procedures to reduce client resistance. This initially may take the form of exploring the client's perception of why she is there.

Determine Appropriateness After determining the source of the referral, the counselor must decide if the referral is appropriate. For instance, referrals for disciplinary action, remedial reading, and employment opportunities are inappropriate and consequently should be referred elsewhere. Sometimes a referral seems appropriate and is accepted, but later it is regarded either as inappropriate or needing further clarification. For instance, a student may be referred to a counselor by a teacher who labels her as being defiant. Upon observation, however, the counselor may find that his definition of defiance and the teacher's definition of it are quite different. To clarify and understand what the problem is, then, it is critical to interview and observe the related members of the system. Similarly, parents may refer their child for counseling because of behavior problems while it is the parents themselves who, because of marital and/or personal problems, are the source of the child's problems. In this case, then, the parents rather than, or perhaps in addition to, the child should receive counseling.

Identify Mediators Tharp and Wetzel (1969) suggest that to modify problem behaviors, it is critical to identify mediators (e.g., peers, family members) in the client's natural environment who might be able to observe and support his desirable behaviors. Often the counselor can work with these mediators in a consulting capacity, i.e., the counselor can assist the second party (parent or teacher) in working with the third party (client). This, of course, often depends upon the accessibility of these mediators and their acceptance of such a role.

In many cases, clients are self-referred, reporting their own behavior as the source of the problem. Even in these instances, it is beneficial to assess the effects that others (peers, family members, etc.) are having on the client's behavior.

Structure the Interview

Describe the Counselor Role In structuring the interview, the counselor begins by describing her role, including in this description a list of problems the counselor typically works with. This often helps to alleviate the client's anxiety regarding the counseling relationship and helps avoid unexpected events which can confuse the client or cause negative feelings. Lennard and Bernstein (1960) found a highly significant association between the degree of discrepancy in counselor and client role expectations and the degree of disharmony or strain in their interpersonal relationship. That is, when both members of a dyad are in agreement regarding their reciprocal responsibilities and there is some similarity of expectations, harmony or stability occurs in their interpersonal relationship.

Role descriptions focus on two major areas. The first area is what the client is to talk about and the second centers on the result of the counselor-client relationship.

Be a Good Listener After explaining her role and the client-counselor relationship, the counselor should attempt to gather information about the presenting problem. In doing this, a positive relationship is essential. There are several things the counselor can do to establish such a relationship. Perhaps the most critical of these is being a good listener to encourage the client's participation.

Satisfactory listening requires that the counselor maintain eye contact and appropriate body posture. In addition, nonverbal responses, such as nodding and smiling whenever the counselor is discussing items related to the problem, are helpful. Ivey, et al. (1968) have demonstrated that listening or attending skills can be taught to beginning counselors.

While attending skills are critical throughout the counseling relationship, they initially serve to encourage the client to talk about his problem. The counselor's attention will help him learn more about the

5

client and also contribute to the client's sense of security or comfort within the counseling situation.

Ask Open-ended Questions Once the client starts talking, the counselor can generally elicit additional information about the client's problem by asking open-ended questions. These questions allow the client to give a wide range of answers, and they promote verbalization because they cannot be answered with monosyllables. In addition, they give the client freedom to discuss various areas of concern. As responses are elicited, the counselor can maintain verbalization by responding to the feeling of the client's message. Such responses facilitate the client's movement toward self-exploration and self-understanding.

Use Clarification An additional technique to facilitate client self-understanding and also to promote more accurate perception by the client is clarification. In clarifying, the counselor attempts to restate what the client is saying or simplify the statement to make the meaning clearer. The client can then validate the accuracy of the counselor by agreeing or disagreeing with the clarification. If listening, responding to feelings, and clarification skills cannot be demonstrated by the counselor trainee at this point, she should receive training in these skills before going further in the counseling process.

Define the Problem

An important task in the initial counseling interview is determining the presenting problem. This information can come from the client or those (parents, teachers, etc.) who have referred him because he is exhibiting problem behaviors.

Identify All Problem Areas Gottman and Leiblum (1974) suggest that in either case it is critical to examine the labels the client uses to describe his own behaviors. The labels often will indicate whether the client is trying to meet his own or others' expectations. For example, if a client is unhappy with his dating patterns, it is critical to determine if he wants to have two dates a week with a specific individual or if he wants to be dating more often than his peers. *It should be noted, however, that the presenting problem may not always be the issue of greatest concern to the client; therefore, it is important to get an indication of all areas in which a client is experiencing major difficulties.* The counselor may sometimes find it hard to get the client to describe problem areas, perhaps because the client's conception of human behavior differs from his own. There also may be a difference in language conception. Either the counselor must be capable of translating the client's language into his own, or the client must learn the interviewer's language. The task of teaching new language to the client often can be facilitated through pre-interview "homework" (Patterson, 1976). Behavior problem checklists also can assist a client or members of his system in specifying what is to be observed and where it is to be observed.

Set Priorities Once several problem areas have been identified, the counselor must begin to set priorities for treatment. Sundel and Sundel (1975) specify that four criteria seem to be critical in making this determination: (1) which problem is of most immediate expressed concern; (2) which will likely have the most negative consequences; (3) which can be corrected most easily, considering resources and constraints; and (4) which requires handling before other problems can be solved.

Operationalize the Problem Once the priority of problems has been established, the counselor should help the client operationalize the label used to describe the problem(s). That is, the counselor should direct the client to give specific, concrete examples of the problem. *When a problem has been satisfactorily operationalized, it is stated in terms so that two or more people can agree when it exists.*

Identify Temporal Elements and Maintaining Conditions After the problem has been operationalized, the counselor must determine the time, place, and situation in which it occurs. When the problem has been defined in behavioral terms and the temporal elements have been specified, the counselor must attempt to isolate those conditions maintaining the problem. *That is, the counselor attempts to identify those stimulus conditions which elicit problem behavior and those conditions which maintain it.*

For some behaviors, such as anxiety or fear, the antecedent conditions are generally neutral stimuli that elicit involuntary behavior. However, for most operant behavior, such as talking or fighting, the controlling conditions are reinforcing or punishing stimuli. With an appropriate set of questions (e.g., when is the problem most severe? least severe?), the counselor can gather this information from the client or others in the client's environment.

7

Observe and Record Behavior

Establish Baseline When problem behaviors have been specified in behavioral terms, the counselor and client are ready to begin observing and recording these behaviors and the events which maintain them. This may involve counting specified behaviors or using self-report data to establish a baseline. This pre-intervention, or baserate, of behavior permits the counselor to tailor the intervention to the client's needs. The baserate indicates how well the client is performing prior to intervention and also permits the counselor and client to evaluate the effectiveness of counseling.

There are generally three attributes of behavior which can be quantified, or measured: frequency, duration, and intensity. However, these attributes differ in terms of how, where, and by whom they can be measured.

Frequency Data Frequency is the generally preferred type of data because people are typically more concerned about how often something happens rather than how long it lasts. The frequency of the problem may be recorded either as total amount per unit time (rate) or percent, but rate is the most used variable. Behavior which is excessive (e.g., excuses) or deficient (e.g., not completing assignments) involves the rate at which something is occurring.

Duration Measurement Duration data are used when one needs to know the amount of behavior, e.g., the length of crying, the amount of on-task behavior. Some behaviors, however, may be best represented by recording both frequency and the duration. For example, behaviors such as attending to the teachers, maintaining a conversation, and eating all can be recorded by duration and/or frequency.

Intensity Data The intensity or severity of behavior often is measured by electronic equipment, but when it is unavailable, clients can be taught to record the severity or intensity of fear, depression, or other behaviors by using rating scales. Ratings over time can be especially valuable if they are annotated by critical incidents which can link variations to specific situations.

Methods of Recording There are several ways to record problem behaviors. Some problems leave evidence that one can count to measure the degree of the problem. For example, percentage of problems, assignments not finished, or days tardy show the degree of the problem. This is a very easy method for recording but is not efficacious in all situations because many behaviors, e.g., many social-behavior problems, don't leave evidence. Problems which don't leave evidence and which occur infrequently (1-10 times per day) should be recorded all day, with the observer making a simple check on a sheet of paper each time the behavior occurs. On the other hand, problem behaviors which occur quite often (four or more times per hour) should be recorded only about an hour each day. When the behavior occurs more than 30 times per hour, the counselor need record for only a half-hour.

Time sampling is an appropriate procedure for observing behaviors which are not discrete (talking). With this approach, the observer looks at the client at specified intervals and records whether the behavior is occurring or not. As noted above, the counselor can decide whether to observe for an hour, half-hour, etc., by determining how often the behavior occurs. If it occurs quite frequently, less observation time is required than if it occurs infrequently.

Reliability of Data Once the data are recorded, reliability of measurement must be established. Reliability refers to the consistency of measurement. It is usually calculated by comparing how well two or more independent observers agree among themselves. Thus, if two observers see the same thing at the same time over a period of time, we can say the observations are reliable.

Graphic Representations At this point the observational data are plotted on a graph. A graph provides the (1) behavior being measured, (2) unit of measurement, and (3) period of time over which the measurement occurred. Graphs give a pictorial representation of the data, often revealing patterns that are not apparent in the column numbers. In addition, graphs which show improvement often provide encouragement to the client to maintain the desired behavior change.

Graphic representation also permits an emphatic illustration of behavior rates as they increase, decrease, or remain stable. If the variability of the data is too great, however, it is difficult to determine how often the behavior typically occurs and consequently, would warrant continued recording to determine what event might be causing the fluctuation.

Formulate Treatment Objectives

Explore Alternatives Once the counselor and client have focused on a problem and the situational factors maintaining the problem, they are ready to specify the behavior the client needs to learn or unlearn. That is, up to this point, the client has been describing "what is" happening. Now she must specify "what should be" happening. However, before the counselor and client set a goal, they must first explore alternative behaviors which would offer possible solutions to the problem. After exploring alternative behavioral solutions, they should evaluate the probable consequences for each solution and select the best alternative or goal.

Although the client usually should actively participate with the counselor in formulating treatment goals, there are some situations for which the counselor must assume major responsibility. Acts which are illegal (stealing) or detrimental to oneself or others (rioting) are goals which counselors cannot sanction. If the counselor and client cannot reach agreement on the goal, the counselor should help the client obtain professional assistance elsewhere.

State in Measurable Terms Once objectives have been specified, they should be stated in measurable terms, i.e., the specific behaviors the client will be performing as a result of counseling. Objectives stated in performance terms can serve as a basis for evaluating current counseling procedures. Clients who know where they are going, how they will get there, and how they will know when they've arrived are more likely to reach their destination, or objectives, than those who do not know.

Identify Intermediate Steps In formulating the terminal objectives, it is often helpful to establish intermediate steps, with each intermediate step, or objective, placed in a hierarchy leading to the terminal goal. Success in reaching intermediate goals provides reinforcement for progress and consequently results in greater achievement.

Specify Conditions and Performance Level After agreeing on intermediate and terminal goals, the counselor and client should attempt to specify conditions under which the goal behavior is to occur, i.e., the specific settings, times, and situations in which the desired behavior should be exhibited. If possible, the goal behavior should occur in a setting where it can be controlled. For example, behavior at home or in the classroom is much more easily controlled than behavior in social situations or behavior outside the neighborhood.

When the goal has been specified in performance terms and the conditions under which the behavior is to occur have been identified, an acceptable level of performance must be established. This is the cri-

10

terion level, which specifies how well and how often the behavior is to be performed.

Determine the Appropriate Intervention

When the goal has been established, a counseling strategy must be selected. The model presented in this book provides guidelines for determining an appropriate treatment and in so doing poses the danger of implying that a suggested intervention is the only one which will work with a given problem. Actually, a rationale could likely be built for any given theoretical approach for almost any given problem, but certain interventions have proven more effective than others in ameliorating certain classes of behavior problems. Consequently, the model guides the trainee toward interventions which have been most successful with the specified problem area.

Often, more than one intervention is necessary to alleviate a problem. A problem behavior that occurs in excess may need to be reduced and a desirable behavior incompatible with the problem behavior may need to be increased.

Decrease Behavior

Covert and Overt Behaviors The problem behaviors which occur in excess in either their frequency or intensity may be either overt or covert. Examples of excessive overt behaviors include stealing, fighting, and crying; excessive covert behaviors include fears or anxieties. The distinction between these two types of behavior is important because this knowledge helps to determine the most appropriate intervention. Overt or operant behaviors are controlled by their consequences, whereas covert or respondent behaviors are controlled by their antecedents.

Extinction by Ignoring If the problem behavior is overt, the counselor must determine if it can be ignored, i.e., if the behavior can be reasonably tolerated for a while. Ignoring a behavior is the easiest extinction approach. In this case, it may be necessary to determine if others (friends, teacher, parents, etc.) are inadvertently reinforcing undesirable behavior and if so, to teach them not to reinforce the behavior. The result should be a decline in the frequency of maladaptive behavior over time unless the target response (fighting, calling others names, etc.) is in itself very reinforcing. If ignoring the behavior proves to be unsuccessful, the client should be removed from the reinforcing situation.

Mild Punishment Procedures On the other hand, when others cannot ignore the behavior or when it is dangerous to self or others, the judicious use of punishment must be employed, although punishment is often ineffectual, resulting in the suppression rather than the elimination of a behavior. Aversive or punishment procedures generally are successful when they are mild and when they can provide for performance of the alternative pro-social response, which can then be reinforced. If desirable behaviors have been substituted for the old behaviors, the case may be terminated; if not, the counselor must determine if the client needs prerequisite skills to exhibit the desired behavior. If this is the case, the counselor then teaches those skills.

Increase Behavior

Sometimes, in addition to reducing or extinguishing undesirable behavior, the counselor strives to increase incompatible desirable behaviors. Other times, an increase in behavior, e.g., social participation, may be warranted without reducing any behavior. Typical behaviors to be increased may be either overt or covert. Examples of overt behavior to be increased would be completion of assignments, participating more in class, etc., while an example of covert behavior to be increased would be self-rewarding thoughts.

Systematic Reinforcement and Desensitization If the behavior to be increased is overt, the counselor must decide whether the client has the necessary skills for exhibiting that behavior. For example, if the goal were an increase in interactions with peers, the counselor would have to determine if the client has the necessary social skills for interacting with others or if he just isn't implementing these. If he does have the necessary skills, and no excessive anxiety seems to be present, systematic reinforcement of the desirable behavior seems to be the treatment of choice. However, if the level of anxiety is high, the counselor needs to determine whether this is a free-floating type anxiety or if it is situation specific. According to Meichenbaum (1973), subjects experiencing situation-specific anxiety respond better to systematic desensitization, whereas subjects experiencing free-floating anxiety respond better to a cognitive or insight approach combined with relaxation.

12

Following reduction of anxiety, then, systematic reinforcement may be used to initiate and maintain desirable behaviors that are incompatible with the old ones.

Teach New Skills In some cases where the goal is an increase in behavior, the client does not possess the needed skills. An example of this would be a subject who wants to increase the number of dates he has but who really doesn't know how to ask for a date or how to behave when he has one. After determining that the client doesn't have the needed skills, the counselor must decide if the skills can be taught in the natural environment (e.g., home, school, neighborhood, etc.). This is preferable, but if treatment agents (friends, parents, employers, teachers, etc.) are unable or unwilling to provide reinforcers for desirable client behaviors, a new environment for treatment needs to be specified. For instance, there is little chance that a child's problem behavior can be ameliorated by parents in an environment where alcohol abuse is prevalent. If the problem is strictly school related, teachers or peers can serve as reinforcing agents and increase selected behaviors, but if the problem is home related and parents are unwilling to modify their own behavior, there is little likelihood that the child's problem behavior will change.

If the counselor is not able to specify an environment to teach the new behaviors or if there is a risk of failure within the actual situation, role-playing procedures are appropriate. Role playing provides an opportunity for the client to practice and anticipate new responses with the opportunity for self-correction and feedback. Once responses have been mastered in the laboratory situation, they can be practiced in other environments (home, school, club, etc.).

It is not always necessary to actively teach new behavior patterns. Rather, the learning can be accomplished symbolically through observation of others. Modeling may be employed to teach new behaviors by providing the opportunity for the client to observe both the behavior and the consequences of that behavior on the individual. Thus, it may serve either to inhibit or increase previously learned responses as well as teach new ones.

If modeling proves to be unsuccessful or the behavior to be learned is too complex, the counselor might utilize shaping procedures. In this approach, the desired total response is broken down into a series of steps which are necessary for mastering the final response. Each smaller response is reinforced until it is under the client's control. Gradually, more accurate approximations of the final response are required before reinforcement is delivered. This continues until the entire response is learned. For example, in teaching a child to interact with others, reinforcement may initially be given to the child for standing near others, then for initiating conversation, later for getting information, and finally for providing information.

Consider Contracts   Regardless of which intervention is used, the counselor must determine the most appropriate procedure for delivering it. To change overt behavior in cases where other parties are directly involved in the client's problem and the client is able to structure her own intervention program, behavioral contracts may be useful. With this technique, each party specifies what behaviors she would like to see the other party modify or increase, and each agrees to comply with the other party's requests concerning changes in her own behavior. This approach presumes client ability to accept responsibility. However, some clients cannot accept such responsibility so they require tokens or points which can be disseminated by others for appropriate behavior. Only when the client engages in the desired behavior does she receive a token or point which may be exchanged for a wide variety of backup reinforcers.

Use Cognitive Restructuring   In situations where covert behaviors need to be increased, cognitive restructuring seems to be an appropriate treatment. Through this intervention, the client is taught more adaptive ways to think about things. That is, he essentially is taught to tell himself more positive or realistic things and to dispute irrational thoughts, replacing them with positive rational thoughts. By modifying the label the client attaches to the situation, it is possible to alter the individual's maladaptive emotional reaction. Whenever the client experiences emotional upset in some life situation, he should stop and ask himself whether some irrational internal sentence may be at the root of this feeling (e.g., I must be liked by everyone). If so, he is encouraged to replace the irrational statement with a more appropriate one (e.g., It would be nice if others liked me). Thus, instead of engaging in self-defeating labeling activities, the client is trained to alter these cue-producing responses (Ellis, 1962).

14

Evaluate Intervention

Because the model directs the counselor to specify goals and objectives and operationalize them in terms of measurable outcomes, evaluation can be conducted. The success of counseling is determined by whether the counselor reaches her objectives. In addition, the counselor can evaluate her progress by comparing the baserate of target behavior with behavior during treatment and/or time of termination.

If objectives are met, the counselor and client must decide whether they want to continue with counseling. In some cases, new objectives may be set, but the counselor should be aware that some clients may generate new objectives only to avoid termination. These issues should be discussed and dealt with prior to termination.

If termination is agreed upon, the counselor and client should plan transfer of learning and follow-up since newly learned behaviors rarely generalize to other environments unless they are supported by others. Follow-up helps the counselor to further evaluate his program and facilitates the client's implementation of skills.

2 Processing the Referral and Structuring the Interview

Crucial to the effectiveness of a counseling intervention is the gathering of pertinent data. The first such item is a referral indicating a perceived problem for which the referring agent requests help. Counselors may receive referrals from various sources including teachers, principals, parents, the courts, and other professionals in the community, as well as from the persons exhibiting the problem (self-referrals). Figure 2 shows steps involved in the referral and initial interview.

DETERMINE THE REFERRAL SOURCE

Methods of Referring

Referral systems are handled in various ways, according to the counselor's preference, but the system should be organized so that referring agents are aware of how to get help from the counselor. Some counselors are amenable to informal referrals. For example, they may get counseling cases through requests by teachers in the teachers' lounge or the lunchroom, or they may accept a client through the request of friends. They then follow up on the basis of the information received in those settings.

On the other hand, some counselors require persons who want to refer clients to fill out a referral form (see Table 1). The purpose of this form is not only to provide the counselor with the necessary information but also to prevent others (teachers, parents, friends) from referring a client without first specifying the problem behavior and secondly, analyzing what, if anything, has been tried to alleviate the problem. By making a referral contingent on completion of this form, the counselor can prevent unnecessary referrals as well as gain relevant information concerning the case.

17

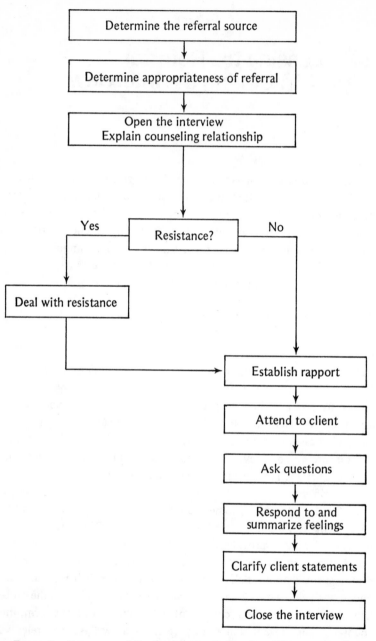

Figure 2. Summary of Processing the Referral and Structuring the Initial Interview

Table 1. Referral Form

Date _____

Name _____

Address _____ Phone _____

Age _____ Birthdate _____ Marital status _____

Sex ____ Race ____ Referral source _____

Highest grade completed in school _____

Family physician _____

Employer (or school) _____

Parent or spouse _____

Children or siblings & ages _____

_____

Physical or health problems _____

_____

Medication, if any, being administered _____

Major problem(s) for which client would like help.

_____

What has already been tried to alleviate this problem(s)? _____

_____

_____

_____

Establishing Who Is Client

The counselor must determine who is the client—the person making the complaint (teacher, parent) or the person exhibiting the problem behavior. This distinction is not always obvious. For example, the counselor may be confronted by a parent or teacher who says, "Tony is always misbehaving. He throws things and won't mind when I tell him to do something. Can you talk to him and put some sense into his head?" If the counselor accepts such a referral, he must ask, "Who is my client? Is

19

it Tony or Tony's teacher?" In most instances, the client is the person who is concerned about the behavior. For example, in this case the teacher is the client because his expectations for Tony's behavior are not being met. The counselor may work with Tony to change his behavior, but to work only with him and not the teacher would be a mistake. Rather, the counselor may say to the teacher, "Yes, that is a difficult problem. May I come into the class and observe him? Maybe we could work on this together." With this approach, the counselor becomes an ally of the teacher and can work with him to discover the nature of the problem and what is maintaining it. Similarly, in the case of agencies, it is crucial to determine who the client is. For instance, a client referred by the court or the Welfare Department may have no goals for behavior change or very different ones from those of the referring agent.

Self-referrals obviously are frequent in community agencies, and consequently, goal setting is easier because the client identifies the problem area she wants to change. In schools, counselors can encourage self-referrals through visiting classrooms and describing the counseling role to students. Classroom guidance programs conducted by the counselor provide an additional way for students to get acquainted with the counselor and consequently result in some self-referrals. Sometimes an individual will seek help from a counselor if she is upset about something or if she needs specific occupational or educational information.

DETERMINE APPROPRIATENESS OF REFERRAL

Appropriateness To Job Description

Upon receipt of the referral, the counselor needs to determine if it is appropriate. That is, she must decide if the problem in question is one which fits within her job description and one with which she can be effective. Some referrals may be labeled inappropriate because they can be handled better by others, perhaps some other staff personnel or other agency. For instance, a student who is referred to a school counselor because he is having a great deal of difficulty in academic subjects may be referred to the school psychologist for a diagnostic work-up or perhaps to a math or remedial reading teacher. A child who exhibits severe withdrawal or some other severe disturbance may be re-referred for therapy at a Mental Health Center, a private clinic, etc. Some cases occurring in agencies may need to be referred to a psychiatric in-patient facility.

Differences in Perception of Problem

Other instances of inappropriate referrals sometimes occur because the counselor and referring agent view the problem differently. For example, after the death of Sally's mother, Sally's father asked a mental health counselor to talk with her. Sally's father said he didn't think she was experiencing "appropriate grief." He further stated that since Sally did not appear to be unhappy, she must be repressing her grief and that it would occur in some inappropriate way at a later time. However, the counselor decided after talking with Sally that she was adjusting well and that counseling was not warranted. Consequently, the case was not continued.

In any social system (e.g., school, family), each member has a different perception of the "real problem" in that system (Gottman and Leiblum, 1974). A student may be referred to a counselor by a teacher who labels him as being defiant. Upon observation, the counselor may find that his definition of defiance is quite different from the teacher's definition of it. At this point, the problem must be discussed in terms of specific undesirable behaviors before the counselor can determine the appropriateness or inappropriateness of the referral.

Inappropriateness of Some Self-Referrals

Like teacher, parent, or community referrals, self-referrals also may be inappropriate. For instance, a student may ask to see a counselor merely to try to get out of a class she dislikes or to tell on someone she doesn't like. Some clients may be inappropriate referrals simply because they're trying to receive drugs and have no other reason for coming or because they want a service (e.g., employment or job training) which is not available through the agency. In the case of desired services, the client and counselor can talk about ways or places to seek them, but if the client is not interested in this, the case should be terminated.

EXPLAIN COUNSELING RELATIONSHIP

Help the Client Begin Talking

If the referral is appropriate, the counselor's task then is to schedule a meeting to explain the counseling relationship. The client is likely to be anxious when he comes to the counselor because of uncertainties about why he's there and what will happen to him while he's there. In some cases, clients are embarrassed about having a problem and therefore are reluctant to discuss it. A counselor can often reduce a client's hesitancy to discuss his problem by inviting him to start the conversation. "Door openers" such as the following are often helpful:

What brought you to see me, Bill?

What would you like to discuss?

I understand you are having some difficulties. Tell me why you are here.

Is there something you would like to talk about?

It is important at the outset of the initial interview to provide minimal structure to the counseling process. That is, the counselor should initially try to avoid defining limits or goals within the counseling relationship (Shertzer and Stone, 1968). If the client remains silent, the counselor may intervene, asking him to discuss anything that might concern him. Other counselor responses might include:

It must be difficult to know where to start.

You may be wondering where to begin.

These responses should help the client begin talking. In some cases the client may begin with small talk by commenting on the weather or other external events. Some younger children will explore their environment by asking questions such as, "What is that hanging on your wall?" or "Is that a picture of your wife on your desk?" These comments are conversational in nature, but counseling is more than a conversation and must be treated so. The counselor may want to listen to these initial comments but should not attempt to encourage them or probe their content deeper (Hackney and Nye, 1973).

Deal with Resistance

The client may be unwilling to talk if she has been referred by a parent, teacher, judge, or welfare case worker and perceives no particular problem. In such a case, the counselor should explain what will be happening in the sessions. For instance, the counselor might say:

Mark, your teacher asked me to talk with you (or your teacher thought you might want to talk with me) about how you're getting along with the other boys and girls in your class. What do you think about this?

This then allows Mark to give his perceptions of his peer relationships as well as to express his feelings about coming to the counselor. However, clients may show resistance in ways other than not talking. Persons referred for poor attandance and fighting, for example, often exhibit resistance manifested in failure to attend sessions and complete homework assignments as well as in long silences.

Another form of resistance is hostility. Statements such as the following are typical:

I wouldn't be here if I didn't have to.

I don't want to see you.

This isn't going to do any good.

A more subtle form of resistance may be manifested by the client who rambles and changes topics. This type of client may seek advice eagerly or agree with anything the counselor might say but not internalize any of it. The counselor must be cautious not to inadvertently reinforce such behavior.

Some resistance can be understood in terms of **approach-avoidance.** While on the one hand, the client wants to alter her behavior, she may not like the resulting loss of certain rewards. For instance, the drug user may want to stop depending on drugs, but she doesn't want to give up the pleasurable results she's experienced under the effects of drugs. Or, the client may want to make better grades, but he may not want to give up some of his time with friends to study. Still another example is the person who wants dates but who gets very anxious even at the prospect of one because of not knowing how to behave. Such approach-avoidance sometimes results in resistance in the counseling situation. This resistance may be handled effectively by the counselor through simply responding to the reluctance. For example:

Your reluctance to get started may be your way of saying you're afraid.

It's pretty tough to talk about these things.

Maybe there are both advantages and disadvantages in leaving things the way they are.

Resistance also may be due to a client's lack of skills. For instance, he may wish to be cooperative but doesn't know how to express himself. Consequently, he appears to be resistive because he's quiet or because his answers are very superficial. In such a case, the counselor might start by modeling self-expression of feelings or thoughts. She can play tapes of how good clients express themselves in a counseling interview and then get the client to practice expressing himself to her (the counselor). Successive approximations to the desired level can be reinforced by the counselor (see Chapter 9).

On the other hand, the client's resistance may be due to factors in the immediate environment. The counselor may be perceived by the client as an institutional representative of the system. For the resistant client, then, cooperation in counseling implies yielding to a value system that is an anathema to his own (Vriend and Dyer, 1973). Willingly interacting with the counselor is like choosing to give into "the system."

It is important to recognize that many clients will be resistive and to note that this does not indicate failure of the counselor. A counselor sometimes assumes that resistance means the client dislikes him and he then feels rejected by the client. Frustration resulting from this resistance may be manifested in veiled anger, such as folding of the arms or looking up in the air. Or it may be expressed in statements, such as, "I wonder what you have to hide." These responses, however, only reinforce the client's resistant behavior rather than decrease it. Consequently, rather than projecting the client's resistance onto himself, the counselor should attempt to question it. What payoff does the client receive from her resistance? Is this the way she usually behaves? Does the resistance prevent her from having to do anything about the problem? Questions such as these may help the counselor to deal with the resistance rather than give up on the client.

Discuss Counseling Sessions

Once the counselor and client have worked through the resistance, the counselor can explain what can happen during counseling. This may be similar to the following:

> When you come to see me, we'll talk about things that concern you and discuss what can be done about them. Maybe we can pool our ideas and come up with some things you can try. If you try something and it doesn't work, we'll talk about it and try to figure out what else might help.

Explain Confidentiality One of the questions the client may ask, either initially or later in counseling, is whether the counselor is going to tell his teacher, parent, probation officer, or welfare worker what he says. In answer to this question or sometimes before the question arises, the counselor will say that what he and the client discuss will be held confidential and nothing will be repeated *except under certain conditions*. A promise without this qualification can prove to be frustrating. There are cases where it is in the best interests of the client that the information be shared. If the client finds out his statements have not been kept confidential, even though the counselor promised total confidentiality, the trust is damaged and the counselor loses some of his effectiveness. Consequently, some qualification of confidentiality usually should be included. For instance, the counselor may say:

> I will try to keep what we talk about here just between the two of us. But if you said you were planning to do something that would be harmful to you or someone else, I probably would tell someone else and try to keep anyone from getting hurt. I promise that I'll let you know if I'm going to tell anyone what we've talked about. And sometimes, if I think it would be helpful for someone to know something you've told me, I may ask you if it's okay for me to mention it. For example, if you told me you were having trouble in school, I might ask you if you minded my discussing this with your teachers.

Questions concerning the counselor's role or the counseling relationship may come up throughout the counseling sessions and should be answered as they arise. The crucial aspect of explaining the counseling relationship is to relieve the initial anxieties the client may have, to give her some expectations about what is likely to happen to her when she comes, and to help her feel at ease in the counseling situation.

ESTABLISH RAPPORT

If the explanation of the counseling relationship is satisfactory, the counselor should then work toward gathering information by first establishing rapport. The initial interview(s) should be given primarily to establishing this rapport and to developing an understanding of the client's perception of the problem. Rapport is important throughout the counseling process, but unless it can be established in the initial interviews, client resistance to change will likely occur. A counselor should never fake a relationship by expressing concerns and feelings she doesn't have. Rather, there are several things a counselor can do to promote a positive relationship.

Attend To Client

Crucial to understanding another person's problem is the ability to attend to him, both to his verbal statements and his nonverbal behavior. Obviously, a lack of attention would make the client feel the counselor isn't interested in him and would likely result in resistance, low expectations for help, or even premature termination.

Physical Relaxation Ivey, et al. (1968) have demonstrated that attending behavior can be taught and have identified three major components of attending.

The first of these components is physical relaxation. When the counselor is seated in a comfortable, relaxed position, she can more readily talk with the client than when she is very tense and rigid. In fact, the relaxed counselor tends to speak and gesture in a more natural manner and communicates to the client that she is ready to help and feels some confidence that she can help. In contrast, the tense counselor is less likely to be able to attend because she is concerned about her own behavior and cannot act in a free and natural manner. When the counselor is ill at ease, this is readily communicated to the client and makes him feel some discomfort as well.

Eye Contact A second factor in effective attending behavior is eye contact. A counselor who looks at the wall, out the window, and doesn't focus on the client not only communicates to the client that he isn't listening, but also he actually has a difficult time listening, even when he tries to do so. On the other hand, a fixed gaze is as undesirable as no eye contact since it is also likely to make the client uncomfortable. Varied eye contact is preferable, i.e., most of the time the counselor should look at the client as they talk with each other, but periodically glancing away will help avoid a fixed gaze.

In short, effective nonverbal attending behavior should include:

1. The counselor should initially be sitting upright in his chair. When he wants to communicate interest to the client, he can lean forward in a 45-degree angle.
2. Hands should be at the side or in the lap in a relaxed position rather than fidgeting with something, which might distract the client.
3. Eyes should be focused on the client, but not in a fixed gaze.
4. The counselor's body should be facing the client, not turned sideways.
5. Feet should be on the floor, not hanging over a chair.

Verbal Following A third component in good attending is "verbal following" of what the client says. That is, the counselor stays with the topic and shows by his responses that he has accurately heard the content of the client's message. Obviously, there are times when the counselor will not hear or will misinterpret the client's statement. If this happens consistently, however, it becomes frustrating to the client and communicates to him that the counselor either doesn't care enough to attend or that he doesn't have the capacity to attend. In either case, it is unlikely that the client will want to continue counseling under such circumstances. Examples of "verbal following" are given below:

Client: I wish I could speak up to people when I disagree with them, but I'm always afraid to.

Counselor: You'd like to express disagreement with other people, but you're afraid of what will happen if you do. Is that right?

Client: I wish I could just run away and avoid all responsibility.

Counselor: It would be good to just get away and forget all the things you have hanging over you now.

When the counselor is able to verbally follow what the client says, she has the choice to attend or ignore (reinforce or extinguish) client responses (Ivey, 1971). The following example demonstrates this:

Client: Well, there isn't much more to say.

Counselor: Silence

Client: I think I'll play ball after school.

Counselor: Silence

Client: I don't know if I want to play if some of those kids are there.

Counselor: It's not too much fun playing when they are around.

Verbal following in this case is more than a technique; it is a highly conscious awareness of what is going on between the counselor and the client (Hackney and Nye, 1973).

Example Exercise

In the following counselor and client dialogue, identify those statements which indicate verbal following:

Client: It seems that people are never around.

Counselor: People just never seem to stop by.

Client: No, I've asked them, but they never drop over.

Counselor: Can you tell me why they never stop over?

Client: Well, maybe they don't have a good time.

Counselor: You're not sure if they enjoy themselves.

Client: No, they never like what I want to do.

Counselor: What do you like to do?

Client: Well, I like to play electric football and Monopoly, but they always want to do something else.

Counselor: They just never want to do what you want to do.

Answers

People just never seem to stop by.

You're not sure if they enjoy themselves.

They just never want to do what you want to do.

Once the client begins to talk about his concerns, the counselor's task is to facilitate the discussion, perhaps by statements such as "Uh huh," "Then?" "So?" "And?" or a nod of the head. This minimal encouragement promotes continued talking and keeps the client on the topic.

Ask Questions

Sometimes it is difficult to get an interview started smoothly. After the counselor has explained the counseling relationship, the client may say nothing. After several seconds, the counselor may say something like:

It's hard for us to get started talking, isn't it?

Is there something in particular you wanted to discuss?

Why don't you tell me how you feel about being here?

You said you wanted to talk about something. It's sometimes hard to know where to start, but feel free to go ahead.

These kinds of encouraging responses can help get an interview started, and they also have the added advantage of letting the client decide what she wants to discuss first.

But what if there's a lull or silence after this initial client statement? Often, when the client doesn't say anything immediately, the counselor begins asking questions. This may be the result of the counselor's discomfort with silence, and all too often, the questions he asks do not aid in the interview. Benjamin (1974) says a good test of whether to question at all is to ask if the question will further or inhibit the interview.

Open-ended and Closed-ended Questions Questioning cannot always be regarded as an inappropriate technique; rather, some consideration should be given to when to question and what kinds of questions to use. Unfortunately, counselors often use closed-ended questions as opposed to open-ended ones. Closed-ended questions can be answered by one word or a short specific answer; they consequently curtail communication. In contrast, the open-ended question requires the client to give views, opinions, feelings, etc. This kind of question elicits more client verbalization since it can't be answered by one or two words. Because the closed-ended question often results in reduced client verbalization, it may lead to bombarding, or further use of closed-ended questions. The following interaction shows how this happens.

Counselor: Did your teacher tell you to come?
Client: Yes.
Counselor: Did you do something she didn't like?
Client: Yes.
Counselor: What did you do?
Client: I didn't get my math done.
Counselor: Was it too hard?
Client: Yeah.
Counselor: Did you ask for help?
Client: No.

With this kind of questioning, the client makes very brief responses, and as a consequence, the counselor almost completely directs the interview. That is, the counselor sets up a pattern of closed-ended questions and answers from which he will unlikely be able to extricate himself. In this case, the counselor is telling the client that he is the authority and knows what is relevant for the client (Benjamin, 1969); the client will likely subject himself to this only as long as he feels that these questions will lead to a solution. On the other hand, because open-ended questions tend not to restrict the client to very narrow answers, they elicit more information. For instance, the counselor could have said, "Tell me what happened that brought you here" and have received most of the information that he received from the five questions in the preceding dialogue. Examples of closed- and open-ended questions follow:

Closed: You hate school, don't you?
Open: How do you feel about school?
Closed: How many sisters and brothers do you have?
Open: Tell me about your family.

Closed: Did Tom get mad at you because you hit him?
Open: Why do you think Tom got mad at you?
Closed: You're upset today, aren't you?
Open: How are you feeling today?

Direct and Indirect Questions Benjamin (1974) makes a further distinction between the direct and indirect question. The direct question warrants a specific answer while the indirect question is actually a statement which indirectly makes an inquiry. Examples of these follow:

Direct: What do you think about your classmates?
Indirect: You must have different feelings about your classmates.
Direct: Do you lack self-confidence?
Indirect: You sound like you're unsure of yourself sometimes.

The indirect question has several advantages. It indicates that the counselor is verbally following and that she understands, but it still leaves the client open to respond or not and to make the kind of response he wants. The indirect question, like the open-ended question, then, is likely to produce greater client verbalization and prevent the client's impression that he's being interrogated rather than understood.

Example Exercise

In the following counselor-client dialogue, categorize each counselor question by (o) open or (c) closed and (d) direct or (i) indirect.

1. *Client:* I just can't seem to tell her what I really think.
   Counselor: Do you lack self-confidence?
2. *Client:* Well, I don't think so.
   Counselor: You sound unsure of yourself.
3. *Client:* Maybe I am, but every time I get near her, I freeze.
   Counselor: Tell me about this.

Answers

1. Question 1 is direct and closed-ended.
2. Question 2 is indirect and closed-ended.
3. Question 3 is indirect and open-ended.

Respond To and Summarize Feelings

Verbal following, or responding to the *content* of a client's message, is helpful in making the client feel comfortable enough to express his concerns. However, it is also important for the counselor to be able to respond to the client's *feelings*. Specifically, this involves listening to how the client says what he does and then responding in such a way that the client knows the counselor understands his feelings. Tone of voice, rapidity of speech, and nonverbal gestures as well as the verbal content of the client's message help the counselor determine the feelings of the client. For instance, slow speech may indicate discouragement, whereas rapid speech may indicate either anxiety or excitement. Tone of voice is a good indicator of the client's emotions; blushes, stammers, etc. also give clues about the client's feelings.

Level I—Responding There are different levels of responding to feelings.* At the lowest level of adequate responding is the simple reflection of feelings the client has explicitly stated. Some examples of this level are given below:

Client: I'm really upset that the teacher picks on me.

Counselor: It upsets you to be picked on by the teacher.

Client: I think it's just great that he invited me to the party.

Counselor: You're really happy that you were invited.

Client: What a rotten way for someone to treat you!

Counselor: You're bothered and upset about the way you were treated.

In these interchanges, the counselor says what could have been said by the client. *The counselor puts it in his own words but doesn't go beyond what has been stated* (Egan, 1975). He does not try to probe deeper into what the client is half saying or stating implicitly.

The purpose of Level I responses is to establish rapport and raise the level of self-exploration of the client. Therefore, the counselor has an excellent criterion for judging the quality of her response—to what extent the client explores his feelings and behavior.

Level II—Responding Once the counselor has established rapport with the client and wishes the client to move toward self-understanding, then he would use a higher level of responding to feelings. *These responses require the counselor to go beyond what the client has expressed and pick up those covert feelings which are neither expressed*

---

*It should be noted that these levels do not correspond to the Carkhuff Levels of Empathic Understanding (Carkhuff, 1969). What is labeled Level I here represents what would be Level 3 on Carkhuff's scale.

nor obviously implied. Here, the counselor gets at feelings which the client may even be unable to express himself. Examples of a client statement and responses at the two levels are given below:

Client: I don't understand it. I've practiced harder than almost anyone, and I think I have as much athletic ability as the other guys on the team. But it doesn't seem to pay off. I always flub the "big play."

Level I: You feel frustrated that even when you work and practice hard, it doesn't pay off.

Level II: It's depressing to put in a lot of effort and still fail. It gets you down and maybe you even feel a little sorry for yourself.

At the lower level, the response is merely a reflection of the client's feelings. At the second level, the counselor picks up on feelings which were implied but not stated and interprets these feelings. This helps the client move from self-exploration to self-understanding (Egan, 1975).

Example Exercise

In the following exercise, indicate the level of counselor response as (0) not responding to client's feelings; (1) responding to explicitly stated feelings; or (2) responding to implicit communication.

1. *Client:* I write a lot, but I'm not sure how good it is. Some of my friends tell me they like it, but they are not critics. I keep writing and sending it off to publishers, but they reject it.

    Counselor: It's pretty disillusioning to put that much work into it with so little success. It kind of makes you wonder whether you have talent, and you don't want to fool yourself.

2. *Client:* I just can't take it anymore. I've got to do something.

    Counselor: You're fed up and have to get out.

3. *Client:* You're listening, but it doesn't seem to help.

    Counselor: You feel I'm paying attention, but it doesn't help you solve your problem.

4. *Client:* I'm really mad at her.

    Counselor: She really upsets you.

5. *Client:* I wish he would get off my back.

    Counselor: Why does he do that?

6. *Client:* I got laid off yesterday . . . strike . . . what do I do now?

    Counselor: You lost your job and now you're not sure what to do.

7. *Client:* I feel like I have to do everything just right.

    Counselor: Sometimes you'd like to forget it and let go.

8. *Client:* I really felt left out at the dance.
Counselor: Did you go to the party with Bob?

Answers

1. 2	2. 1	3. 1	4. 1
5. 0	6. 1	7. 2	8. 0

Undershooting and Overshooting The ability to respond to feelings is an important skill which is appropriate to use throughout counseling. It makes the client feel understood and helps him engage in self-exploration. In using this skill, however, it is easy to make some errors. One basic error is that of "undershooting" or "overshooting." That is, the counselor sometimes responds with much less or much more intensity than the client feels. Examples follow.
Client: I'm so mad at him that I feel like killing him!
Counselor: You feel a little irritated with him.
Client: A little irritated! I'd like to break his neck!

When the counselor "undershoots," as in the preceding example, the client is not likely to view the response as an understanding or perceptive one. Or if the counselor "overshoots," as in the following example, the client likewise feels that the counselor doesn't understand.
Client: I think maybe if I could just be by myself for awhile, I could think it through and make a decision.
Counselor: You'd like to just run away and be alone so you could make decisions.
Client: No, I don't want to run away. I just think I could make this decision about Charlie easier if he weren't around.

An Inappropriate Probe Another error that sometimes occurs is the use of a probe when the counselor should be communicating understanding. For example:
Client: I'm never allowed to do anything. I get so mad because I'm treated just like a little child all the time!
Counselor: What do you want to do?
Here, it would be more appropriate to respond to the feelings of the client. For example:
Counselor: It is really upsetting to be treated as a child who can't make decisions for himself.
The client can appreciate such a response.

Summarizing Feelings **Summarization of feelings** is similar to responding to or reflecting feelings. The only difference is that reflection responds to only one portion of the client's communication while summarization involves bringing together several feelings in a meaningful pattern. It is helpful to use summarization at two or three points during the interview and also at the end. By periodically summarizing feelings, you communicate to the client that you understand what he's saying and that you are concerned about helping.

Clarify Client Statements

Clarification is the process whereby the counselor gives the client his observations and perceptions of what the client has told him (Edinburg et al., 1975). The counselor can clarify either by simplifying the message to make it clearer or by expressing for the client what he has had difficulty in communicating clearly by himself (Benjamin, 1974). For example:

Client: I just wonder if it's worth it. I want to have friends, but I just can't seem to make people like me. If I just knew a simple—maybe a magic way—to suddenly be popular . . . .

Counselor: You know you want friends, but you don't know how to make people like you.

Client: I love my children, but sometimes I just really wish I didn't have them around. They get into fights and . . . . Oh, do you know what I mean?

Counselor: The bad behavior of your children really bothers you. You love them, but you get angry with them too. Is that right?

Clarification should be used when the client needs help in expressing herself or when it would be helpful to draw some statements together for her. The counselor cannot be expected to understand everything. Rather than guess at what the client is saying, he should stop and ask the client to clarify her response. This often seems to communicate to the client that the counselor is interested in what she is saying.

Use Silence

In a counseling interview, silence can be very anxiety provoking for the counselor. Even a few seconds seem long, and the counselor may feel compelled to say something. Often, he breaks the silence with questions, many of which are not very well thought-out or relevant. Silence usually produces similar anxieties for the client, but it can be productive in that it may cause the client to initiate conversation to reduce his discomfort.

There are other times when silence is productive. If the client pauses, it may mean that he's thinking about something or considering an alternative direction to take. On the other hand, it may mean he's trying to avoid the topic or perhaps that he's shy, hostile, or resistive. One way to decide whether to break such silence is to determine if the client's eyes are fixed without being focused or if he's looking from one object to another to avoid eye contact with the counselor. If the former is the case, he is likely thinking about something; if the latter is true, he likely is trying to avoid the topic. It seems sadistic to remain silent when the client is extremely anxious and hasn't said anything for several minutes. Yet, the counselor should learn to be comfortable with silences up to 30 seconds, refraining from interrupting them. Longer silences may be unproductive. They can be broken by comments such as:

What are you thinking about?

You seem shy about discussing this.

Maybe this is difficult for you to talk about.

If no verbalizations result from this, the counselor may say:

I'm not sure what your silence means.

I'm wondering what you're thinking about.

In short, silence may be another effective counseling technique when used appropriately. Like other techniques, it requires practice. One way to feel more comfortable with silence is to use a role-playing situation to practice a 30-second pause before responding to the client. This gives the counselor a more accurate notion of how much time is elapsing between verbalizations and helps him pace his responses better.

CLOSE THE INTERVIEW

There is often a question about when to close the interview. One method of handling this is to specify a time period for counseling and stop at the end of that time. This may run from 15 to 60 minutes or more, depending on the age level of the client. Given this procedure, the counselor may close the interview by saying:

It looks like we have run out of time today.

I think our time is up.

Another approach to closing the interview is to summarize the main points discussed. Here the counselor should be concise, summarizing without a great deal of elaboration. For example:

> We've talked about your concern that your grades are down and that your friends don't come around any more. You also said you aren't making yourself as available to friends as you have in the past.

On some occasions, the counselor can ask the client to summarize the session, "Since our time is up, I'm wondering if you could summarize the main points we have been discussing." Following the summarization, the counselor and client can discuss how the homework assignments, if any, can be implemented and then verify the next meeting time.

CHECKLIST FOR PROCESSING THE REFERRAL AND STRUCTURING THE INTERVIEW

Check yes in the spaces below as the procedure is completed. Then go on to the next step.

	yes	no	Completed?
1. *Determine the referral source.*			_____
a. Receive referral form.	___	___	
2. *Determine appropriateness of referral.*	___	___	_____
3. *Explain counseling relationship.*			_____
a. Open the interview.	___	___	
b. Respond to resistance.	___	___	
c. Explain counselor role.	___	___	
d. Discuss confidentiality.	___	___	
4. *Encourage client talk.*			_____
a. Attend to client.	___	___	
1. Eye contact	___	___	
2. Body posture	___	___	
3. Verbal following	___	___	
b. Ask open-ended questions.	___	___	

c. Paraphrase client's feelings.   —— ——
d. Reflect client's feelings
   (explicitly).   —— ——
e. Reflect client's feelings
   (implicitly).   —— ——
f. Clarify client's statements.   —— ——
g. Use silence.   —— ——

5. *Close interview.*   ——————

PROGRAMMED EXAMPLES

Choose the most appropriate phrase(s) to complete the statements. Sometimes more than one answer should be identified.

1. Counselors often request teachers or parents to complete a referral form before referring a student because
   a. it provides the counselor with a specification of the problem.
   b. it often helps in determining the appropriate intervention.
   c. it helps to determine what, if anything, has been tried to alleviate the problem.
   d. it often determines the cause of the problem.

   You're on target if you answered (a) and (c). The referral form should specify the problem and what, if anything, has been done to reduce it. Although it is important to understand what is causing the problem (d) and what intervention is necessary to alleviate it (b), the referral form generally does not provide this type of information.

2. A referral is generally appropriate if
   a. the counselor knows who the referral source is.
   b. the referral problem fits within his job description.
   c. the counselor has the skills to effect behavior change.
   d. the counselor and referral source agree on the problem.

   If you answered (b), (c), and (d), you are correct. When the problem is related to the counselor's role (b), he is competent to treat it (c), and the counselor and referring person agree on the problem (d); the referral is appropriate. (If the counselor feels unqualified to handle the referral problem, he should offer information about other sources of help.) While it may be helpful to know the referral source (a), it is not necessary.

3. When the client has been referred by someone else, the counselor should always
   a. provide the client an initial explanation of why he is there and what will be occurring in the sessions.
   b. discuss the problem immediately.
   c. discuss the behavior of the referral source.
   d. ask him why he was asked to come to the counselor.

   A is the best response because the client will often be less anxious or resistive if he knows why he is there and what he can expect. Asking him why he is there (d) or discussing the problem immediately (b) may only increase client resistance.

4. The counselor should communicate to the client that he will keep information confidential except when
   a. the client has been terminated.
   b. his parents request the information.
   c. he (the client) describes behavior or plans which would be harmful to himself or others.
   d. the counselor thinks it would be helpful information for someone else to have.

   If you answered (c) and (d), you are correct. When the client is behaving in a way which is harmful to himself or others, the counselor should try to keep anyone from getting hurt. Also, there are times when shared information may bring about more rapid change. In either case, the counselor should let the client know in advance that he is going to release confidential information.

5. The three major components of attending behavior are
   a. physical relaxation, eye contact, and verbal following.
   b. eye contact, verbal following, and open-ended questions.
   c. eye contact, verbal following, and clasped hands.
   d. physical relaxation, verbal following, and indirect questions.

   If you answered (a), you are right. These three factors communicate to the client that the counselor is interested in what the client is saying and will likely increase his expectations for being helped. While open-ended questions (b) are helpful in promoting client verbalizations, they are not necessary for attending and clasped hands (c) and indirect questions (d) are not necessarily related to attending behavior.

6. Indicate which of the following questions are open-ended:
   a. Do you like Bill?
   b. How do you feel about your parents?
   c. Where does this occur?
   d. What do you think makes him do that?

You're correct if you answered (b) and (d). Open-ended questions require the client to express feelings (b) and views or opinions (d). Closed-ended questions, on the other hand, can be answered by one word (a) or short specific answers (c).

7. An example of a Level I reflection of feeling might be:
   a. *Client:* I am really mad at her.
      Counselor: Why do you feel that way?
   b. *Client:* Mom just doesn't understand me.
      Counselor: Your relationship with your mother is bothering you.
   c. *Client:* I would like to kill him!
      Counselor: You feel a little upset.
   d. *Client:* I am really upset that my brother calls me names.
      Counselor: It upsets you to be called names by your brother.

If you answered (d), you are correct. At this level, the counselor paraphrases or restates the feeling the client has already expressed. At a higher level, the counselor reflects feelings which are implied but not stated (b). The third statement (c) is a good example of "undershooting" the client's feeling level. Statement (a) does not respond to the client's feelings.

8. Clarification is a skill the counselor might use when
   a. he wants to identify the controlling conditions.
   b. the client needs help in expressing himself.
   c. the counselor wants to terminate the client.

d.   the counselor is unclear about what the client said.

If you answered (b) and (d), you are correct. The counselor can often simplify the message or attempt to make it clearer by restating the client's response and checking it out with him. Clarifying the client's response may or may not have anything to do with identifying conditions controlling the client's behavior (a).

9. The use of silence can be productive because it allows the client to
   a.   think about what the counselor is going to say next.
   b.   think about what he is going to say or consider an alternative direction.
   c.   avoid anxiety-provoking topics.
   d.   identify the problem.
   B is the best answer because silence often helps the client process information and decide what he's going to say or perhaps consider an alternative course of discussion. While he may be concerned about what the counselor will say (a) or want to avoid anxiety-provoking topics (c), this is not a productive use of silence. Identifying the problem (d) usually does not occur this way.

10. To break a silence that persists beyond 30 seconds, the counselor might say:
   a.   You seem awfully quiet today.
   b.   Why don't you say anything else about that topic?
   c.   Maybe you would like to come back another time.
   d.   I'm wondering what you are thinking about.
   D is the best answer because it is important to determine what the silence means. The other alternatives may make the client more anxious and increase periods of silence.

11. Given the following client response, indicate a counselor's statement of verbal following: "Well, they never call or come over."
   a.   How are you feeling at the time?
   b.   When does this happen?
   c.   They just don't keep in touch with you.
   d.   Tell me some more about this.
   If you responded (c), you are correct. Here the counselor is attending to what the client has just said. The other statements ask

for additional information but give no indication that the counselor has accurately heard what the client is saying.

12. Generate a Level I and II response to the following client statement: "I just don't seem to care. My grades are okay—but I could do better if I wanted to—it just doesn't seem worth it."
Level I:

Level II:

Suggested responses:
Level I: You don't feel concerned enough about your grades to put out the extra effort necessary to do better.
Level II: You seem to be feeling a lot of conflict. On the one hand you want better grades, but you are not sure you are willing to do the extra work to get them.

CRITERION TEST

Choose one or more phrases that accurately complete the following statements and follow additional instructions for the last problem.

1. When the client is referred by a teacher, principal, or parent, the counselor should
   a. explain to the client why he was referred and what he might expect in the counseling sessions.
   b. discuss the problem immediately.
   c. discuss the behavior of the referral source.
   d. ask the client why he was referred.

2. Teacher referral forms help the counselor
   a. discover who is concerned about the problem.
   b. specify the problem and discover what has been tried to alleviate it.
   c. determine the cause of the problem.
   d. keep appropriate records.

3. Appropriate referrals are determined by
   a. the counselor's skills and role responsibilities.

    b.   when the referral is made.

    c.   who makes the referral.

    d.   what the referral source has done to alleviate the problem.

4. When client silence persists, the counselor might say:
   a.   Why don't we take a break?
   b.   I'm not sure what this silence means.
   c.   You seem a little anxious.
   d.   What would you like to talk about?

5. Silence can be effective in helping the client
   a.   identify problem behavior.
   b.   think through a situation and perhaps take a new direction.
   c.   decide what is causing the problem.
   d.   reduce anxiety.

6. Which of the following questions are open-ended?
   a.   When does the problem occur?
   b.   Do you like him?
   c.   How do you feel about your marital relationship?
   d.   Who sits next to you?

7. Three important elements of attending behavior are
   a.   eye contact, verbal following, and head nodding.
   b.   eye contact, open-ended questions, and arms at sides.
   c.   eye contact, physical relaxation, and verbal following.
   d.   eye contact, verbal following, and perception checking.

8. Clarification is a skill which helps the counselor
   a.   better understand what the client has said as well as to draw ideas together for the client.
   b.   open the interview.
   c.   determine an appropriate intervention.
   d.   identify what is controlling the problem behavior.

9. Information should be kept confidential except when
   a.   the case is terminated.
   b.   the behavior described by the client is destructive to himself

or others.
c. the case is a difficult one.
d. the counselor needs additional information.

10. An example of a Level I response is:
   a. *Client:* That girl makes me sick.
      Counselor: What do you do when you get sick?
   b. *Client:* I'm just really confused about whether to go to college or get a job.
      Counselor: You feel like making a choice.
   c. *Client:* Oh, what's the use? Everything I touch is a failure.
      Counselor: You're really discouraged and feel like giving up.
   d. *Client:* Oh, what's the use? Everything I touch is a failure.
      Counselor: Everything you touch is a failure?

11. Given the following client response, indicate a counselor statement of verbal following: "Who cares what they think? They are not important."
   a. Why do you say that?
   b. Their opinions don't matter to you.
   c. Whose problem is this?
   d. Tell me more about this.

12. Generate a Level I and II response to the following client statement: "My husband and I are off and on. I don't know what is the matter; we just never seem to stay together."
   Level I:

   Level II:

CHAPTER 2
CRITERION TEST ANSWERS
   1. a
   2. b
   3. a

4. b
5. b
6. c
7. c
8. a
9. b
10. c
11. b
12. Level I: You and your husband just can't stay together. You get along for awhile and then you begin having problems.

Level II: You're confused and bothered by your relationship with your husband. Sounds like you're worried that you can't maintain a good relationship over a long period of time.

3 Defining the Problem

Defining problems in behavioral terms has a multifaceted purpose, or rationale. Using these terms helps the client describe the problem as he views it and allows the counselor to understand the specific behaviors or situations which are causing the client distress. In addition, it allows the counselor to determine exact behavioral referents of the labels used by the client and others in describing the problem. It also helps the client discover desirable behaviors that may be incompatible with the undesirable ones. *Once the problem is translated into behavioral terms, those events which appear to be maintaining or controlling the problem can be determined.* By discovering what behaviors the client is able to perform satisfactorily and the conditions under which the problem behavior occurs, the counselor and client can formulate mutually agreeable goals. See Figure 3 showing steps of defining the problem.

Clients seldom begin counseling by articulating specific goals or behaviors they want to change. Instead of saying, "I am uncomfortable when I meet new people," the client will likely say, "I am shy" or "I am backward." That is, she often describes characteristics or traits rather than the ways in which these characteristics or traits are manifested. Many clients place labels on themselves and then enter counseling to have the counselor remove the labels (Krumboltz and Thoresen, 1969). Here, the counselor must help the client identify those behaviors which led him to the label (shyness, low self-confidence, etc.) and help him modify those behaviors so he can assume a more desirable label for himself (assertive, popular, etc.).

IDENTIFY ALL CONCERNS
Client problems often are complex and may involve several areas. For instance, the child who is experiencing difficulty with peer relationships also may be making poor grades at school and may be exhibiting dis-

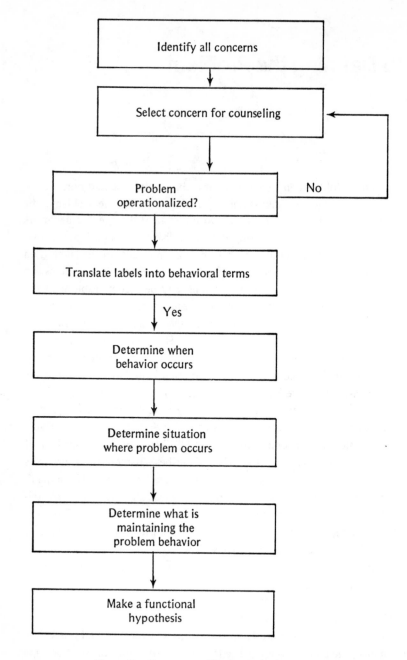

Figure 3. Summary of Defining the Problem

ruptive classroom behaviors as well. Sometimes, these varied problems are related, and improvement in one area will bring improvement in another. For example, a client may be disruptive in math or history. If the client shows improvement in math, he may also improve in history. It's critical to identify all the areas where the client is experiencing major difficulties so the counselor and client can determine which areas are most important and need the most immediate attention. In some cases, this information will come from the client; in others, the information will come from teachers or parents who have referred the client because he is exhibiting problem behaviors.

Overcome Obstacles To Identifying Problems

There are two major obstacles, however, in identifying all client concerns. First, the presenting problem may not be the issue of greatest concern to the client. That is, clients often present a false or minor problem to determine how it will be handled by the counselor. If they regard the counselor's responses positively, then they're more likely to present the real problem.

The presenting problem is easily determined by asking questions such as, "What do you want to talk about?" or "What brings you here today?" (It should be noted that these questions are also helpful in opening the interview.) Of course, some information may be available via a referral form received prior to the first interview. In this case, the question may refer to such information, e.g., "I understand you're concerned because you feel uneasy around girls and have trouble getting dates" or "I see from the referral form that Johnny is disruptive in your classroom."

A second major obstacle is clients' frequent difficulty in describing their behavior and the particular subsetting (classroom, dinner table) in which it occurs. Clients often distort events to meet counselor approval or to justify their own actions. In these instances, the counselor may be unable to determine the specific nature of the problem. For example, an attractive girl may be able to attract many men for initial dates but may be unable to get them to ask her out after that. She blames men for being inconsistent but is unable to describe any negative interactions during the date. The first step here would be for the client to observe and record any instances of negative interactions with her dates (see Observing and Recording Behavior). If she is unable to do this, she might ask a friend to interview previous dates and identify specific reasons why males do not want to go out with her anymore.

Use Checklists and Interviews
However, if the client or others appear to be aware of the problem(s), it may be more appropriate for them to complete a behavior problem checklist. Some clients may fill out the checklists independently; for others, the counselor may ask questions to determine the areas of difficulty. For example, a client who expresses difficulty in getting along with people may be asked specifically, "How do you get along with your parents, your brothers and sisters, classmates, teachers, etc.?" to better determine the context within which problem situations occur and with whom the most severe problems arise.

Examples of behavior problem checklists designed by Guthrie and Hardman are shown in Tables 2 and 3. The first checklist (Table 2) is appropriate for adult clients, and the second (Table 3) is useful for gaining additional information concerning problem behavior of students. It is to be completed by teachers.

Table 2. Checklist for Problem Identification
of Adult Clients*

Name _____ Date _____

Yes	No		Do you want us to help you with:
____	____	1.	Getting along better with other people?
____	____	2.	Getting along better with your spouse and family?
____	____	3.	Managing your money?
____	____	4.	Maintaining a better personal appearance?
____	____	5.	Learning to express yourself more.easily?
____	____	6.	Learning to think and behave in more rational ways?
____	____	7.	Using your leisure time better?
____	____	8.	Making friends?
____	____	9.	Controlling your temper?
____	____	10.	Learning how to relax (or getting rid of tense, nervous feelings)?
____	____	11.	Learning to concentrate and think more clearly?

48

___	___	12.	Getting rid of (or dealing more effectively with) angry feelings or other upsetting emotions?
___	___	13.	Learning to worry less?
___	___	14.	Learning to become more cheerful and optimistic and less depressed?
___	___	15.	Feeling better physically?
___	___	16.	Feeling more self-confident?
___	___	17.	Increasing your self-respect?
___	___	18.	Making decisions and solving problems?
___	___	19.	Understanding others?
___	___	20.	Getting along with your boss?
___	___	21.	Getting rid of resentment?
___	___	22.	Learning to live with an alcoholic.
___	___	23.	Finding or holding a job?
___	___	24.	Getting into school or job training?
___	___	25.	Finding a place to live?
___	___	26.	Controlling (stopping) use of alcohol/or drugs.
___	___	27.	Applying for Social Security, veterans pensions, welfare, or other financial assistance?
___	___	28.	Obtaining high school equivalency certificate?

Other goals or problem areas you would like help with:

29. _____

30. _____

31. _____

32. _____

33. _____

34. _____

*Reprinted with permission from Connie Guthrie, Southern Indiana Mental Health and Guidance Center, Jeffersonville, Indiana.

An example of an interview in which the counselor takes an inventory of problem behaviors follows:

Client: I've been upset lately.

Counselor: How long have you been feeling this way?

Client: I guess for about the last four months. My boy friend has been studying for the bar exam. I really want him to pass so he can get a job.

Counselor: How has your upset been related to his studying?

Client: Oh, I've been feeling alone and have nothing to do in the

Table 3. Behavior Checklist*

Student's name _____

Completed by _____
(include title)

Date _____ Date _____

Is this a problem?			(Fill in this side at termination): Observable improvement		
Yes	No		None	Some	Much
___	___	1. Failure to begin assignments on time	___	___	___
___	___	2. Incomplete assignments	___	___	___
___	___	3. Daydreaming	___	___	___
___	___	4. Walking around the room	___	___	___
___	___	5. Hitting other children in the classroom	___	___	___
___	___	6. Hitting other children on the playground	___	___	___
___	___	7. Makes noises for attention	___	___	___
___	___	8. Does not mix well with other children	___	___	___
___	___	9. Seems to have no friends	___	___	___
___	___	10. Steals	___	___	___
___	___	11. Lies	___	___	___
___	___	12. Resents authority	___	___	___
___	___	13. Does not respond to praise	___	___	___
___	___	14. Unusually shy and withdrawn	___	___	___
___	___	15. Very negative attitude	___	___	___
___	___	16. *Other:*	___	___	___
___	___	17. _____	___	___	___
___	___	18. _____	___	___	___

Comments: _____ Comments at time of termination:

_____   _____

_____   _____

*Reprinted by permission from Ann Hardman, Southern Indiana Mental Health and Guidance Center, Jeffersonville, Indiana.

evenings. I don't like being alone, and I don't get to see him often.

Counselor: Your time with him seems pretty limited.

Client: Yeah. I really miss talking with him. I like to be near him. But recently, even when I am with him, he's either very quiet or very crabby.

Counselor: So one of your concerns is the limited contact with him, and a second concern is the kind of relationship you have when you are with him.

Client: Yes, I guess I feel lonely. I would like to have something to do. I like being with my friends, too.

Counselor: So it's not just being without your boy friend. You would like to be with others, too.

In this case, the client's problems included the desire for more social interaction in the evening, more contact with her boy friend, and better communication with him.

After identifying related problem areas, the counselor can ask about situational events in which the client may perceive problems. For example, she may say, "Tell me about some times when you have been really upset or some things which really bother you." *In short, the counselor must attempt to identify the major problems and subsettings where the problem behaviors occur.*

SELECT CONCERN FOR COUNSELING

If the client presents several problem areas, the practitioner must begin to set priorities for treatment. There are four criteria which appear to be critical in making this determination (Sundel and Sundel, 1975). *The first criterion is choosing the problem of most immediate expressed concern of the client or significant others* (e.g., family, friends, etc.). At this point, a profile of problems can be read out loud to the client or presented to him in a written list. The client can then be asked to select the problem that is of greatest immediate concern to him. For example, a mother may want her child to stop screaming. A client may wish to get a job before he considers other problem areas. Some examples of what the counselor might say are:

Which problem is of most immediate concern to you?

Which problem must you solve now?

The first problem we need to take care of or resolve is . . . .

Unless the counselor has other reasons for choosing a different problem, the client is told that the one he selected will be addressed first. In many cases, however, additional criteria are considered in determining problem priorities for treatment. *A second criterion or way of determining a problem priority is to specify a problem which has the greatest negative consequences if not handled immediately.* While a client or consultee may feel that a specific problem is of the greatest concern to him (e.g., loss of friends), another problem may have greater negative consequences (e.g., loss of job, marriage breakup, etc.). A pupil may feel he needs to get along better with others but unless he attends more classes, he will be expelled from school. The counselor might ask the client or consultee what would happen if the problem were not resolved. Here, the consequences seem more severe for expulsion than for lack of friends and so it warrants more immediate intervention.

Aversive consequences will be different for different people. Because individuals differ in their tolerance for stimulation, examining the aversive or negative consequences of the problematic behavior for the client and significant others provides a useful method for judging the intensity of behavior. For example, the degree of noisiness of Jerry's playing in the classroom is determined by the teacher who reprimands him. While one teacher may ask him to "be quiet," another may send him out of the room.

By examining what has happened in the past with the same people under similar conditions, the counselor and client can better predict the consequences of the client's behavior and weigh them accordingly. Some possible counselor statements might be:

What might happen if this problem is not resolved?

What happens after this specific behavior occurs?

What would likely happen to you if _____ occurred?

Once this is determined, it is helpful to know which problem can be corrected most easily, considering resources and constraints (Criterion 3). What forces (people, situations) stand in the way of problem resolution? What resources exist that could help solve the problem? For example, a mother who feels trapped by her children may list going to school to complete an advanced degree as a goal. Lack of money for a baby sitter and her husband's resistance are obstacles, however. Some possible counselor statements are:

What are some things that might prevent this problem from being solved?

What are some things that will help you resolve the problem? *The fourth and last criterion for prioritizing concerns is the identification of problems which require handling before other problems can be solved.* For example, it makes little sense to work on improved academic behaviors (assignment completion, grades) if the child attends school infrequently. Likewise, before a child can learn to play with others, he must stop calling them names. The counselor might ask: "What would happen if this problem were solved? Would the client make more friends, make better grades, feel better about himself?"

OPERATIONALIZE PROBLEM

Translate Labels Into Behavioral Terms

Often, the client expresses her concern(s) through the use of a label or labels. For instance, she may state feelings of "depression" or "nervousness"; or a teacher may refer a child who is "rude" or "aggressive." While these labels offer a general indication of the problem area, they have different meanings for different people. They can be used, however, as a beginning place to get to behavioral definitions. For example, the client may say she's depressed, by which she means she can't get out of bed, doesn't eat, and doesn't get dressed. *After labels are identified, specific behaviors which are observable and whose presence or absence can easily be confirmed by two or more people can be determined.* Examples of labeling rather than describing specific behaviors are as follows:

disruptive	rude	anxious
depressed	unmotivated	anti-social
aggressive	incorrigible	nervous

Example Exercise

From the referring problems listed below, determine the ones which make use of labels.

1. Girls say no when I ask them for dates.
2. I'm just miserable and figure there's no use in trying anymore.
3. I'm really nervous all the time.
4. Jack gets out of his seat during discussions, talks out in class, and writes on other students' papers.

5. Jack is a bully.
6. Susan can't get along with other children.
7. John is a show-off.

Answers

Examples 2, 3, 5, and 7 use labels. Examples 1 and 4 describe specific problem behaviors.

In an intake interview with a client or an initial interview with a teacher or parent who is referring a client, behavior labels will be used. Initially the client or referring agent should be allowed to speak of the problem behavior in his own terms. This will help establish rapport and, at the same time, give the counselor a general idea of the type and range of problems experienced. After this has been done, the counselor should determine if the behavior has been discussed in terms of labels or specific behaviors. If the former is the case, she should translate the label into behavioral terms.

When only behavior labels are used, the counselor really doesn't know the specific problem behaviors to be changed nor the behaviors which the client or referring person wants to promote. This obviously makes the goal of counseling somewhat vague. On the other hand, a behavioral analysis specifies the undesirable behavior, helps elucidate some of the factors maintaining the undesirable behavior, and specifies the desirable behaviors which should replace the undesirable ones. This kind of analysis is beneficial in designing a treatment plan because the goals are clearly articulated.

In operationalizing the label, the counselor directs the client to give specific, concrete examples of behavior which led him to use the specific label he chose. For instance, if the client says he's too aggressive, the counselor may ask exactly what is meant; e.g., "Give me an example of what you mean by aggressive or describe a situation in which you were too aggressive." This proceeds until the counselor has a clear idea of what is meant by "aggressive." An example of operationalizing the label "too aggressive" follows:

1. The client verbally disagrees with others' statements of opinion, contrary to what he actually believes.
2. The client calls people who disagree with him "misinformed" or "stupid."

3. On occasions, the client asks persons who disagree with him if they'd like to "settle it outside."

An example of a behavioral translation in a counselor-client interchange follows. The teacher is referring Johnny because of "disruptive classroom behavior."

Teacher: Johnny has been disturbing the whole class more and more. He's driving me crazy.

Counselor: When you say Johnny disturbs the class, what do you mean? Does he throw things, scream, hit students? Tell me exactly what he does.

Teacher: He usually gets very aggressive with people around him.

Counselor: Un-huh. Do you mean he hits someone, calls names, takes things from other students, or what?

Teacher: Well, he usually calls someone a name and if the person calls him something back, he either starts punching or says, "I'll beat you up after school."

Counselor: Okay, I'm getting the idea now. When he starts name calling or hitting, what do you do?

Teacher: Well, I used to tell myself I should be patient and try to help him, but now I just can't stand it any longer. He keeps the room in constant uproar.

Counselor: Uh-huh, but what specifically do you do? Do you take him to the principal's office, punish him, or just tell him to stop?

Teacher: When he calls someone a name, I say, "Please stop the name calling," and if he starts hitting, I get his hands and hold them if I can. When he's so angry that I can't control him, I send him to the office.

Counselor: Okay, this helps me understand what's going on. Now, when Johnny is doing what you want him to, what do you do?

Teacher: Just cross my fingers and hope it will last. I ignore him really because I'm afraid I may say something that will set him off again.

Example Exercise

For the following labels, substitute two specific behaviors which are directly observable and can be validated by two or more persons.

1. rude

2. depressed

3. anxious

4. anti-social

5. disruptive

Answers

1. a. interrupts a conversation when two or more people are talking
   b. pushes other students back so he can be first in line
2. a. says, "I'm depressed"
   b. cries at least three times a day
3. a. talks rapidly
   b. talks about something else when asked about his family
4. a. steals objects from stores
   b. has vandalized public property three times in the past month
5. a. throws objects at other children
   b. slams books on desk

IDENTIFY STIMULI AFFECTING PROBLEM

Once the problem behaviors have been defined in behavioral terms and prioritized according to importance, the counselor must isolate those stimuli which precede and follow the problem behavior and control its occurrence. *That is, the counselor attempts to identify those stimuli which elicit problem behavior and specify the reinforcing or punishing stimuli which follow it.* For example, a student may be trying to study, but every time he opens a book, he thinks of an argument he's had with his girl friend. His thoughts are punishing, then, and prevent him from concentrating.

Determine When Behavior Occurs

It is sometimes difficult to specify the antecedents which set the occasion for problem behaviors. By determining when the problem occurs, however, the counselor can often detect what causes or at least precedes the problem behavior. For example, a child may receive negative statements from Father only when he yells while Father is trying to watch the news. The time when the child yells (while Father is reading) elicits or sets the problem off in this situation.

    The time of the problem can serve also as a cue in identifying situational events. For example, a wife may initially report that little interaction takes place from Monday through Friday when her husband arrives home from work. If interactions do occur about this time on the weekend, it might suggest that the husband is tired or fatigued during the week when he gets home from work and just doesn't feel like talking. Often, the time of the event (e.g., noon, evening) and the situation (e.g., dinner) are related.

Determine Situation Where Problem Occurs

In some cases, the situation or place the problem occurs elicits or sets off the problem behavior. These antecedent conditions are often neutral stimuli which become conditioned as a result of being paired with an aversive stimulus. For example, a bicycle may initially be a neutral stimulus for a child, but every time he climbs on it, some big kids threaten him and say they will take the bike. Thus, whenever he sees his bike, a fear reaction is elicited. Similarly, students who have had a negative test-taking experience may generalize this anxiety to all test-taking situations. For this reason, it is important to determine the situation in which the problem occurs. Furthermore, by determining where the problem occurs, one can identify the appropriate setting for intervention.

Determine What Is Maintaining the Problem Behavior

For operant behavior, such as talking and many motor reactions of the skeletal-muscular system, the controlling conditions are reinforcing or punishing stimuli. For example, when Bill cuts into line ahead of other children, he is positively reinforced by receiving his ice cream before others. Aversive or punishing consequences might occur in the form of Bill's cutting into line and the teacher's requiring him to stay in for recess. Sometimes there can be both reinforcing and punishing consequences for the same behavior. In the above example, Bill may receive the ice cream cone (positive consequence) and then be sent home or reprimanded (negative consequence). Likewise, a child may avoid punishment by not admitting a misbehavior while another child who admits it is punished. Thus, lying or cheating may be maintained by the conditions which follow it. When the child is caught emitting certain behaviors, she is severely punished; aversive consequences or punishment often provide an incentive for the client to modify the problem behavior.

57

The counselor might gather information concerning what is maintaining the problem behavior with the following questions:
When is the problem most severe; least severe?
Why do these situations differ?
What people are part of this problem?
Why are these people, and not others, involved in the problem?
What sets the problem off?
What happens that is good or positive after the problem occurs?
What happens that is negative or bad after the problem occurs?

The counselor can listen to the client's narrative and then transform it into a three-column table. The following narrative is an example:

Mr. Zerface complained of the attention-seeking behavior of one of his pupils, Jim. Whenever Mr. Zerface discussed a math problem, Jim talked out loud. Mr. Zerface told him to be quiet. Jim continued to talk out and Mr. Zerface threatened to send him to the office. Jim attended to the lesson then, but Mr. Zerface did not respond positively to his attentiveness; he just expressed that he was happy for some relief. Jim got up to go stand at the pencil sharpener, and Mr. Zerface told him to sit down. Jim walked slowly to his seat, thumping boys in the back of the head. Mr. Zerface sent Jim to the office, and Jim was placed in isolation. This type of scenario occurred about five times over a one-month period.

The counselor, using this case, can record the narrative in terms of antecedent (stimulus) events, behaviors, and consequent events. See the chart in Table 4.

It is important to note that the consequent event (e.g., Mr. Zerface said, "Sit down") may also serve as the antecedent for Jim's next response (e.g., Jim thumped boy next to him). In addition, when Jim listened to Mr. Zerface, the teacher ignored him and the positive behavior was extinguished. When Mr. Zerface threatened Jim, he behaved inappropriately. As shown here, a pattern of events which occurs repeatedly likely will produce conditions which are maintaining the undesirable behavior.

In this instance, the counselor could identify the pattern by recording Jim's behavior and its consequences. For example, Jim exhibited problem behaviors on four occasions, and in each instance the

Table 4. *Identifying Patterns That Maintain the Undesirable Behavior*

Time	Antecedent event	Behavior	Consequent event
9:10 - 15	1. Mr. Zerface discussed math problem.	2. Jim talked out loud.	3. Mr. Zerface said, "Be quiet."
9:15 - 25	3. Mr. Zerface said, "Be quiet."	4. Jim talked out loud.	5. Mr. Zerface said, "You're going to the office."
	5. "You're going to the office."	6. Jim attended to lesson.	7. Mr. Zerface ignored him.
	7. Mr. Zerface ignored him.	8. Jim sharpened his pencil.	9. Mr. Zerface said, "Sit down."
	9. Mr. Zerface said, "Sit down."	10. Jim thumped boys in head.	11. Mr. Zerface said, "Go to the office."
	11. Mr. Zerface said, "Go to the office."	12. Jim went to the office.	13. Isolation.

problem behavior was attended to by the teacher. Furthermore, when the desirable behavior occurred on two occasions, it was either ignored or punished. This illustrates how a quantifiable assessment of those conditions which are controlling the positive and negative behavior can help to generate hypotheses for the most appropriate intervention.

Example Exercise

In the following statements, identify the antecedent condition, behavior, and consequent event.
1. During lunch time, others laugh and duck when Bobby throws objects.
2. Jack gets his way in the hall when he threatens others.
3. When the teacher asks a question, Mary responds and the teacher praises her for participating.
4. When John's parents criticize him, he goes out with a friend and sniffs paint.
5. When Charles wants to go out with the boys, he starts an argument with his wife, acts more and more angry, and then storms out of the house.

Answers

In the first statement, *eating lunch* is the antecedent condition which elicits *object throwing* (behavior) and is followed by others *laughing and ducking* (consequent event). In the second example, the *hall* may be a condition eliciting *threats* which are reinforced when *Jack gets his way*. In example 3, when the teacher asks a *question* (antecedent), it elicits a *response* (behavior) from Mary and is followed by a reinforcing consequence, *praise*. In the fourth example, *parental criticism* is the antecedent condition for *paint sniffing* which results in *good feelings or escape*. Finally, in the last example, the *desire to go out* elicits *initiating an argument* which is reinforced when Charles *storms out* and feels justified in doing so.

Make a Functional Hypothesis

A functional hypothesis is simply a determination of the stimulus conditions controlling the target behavior. If behavioral observations vary with particular stimulus conditions in more than one instance, then we hypothesize that those conditions are maintaining the behavior (e.g., Mr. Zerface reinforces Jim's inappropriate behavior and ignores his attending behavior).

When a functional analysis has been determined from the interview or preliminary observations, additional observations should be made to evaluate the validity of the hypothesis. It is possible that more than one type of antecedent or consequence is acting to maintain the behavior (e.g., teacher's attention and children's attention). In this case, the next step is to gather further observational data to determine whether the hypothesis is adequate.

CHECKLIST FOR DEFINING THE PROBLEM

Check yes in the spaces below as the procedure is completed. Then go on to the next step.

Completed?

1. *Identify all concerns.* _____

                              yes   no

  a. Administer checklists. ___ ___

2. *Select concern for counseling.* _____
  a. Identify problem of most immediate concern. ___ ___
  b. Identify problem, if any, that must be solved now. ___ ___
  c. Identify problem which requires handling before other problems can be solved. ___ ___

3. *Operationalize problem.* _____

4. *Determine when (time) behavior occurs.* _____

5. *Determine setting where problem occurs.* _____

6. *Determine what is maintaining the problem.* _____

61

a. Identify what elicits or sets off
the problem. _____ _____
b. Identify the positive consequences
of the problem. _____ _____
c. Identify the negative consequences
of the problem. _____ _____

PROGRAMMED EXAMPLES

Choose one or more phrases that most accurately complete the statements or answer the questions.

1. If a client says, "I can't get along with others," the counselor might first respond:
   a. Give me an example of what you mean by not getting along with others.
   b. Why does this happen to you?
   c. When does this occur?
   d. What are you doing to cause this to happen?

   You're correct if you answered (a). This response helps to provide a behavioral definition of "getting along with others." You might have asked, "What do you mean by getting along with others?" Each of these questions elicits concrete examples of the problem. The other responses ask questions which presuppose or assume a problem (b) and (d) or ask a secondary question (c). Unless one can specify the problem in behavioral or concrete terms, it makes little difference why or when it occurs.

2. Two major obstacles in identifying all client concerns are:
   a. the presenting problem may not be the issue of greatest concern.
   b. effective checklists are not available.
   c. the client frequently has difficulty describing problem behaviors and the settings in which they occur.
   d. clients don't know what their chief problems are.

   You're correct if you answered (a) and (c). Alternative (b) implies that clients must have a checklist from which to identify concerns, and statement (d) says clients don't know what their problems are. Neither of these statements is accurate.

3. When the client presents several problem areas, the counselor must establish priorities for treatment. To determine the problem of most immediate concern, the counselor might say:
   a. What problem would you like to talk about?
   b. Where does the problem occur?
   c. Have we discussed everything?
   d. Which problem is most important to you now?
   You're correct if you answered (d). This one asks the client which problem should be addressed first. Another way of determining problem priority is to specify a problem which has the most negative consequences if not handled immediately (e.g., what would happen if this problem were not solved?). The other responses (a), (b), (c) are unrelated to determining the most significant problem.

4. Once the problem behavior has been identified, the counselor must specify people or situations *which stand in the way of problem resolution*. The counselor in this case might say:
   a. What are some things that are getting in the way of this problem being solved?
   b. What is the problem?
   c. What seems to be causing this problem?
   d. How can we solve this problem?
   If you answered (a), you're correct. The other answers focus on the problem (b), the antecedent conditions (c), and possible solutions (d) while not addressing themselves to obstacles in the way of problem solution.

5. From the referring problems listed below, indicate those which are behaviorally stated:
   a. can't get out of bed in the morning
   b. feels anxious
   c. has low self-respect
   d. doesn't complete assignments
   If you answered (a) and (d), you are on target. Not getting out of bed and failing to complete assignments are problems which are behaviorally stated. That is, one can *see* or *hear* these behaviors and two or more people are likely to agree that they exist. The other two problems (b) and (c) fail to meet these criteria. One

cannot see or hear anxiety, but one may be anxious as determined by his avoidance of interpersonal situations.

6. Once the problem behaviors have been defined in behavioral terms and prioritized according to importance, the counselor must isolate those stimuli which precede and follow the problem behavior and control its occurrence. From the following list, determine those statements which might identify the conditions which maintain the problem behavior:
   a. What happens that is good after the problem occurs?
   b. When does this problem occur?
   c. Why does the problem occur?
   d. What do you think they were feeling in the situation when this occurred?

   You're correct if your answered (a) and (b). These responses identify those controlling conditions which precede and follow the problem behavior. The other responses, while asking why or what others were feeling, fail to identify the controlling conditions.

7. Given the following client narrative, answer the following questions. (If information is not provided, indicate this.)

   Jack was always complaining to his dormitory roommate, Jim. He would complain when he received a poor grade or when the food in the cafeteria didn't please him. This bothered Jack because the complaints often interrupted his studying. When the complaining occurred, Jim would sit and look at him or leave the room. Nevertheless, the complaints persisted.
   a. Where did the problem occur?
   b. When did the problem occur?
   c. What was the problem (stated in behavioral terms)?
   d. What were others doing that might be eliciting the problem behavior?
   e. What seemed to be maintaining the problem behavior?
   Answers:
   a. In their dormitory room.
   b. Information not provided.
   c. Jim's complaints of poor food and grades.
   d. Jack was studying.

e.   Jack would sit and look at him or leave the room.

CRITERION TEST

Choose one or more phrases that accurately complete the statements and follow other specific instructions.

1. If a client says, "I am depressed," the counselor might first respond:
   a.   Do you feel this way often?
   b.   What do you mean by the term depressed?
   c.   Why does this occur?
   d.   Who was present when you began feeling this way?

2. Because the presenting problem is often not the primary concern, the counselor's next step should be to:
   a.   determine the most important problem.
   b.   determine when the problem occurs.
   c.   determine an appropriate intervention.
   d.   specify other related problem areas.

3. To determine the easiest problem to treat, the counselor must ask:
   a.   Where does the problem occur?
   b.   What sets the problem off?
   c.   What forces stand in the way of this problem being resolved?
   d.   How have you been dealing with the problem?

4. To determine the most immediate concern, the counselor might ask:
   a.   When does the problem occur?
   b.   What would happen if this problem were not solved now?
   c.   What do you think is causing the problem?
   d.   Why do you think the problem is occurring?

5. The counselor often can determine what is controlling the problem by asking:
   a.   Why does the problem occur?
   b.   What happens before and after the problem occurs?
   c.   What would happen if this problem were not resolved?

    d.   What are some areas related to the problem?
6. The counselor often can determine what sets off the problem by identifying
    a.   how the client wants to resolve the problem.
    b.   what causes the problem.
    c.   when the intervention should be administered.
    d.   where the problem occurs.

7. Given the following client narrative, answer these questions:
(If information is not provided, indicate this.)
Marilyn, an employee at Job Corps, never seemed to get her work done. Her boss reported that she often arrived late to work and turned in incomplete assignments at the end of the day. When her boss received the incomplete work, he would ask why it hadn't been finished, and Marilyn would say that she or one of her family had been ill and that she hadn't had time to get everything done. Her boss would nod and tell her he was sorry about the family difficulty.
    a.   Where did the problem occur?
    b.   When did the problem occur?
    c.   What was the problem (stated in behavioral terms)?
    d.   What seemed to be maintaining the problem?

CHAPTER 3
CRITERION TEST ANSWERS
1. b
2. d
3. c
4. b
5. b
6. d
7. a. work; Job Corps
    b. early morning and end of day
    c. late arrival and incomplete assignments
    d. excuses and boss's sympathy

4 Observing and Recording Behavior

CHOOSE OBSERVATION METHOD

After learning to specify problem behaviors, the next step is to begin observing and recording important aspects of the behavioral change program (see Figure 4 showing steps). Systematic observation tailored to events of particular interest is a valuable and versatile technique that may be employed in the natural life settings of the home, school, and hospital, as well as clinics and community agencies.

Observers can range from indigenous community members (Wahler and Erikson, 1969) to the client himself (Lovitt and Curtis, 1969). But before any observational system can be implemented, the participants must be told what to observe and where to do it. However, it is not simply a matter of observing the client in the home or school; rather, settings within these environments should be specified in terms of the likelihood that they may provide the occasion for the client's deviant actions. Some preliminary investigations by Wahler and Cormier (1970) indicate that systematic interviewing of parents, teachers, and others who are in the client's presence on a daily basis can produce this kind of information. The interview checklist discussed in the previous chapter offers special guidelines for interviewers in conducting analyses of home, school, and community environments. Whereas informal parent, teacher, or peer reports of client behavior are not always reliable, reporting is more likely to be reliable when the observers use checklists as guidelines on where to begin their observations.

Observing behavior in the natural environment can present special problems. For example, parents and teachers often complain about the difficulties of recording a child's behavior at home and school. A teacher may find it extremely hard to monitor on-task behavior during a reading lesson, while this difficulty may not exist during a silent reading period. Therefore, it is advisable to select a setting that presents

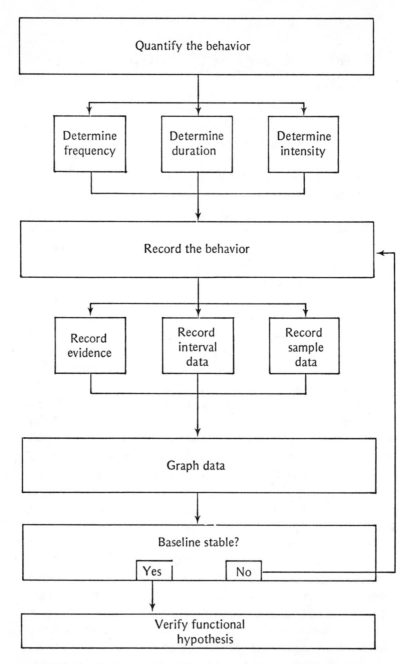

Figure 4. *Summary of Observing and Recording Behavior*

the fewest problems. As the observer becomes more competent in recording data, the observations may be shifted to more complex settings. When others in the client's environment cannot observe his behavior, the client can be taught to observe his own behavior.

ESTABLISH BASERATE

Once the counselor has identified a setting where behavior may be observed, he must establish a level at which the behavior typically occurs. The record of this level is usually referred to as a **baseline** or **baserate**. Knowledge of the client's baserate of behavior strengthens the counseling process in two ways. First, it permits the counselor to tailor the intervention to the client's needs. For example, there may be a number of children referred because of poor peer relationships. Observation of one child's interaction may reveal that she can initiate an interaction (e.g., "Hey, what are you doing?") but can't provide information (e.g., "None of your business"). Another child, however, may be watching what others are doing but won't stand near where others are playing. Thus, while the ultimate goal of both children is to play with others for a period of time, the baserates for these children may indicate that they are at different levels in relationship to their goal. Consequently, an appropriate starting point for one child would be to encourage close physical proximity to others, while the other child may need to be taught how to give information in a positive manner.

A second reason for establishing a baserate is to help the counselor and client monitor the client's progress in reaching his goal and to evaluate the effectiveness of counseling. For example, a client may be attempting to increase the number of positive self-thoughts he has. If the number of positive self-thoughts the client has before treatment is instituted has been recorded, this baserate can be compared to the average number of such thoughts per day during treatment and at end of treatment. This helps the counselor and client to determine whether the intervention has been effective.

In agencies where counselors want to get a baserate of behaviors, a modified natural setting may be used. For example, a child client and her parents may be placed in a room where the counselor can observe through a one-way mirror. Later, the counselor may teach the parents to observe and record the child's behavior at home. Then, observation of the client's behavior near termination of counseling can be compared with the baserate to provide an objective measure of the treatment. If little or no behavior change occurs, the intervention should be re-evaluated (see Chapter 11).

Quantify the Behavior

There are three attributes of behavior which can be measured: frequency, duration, and intensity. **Frequency** is the number of times a behavior occurs. **Duration** is the length of time a behavior occurs, and **intensity** is the degree to which a behavior occurs. While there is no one perfect measure of behavior, the efficacy of using these three attributes to measure it depends on the type of behavior under observation, the time available, and the setting in which it occurs. Furthermore, there is some evidence to suggest that several measurement operations used together are better than a single measurement operation used alone (Eyeberg and Johnson, 1974).

Determine Frequency Frequency is the generally preferred type of data for several reasons (Froehle and Lauver, 1971).

1. Frequency involves only counting.
2. Frequency is the attribute of most importance in a problem situation.
3. Observations can be made any place since no equipment is needed.

Frequency can be recorded and expressed in three ways: as total amount, as an amount per unit time, or a percent. The total amount is usually of less interest than the amount per unit of time (rate of behavior) and the amount per unit of opportunity (percent of behavior).

Many problems are definable in terms of rate. Behavior which is excessive (excuses) or deficient (low number of positive statements to spouse) involves the rate at which something is occurring. Having dates, missing spelling words, or complying with parental demands may be best expressed as a percentage. If a parent were concerned about the rate at which children ignored parental commands, she might chart the behavior as shown in Table 5.

To compute the rate of behavior, merely divide the number of times a behavior occurs (frequency) by the amount of time. For the data shown in Table 5, the ratios would be 2, 2¼, and 3. If the observer has reason to believe that a behavior varies according to the time of day, he should record the behavior during the same time period each day.

Table 5. Charting To Determine Rate of Behavior

Date	Time observed	No. of hours	No. of target behaviors	Rate
10/4	6:00 p.m. - 8:00 p.m.	2	4	
10/5	5:00 p.m. - 9:00 p.m.	4	9	
10/6	4:00 p.m. - 9:00 p.m.	5	15	

Determine Duration   The duration measures the length of time a behavior occurs. Behaviors such as crying, sleeping, or studying may be best measured by duration. However, sometimes the criteria for the occurrence of a behavior may include both frequency and duration. For example, the frequency of crying may be tallied, with crying behaviors defined as "crying noise" which lasts for five seconds or more. Similarly, it may be important to know that someone studies, but it is not as important as knowing how long that person studies.

In the following example, the counselor and a college student discuss a strategy for monitoring study behavior:

Client: Once I get to the library, I have trouble staying in my seat.

Counselor: How long are you able to stay in your seat?

Client: Oh, I don't know. Maybe 10 minutes, maybe 15.

Counselor: Okay, our time is just about up. We've been talking about your inability to stay in your seat. I'm wondering if before our next session you could take this timer and start it each time you sit down to study. Each time you get up, stop the timer and record the amount of time you were in your seat. On this chart, you might jot down what is happening or what you are thinking when you get up.

A sample chart is shown in Table 6; this chart provides not only the frequency but also the duration of time spent studying. In addition, the counselor can determine from it what the client is thinking or what others are doing to cause the client to stop studying.

Determine Intensity   Accurate measures of intensity of a behavior generally require electronic equipment. However, while there are physiological measures for recording tension, these instruments are often expensive and not available to the practitioner. Until such instruments are available, the counselor can use several inexpensive measurement operations which have a fair degree of validity and reliability. For

71

*Table 6. Client Self-Observation To Determine
Frequency, Duration, and Circumstances*

Date _____

	Time started	*Time got up*	*Remarks*
1.	_____	_____	_____
2.	_____	_____	_____
3.	_____	_____	_____
4.	_____	_____	_____
5.	_____	_____	_____
6.	_____	_____	_____
7.	_____	_____	_____

example, the counselor can develop rating scales which measure the intensity of fear, depression, or other covert behaviors. These ratings can be made by the client or others periodically as a regular part of treatment.

Ratings over time can be valuable if they are annotated by critical incidents that can link variations to specific situations. Figure 5 shows

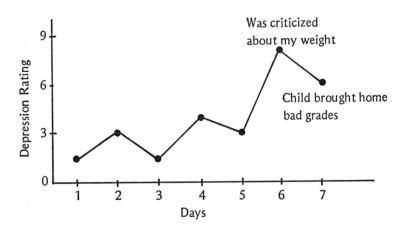

Figure 5. Linking Behavior Ratings To Specific Situations

how this can be done. Such an annotated record can be used by the counselor to generate hypotheses about events which may control the problem. For example, in the above illustration, the client felt more depressed when she was criticized about her weight and when her child brought home bad grades. A record of these incidents can be facilitated by having the client keep a daily log.

There are a number of other salient behavioral dimensions which can be charted over time. Some examples follow.

1. Extent to which client feels anxious

1	2	3	4	5	6	7	8	9
Not				Somewhat				Very
anxious				anxious				anxious

2. Extent to which the client feels he is understood

1	2	3	4	5	6	7	8	9
Not				Somewhat				Very
understood				understood				understood

3. Extent to which client feels sad or depressed

1	2	3	4	5	6	7	8	9
Not				Somewhat				Very
sad				sad				sad

4. Extent to which client feels he is appreciated or liked

1	2	3	4	5	6	7	8	9
Not liked				Somewhat				Very much
at all				liked				liked

In some instances, intensity becomes a critical factor in determining the definition of the target response. For example, in a study by Hart et al. (1964), crying was defined in a way to distinguish it from whining by requiring the observer to record an instance of crying only when it was loud enough to be heard at least 50 feet away.

Record the Behavior

When the counselor looks at behavior and makes a record of what he sees as it occurs, he is engaging in observational recording. There are three principal ways to record behavior:

1. Record evidence
2. Interval data
3. Sample data

At least one of these will be appropriate for a given client problem. After learning about each of these methods, the counselor can choose the best one for a given problem and use it, ignoring the others.

Record Evidence Some academic problems *leave evidence* that you can count to measure the degree of the problem. Incorrect problems on work sheets can be counted, and the number incorrect or percentage incorrect shows the degree of the problem. Attendance, achievement test scores, percentage of problems not finished, number of homework assignments not completed, and pages of work not finished all measure low skill levels, low academic ability, or low motivation. For problems of this sort, it is helpful to arrange for the client to have about the same amount and kind of work each day and to keep a record of the unsatisfactory performances (number unsatisfactory/number assigned) each day for several days (preferably successive days).

Example Exercise

Given the following, indicate those which leave evidence:
1. positive thoughts
2. destroyed property
3. positive interactions
4. smoked cigarettes
5. negative statements
6. assignments completed
7. anxiety

Answers

Numbers (2), (4) and (6) are correct. In each instance one can see evidence of something tangible that indicates a problem.

Evidence is an inexpensive, unobtrusive measure which doesn't affect the way the client normally responds in a situation. For example, the presence of a counselor in a classroom may alter the typical behavior of the children. On the other hand, the counselor might infer the child's on-task behavior from the number of assignments she completed and the recorded grade. In the latter example, the student would be unaware that her behavior is being observed. The best measurement in this case might be both the unobtrusive measurement (grades, assignments completed, etc.) and the obtrusive measurement (on-task behavior).

Example Exercise

Given the following three examples, indicate which measurement procedure(s) might bias the observation:

1. Mrs. West, the counselor, is trying to determine if Billy is working at his seat. She sits in the corner facing him and records a mark each time he is off task.
2. Mrs. Stotler, Billy's teacher, keeps a record of the number of assignments Billy has completed and the number correct.
3. Mrs. Stotler looks up each hour and records whether Billy is on or off task.
4. The counselor from the Mental Health Clinic goes to Billy's home to observe interactions between him and his mother.

Answers

Numbers (1) and (4) are correct. The first example characterizes an obtrusive measure which would likely bias the observation. The last example also would be an obtrusive measure because the mere presence of the counselor would likely contaminate the interactions. In the second example, the teacher is recording evidence that is already there, and Billy is unlikely to know that special attention is being given to him. Likewise, in the third example, unless the teacher looks at Billy in a very conspicuous manner, he is unlikely to know that she is observing him.

Record Interval Data *The chief advantage of the interval recording method is that it gives an indication of both the frequency and duration of the behavior observed.* Each observation session is divided into equal time periods to make an interval recording. The observer then records the occurrence of a behavior during these intervals. In Figure 6 that follows, the observer has recorded whether a student was on or off task during a two-minute observation period. If the student was off task at any point during each 10-second interval, it was scored as off task; otherwise, the student was on task. *The major disadvantage of the interval recording method is that it usually requires the undivided attention of the observer.*

The interval size will generally vary from five seconds to one

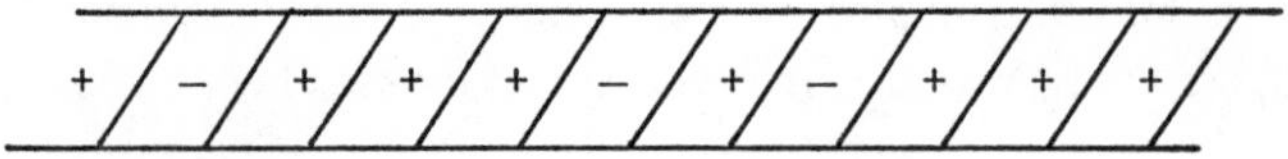

+ = On task
− = Off task

Figure 6. An Example of Interval Recording

minute in duration, depending upon (a) the rate of the response and (b) the average duration of a single response (Gelfand and Hartmann, 1975). For high-rate behaviors (e.g., behaviors which occur 20 to 30 times per hour), the interval should be sufficiently small so that two complete responses could not occur in a single interval. On the other hand, the interval should be as long as the average duration of a single response (e.g., social interaction). Intervals of three to five minutes would likely result in an underestimate of the frequency of the target behavior and might also result in an underestimate of behavior change.

There are two primary ways data can be counted by using the interval approach. Target behaviors can be (a) counted on the basis of the proportion of the interval (e.g., a check (✓) or yes might be recorded if the behavior occurred during 50 percent of the interval) or (b) a yes or check (✓) could be recorded if the target behavior occurred at any time during the interval. The latter method requires less judgment on the part of the observer and thus is likely to be a more reliable method (i.e., two or more people are likely to agree when the behavior does or does not occur.)

Record Sample Data   This technique is similar to interval recording, except that it does not require continuous observation. Data sampling or time sampling is a good way to record behaviors which occur infrequently but may last over a long period. Many behaviors (talking) are continuous, i.e., difficult to tell when they start or stop. For example, observers (counselor, supervisors, teachers) often cannot be present the entire time a problem is occurring. Instead, they can observe or sample the behavior at fixed time intervals by scoring the presence or absence of such responses within a short time interval.

There is a variety of ways to count behaviors, depending upon the rate of behavior. For low-rate behaviors, such as fighting or enuresis, each instance may be tallied as a complete event. For high-rate behaviors, such as talking or playing with others, another approach may be

76

necessary. One procedure is to make one observation per unit of time and simply record yes or no. That is, the observer (counselor, teacher, other) might look up each 10 seconds and record whether the behavior exists or doesn't exist (see Figure 7).

Playing With Others	Seconds	10	20	30	40	50	60
	Yes						
	No						

Figure 7. Recording Behavior by Time Sampling

The preceding example also permits the observer to monitor several things during one period so long as the schedules of these events are different. That is, if three behaviors (crying, hitting, and screaming) are occurring simultaneously, it is more difficult to reliably record each behavior than if each behavior occurs separately. If two or more behaviors occur concurrently, it might be appropriate to include both behaviors for a response definition. Nevertheless, single response classes (talking to someone) tend to be more reliable than multiple response classes (aggressive behavior composed of hitting, throwing objects, screaming, etc.).

Graph Data Discrete behaviors often can be recorded on prepared forms so that a tally is made each time the behavior occurs. This type of chart is similar to the one described in Figure 7. Each chart should contain the date, name of the client, operational definition of the target behavior, time(s) of observation, length of interval, and the frequency or duration of the target behavior.

Once the behavioral data has been recorded for several recording periods, graphing it is quite simple. The first step is to draw two lines at right angles, one horizontal and vertical, so that they meet at the lower left-hand corner, as in Figure 8.

The next step is to enter consecutively the time periods for recording, with the first on the far left and the last on the far right. Usually a summary label which describes the recording period (e.g.,

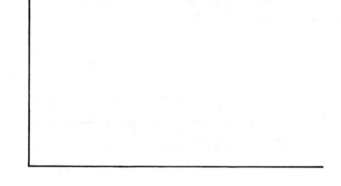

Figure 8. Axes for Graphing Behavioral Data

minutes, hours, days, months) is entered and then the recording periods are represented by numbers, as in Figure 9.

It is also essential to determine the maximum number of target behaviors noted during any recording period. For example, if one were to record 17 instances of a target behavior on day 5 and no other day

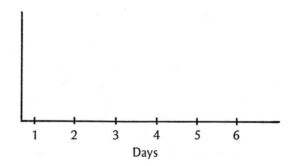

Days

Figure 9. Axes for Graph with Recording Periods Entered

had a greater number, then 17 would be the maximum number to show on the vertical axis. The vertical axis would be divided, then, into 17 equal units starting with 17 at the top of the axis and running to 0 at the bottom, as in Figure 10.

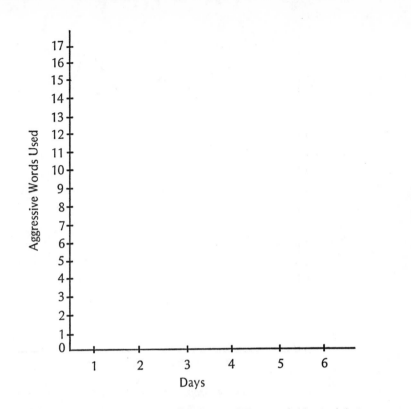

Figure 10. Axes for Graph of Behavioral Data with Vertical Axis
Numbered and Labeled

To the left of the vertical axis one should enter the target behavior (i.e., aggressive words). The final step is to enter the data. Above the number representing the observation period, a dot should be entered opposite the number of target behaviors observed in that recording period. Similarly, above the representation for the second observation, a dot should be entered opposite the number of target behaviors observed in that period. This process is continued until all the periods are presented. Figure 11 shows an example based on target behavior rates of 10, 12, 15, 13, 17, and 11.

Once the data have been plotted, lines should be drawn to connect the observation points. Assuming that these are pretreatment observations, it is customary to print Baseline or Baserate above the graphic analogue.

79

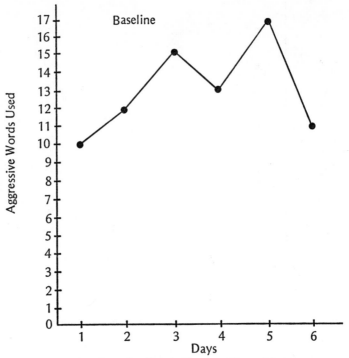

Figure 11. *Axes for Graph Showing Plotted Behavior*

Example Exercise

Examine the following graphs and then answer the questions:

1a. What is the unit of measurement in the graph shown in Figure 12?

1b. What is the length of time measurements were taken?

2. Given the following information, label the axis and plot the data on the graph in Figure 13.

   Joe smoked 10 cigarettes on Monday, 8 on Tuesday, 9 on Wednesday, 14 on Thursday, 11 on Friday, 8 on Saturday, and 11 on Sunday.

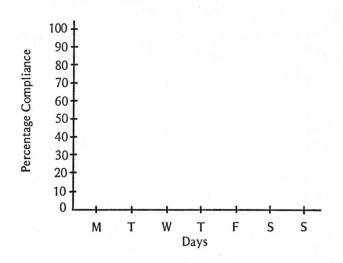

Figure 12. Graph Showing Measurement Units (Question 1)

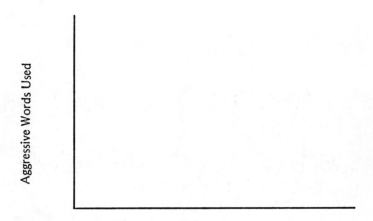

Figure 13. Graph for Labeling and Plotting (Question 2)

Answers

1a. percentage of compliance
1b. seven days

2.

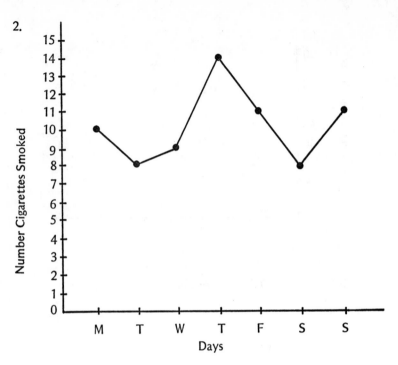

Figure 14.   Graph Showing Labeling and Plotting
(Answer for Question 2)

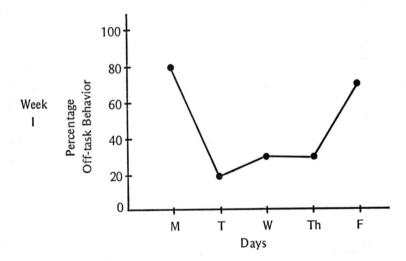

Figure 15.   Recording To Establish Baseline—Week I

amined. For example, if a counselor were to chart a child's on-task behavior over a three-week period, she might get the data shown in Figures 15, 16, and 17.

During the first week, the child's behavior fluctuated greatly. On Tuesday, the percentage of off-task behavior dropped from 80 percent to 20 percent (well within the acceptable range). The behavior remained stable through Thursday but then rose sharply to 70 percent on Friday. This baserate would be inappropriate since there are sharp fluctuations on Monday and Friday. In addition, there appears to be a general increase in off-task behavior from Tuesday through Friday. If the counselor is to obtain a stable rate of behavior, she should continue to observe the child's behavior (see Figure 16).

During the second week, the baseline of behavior declined. This is often characteristic of a client who is recording his own behavior. The act of recording a behavior (e.g., smoking, eating, studying) makes one more aware of his behavior and causes him to engage in it less or more frequently, whichever is more desirable. In effect, the reactive effect of self-observation serves as an intervention to reduce the problem behavior. Once again, the counselor would want to continue to observe the child's behavior to see if it can reach a stable level.

In the third week, the child's behavior finally reached a stable level. That is, there was little deviation from the mean and no upward or downward trends (see Figure 17).

The dotted line indicates that the mean level of off-task behavior is 40 percent. This appears to be a reliable frequency of the target behavior. With this established, the counselor, teacher, child, or other concerned parties can then decide if they wish to intervene. It might be noted here that while this example provides an illustration of different trends in the data, it may be unrealistic to assume that a counselor can spend three weeks getting baseline data. Counselors are often pressured by others (principals, parents, courts) to intervene and alleviate the problem immediately.

For behaviors such as time off task, a period of five to seven days is generally adequate to establish the typical frequency of the client's behavior. For other behaviors, however, the fluctuation across time may be more extreme. Fighting, negative comments, or drinking may depend upon influences in the client's environment and consequently

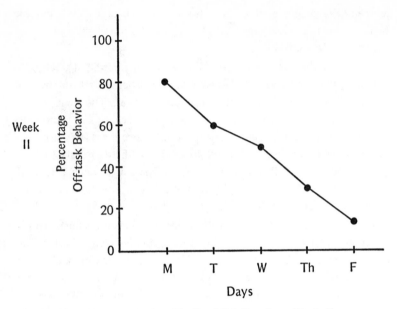

Week
II

Figure 16. Recording To Establish Baseline—Week II

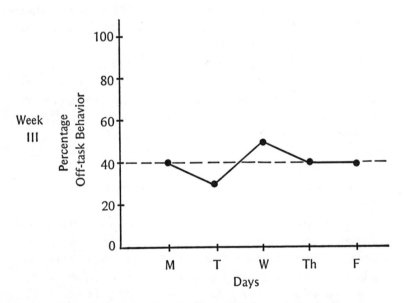

Week
III

Figure 17. Recording To Establish Baseline—Week III

warrant an extended baseline period and greater sampling of behavior. Baseline observations should be recorded until stability of frequency has been established (Tharp and Wetzel, 1969).

VERIFY FUNCTIONAL HYPOTHESIS
Once the baseline has stabilized, the counselor and client should verify the functional hypothesis (see page 60). That is, if the antecedent (e.g., child talk) and consequences (e.g., teacher reprimand) occur in more than one instance, then the hypothesis (e.g., the child's off-task behavior is elicited by child talk and maintained by teacher reprimands) has some verification. In some cases where the counselor may only be able to observe the consequence of the target behavior, those events (e.g., cues) which precede the behavior may be difficult to determine. If the hypothesis is not verified, however, observation should continue. Otherwise, a new hypothesis should be stated.

CHECKLIST FOR OBSERVING
AND RECORDING BEHAVIOR
Check yes in the spaces below as the procedure is completed. Then go on to the next step.

Completed?

1. *Quantify the behavior.*   _____

                                    yes   no
   a. Determine frequency.   ___   ___
   b. Determine duration.   ___   ___
   c. Determine intensity.   ___   ___

2. *Record behavior.*   _____
   a. Record evidence.   ___   ___
   b. Record interval data.   ___   ___
   c. Record sample data.   ___   ___

3. *Graph data.*   _____

4. *Establish stability of baseline.*   _____

5. *Verify functional hypothesis.*   _____

PROGRAMMED EXAMPLES

Choose one or more phrases that accurately complete the statements and follow individual instructions for other problems.

1. Self-observation is most effective when
   a. the client can accurately discriminate between problematic and nonproblematic situations.
   b. others cannot observe the client's behavior.
   c. the client wants to observe his behavior.
   d. the behavior is of interest to the client.

   You're correct if you answered (b). Unless this condition is met, the other alternatives are not important.

2. Jack has three dates the first month, five dates the second month, two dates the third month, and two dates the fourth month. What is his rate of dating behavior?
   a. 3.5 per month
   b. 3 per month
   c. 4 dates per month
   d. 4.5 per month

   If you answered (b), you are correct. The rate of behavior is computed by dividing the number of times a behavior occurs (12) by the amount of time (4).

3. The easiest way to record the intensity of a behavior is to teach the client
   a. to locate the appropriate electronic equipment.
   b. to count the behavior.
   c. to rate the behavior.
   d. to describe the behavior.

   If you answered (c), you are correct. Ratings are easy to tabulate over time. While equipment may produce an accurate estimate of the severity of the problem (a), it is also expensive and difficult to locate. The second and fourth alternatives (b) and (d) provide only indirect measures of severity.

4. Data sampling (or time sampling) is a preferred recording procedure

a. when behaviors are continuous.
b. when duration of the problem is in question.
c. when evaluation is necessary.
d. when conditions prohibit continuous observation.

If you answered (a) and (d), you are correct. When it is difficult to determine the onset and termination of a behavior (a), or when there is little time to observe the behavior (d), time sampling is preferred. The second and third alternatives bear no direct relationship to the time sampling procedure.

5. One advantage of a graphic representation is that
   a. it offers an illustration not found in narrative of behavior.
   b. it tests the significance of the behavior change.
   c. it tests the reliability of the data.
   d. it tests the validity of the data.

Hope you selected (a). Graphs provide a representation of the behavior not found in a narrative. The other three alternatives are unrelated.

6. List two factors which are important reasons for establishing a baserate of the client's behavior.

   a.

   b.

The two factors are: (a) to determine how often the behavior occurs and (b) to compare baseline level with the intervention level to determine the effectiveness of the intervention.

7. List three reasons why frequency is the preferred mode of observation:

   a.

   b.

   c.

Three reasons are: (a) it involves only counting; (b) it is the attribute of most importance; and (c) it can be made without equipment.

8. List three attributes of behavior which can be measured (observed and recorded):

   a.

   b.

   c.

   Three measurable attributes are (a) frequency; (b) duration; and (c) intensity.

9. Given the following information, draw a graph, labeling the axis and plotting the data. Mrs. Hougler had frequent headaches. During Week 1, she had 5 headaches, 4 during Week 2, 10 during Week 3, 3 during Week 4, and 5 during Week 5.

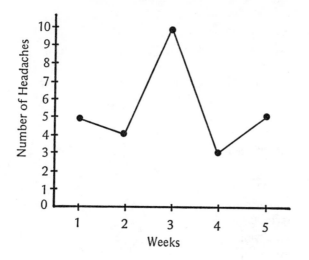

Figure 18. Graph Plotting Frequency (Answer for Question 9)

10. Using information from Question 9, decide if baseline should be continued or stopped. Why or why not?
    Answer:
    Baseline should be continued because there appears to be a sharp fluctuation in headaches from Week 3 (10) to Week 4 (3).

CRITERION TEST

Choose one or more phrases that accurately complete the statements and follow individual instructions for other problems.

1. When others are unable to observe the client's behavior, the counselor might
   a. set goals for counseling.
   b. design the intervention.
   c. teach the client how to observe his behavior.
   d. terminate counseling.

2. Willie got into 6 fights the first week, 8 fights the second week, 4 fights the third week, 4 fights the fourth week, and 5 fights the fifth week. His rate of behavior is
   a. 4.6 fights per day.

89

b. 5.4 fights per week.

c. 4.8 fights per week.

d. 2.7 fights per month.

3. Rating a behavior on a scale is another way to measure the
   a. frequency of behavior.
   b. duration of behavior.
   c. intensity of behavior.
   d. rate of behavior.

4. When behaviors are not discrete, _____ is a preferred procedure.
   a. recording evidence
   b. time sampling
   c. interval recording
   d. baseline recording

5. Graphing behavior is desirable because it
   a. provides an illustration of behavior not found in a narrative.
   b. provides a measure of validity and reliability.
   c. describes the behavior.
   d. quantifies the behavior.

6. List two factors which are important for establishing a baserate of behavior.

   a.

   b.

7. List three reasons why frequency is the preferred mode of observation.

   a.

   b.

   c.

8. List three attributes of behavior that can be measured (observed and recorded).

   a.

   b.

   c.

9. Given the following information, label the axes and plot the data on the graph below. Mrs. Fansler was frequently anxious. On a scale from 0 (low) to 10 (high), she rated the degree of her anxiety as 6 on Monday, 4 on Tuesday, 7 on Wednesday, 4 on Thursday, and 6 on Friday.

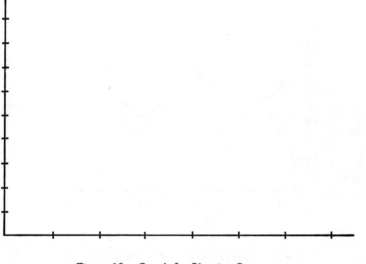

Figure 19. Graph for Plotting Data
(Criterion Question 9)

10. Should baseline be stopped or continued? Why?

CHAPTER 4
CRITERION TEST ANSWERS

1. c
2. b
3. c
4. b
5. a
6. a. to determine how often the behavior occurs.
   b. to compare the baseline level with the intervention level to determine the effectiveness of the intervention.
7. a. it involves only counting
   b. it is the attribute of most importance
   c. it can be made without equipment
8. a. frequency
   b. duration
   c. intensity
9.

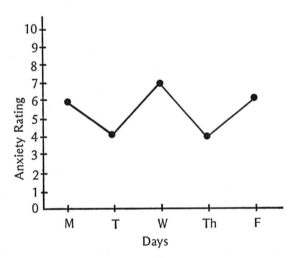

*Figure 20. Labeling Axes and Plotting Data
(Answer for Criterion Question 9)*

10. Baseline should be stopped because there appears to be little fluctuation in anxiety.

5 Formulating Treatment Goals

The third chapter described how the counselor can help clients operationalize their concerns, i.e., express them in terms of specific behaviors. This chapter is designed to help the counselor determine behaviors the client wants to learn or unlearn. That is, the third chapter focused on "what is" happening with the client while this chapter focuses on "what should be" happening. See Figure 21, showing steps for formulating treatment goals.

The performance discrepancy between "what is" and "what should be" generally takes two forms. Either (a) the client is not performing the way *she* expects to perform, or (b) the person is not performing the way *others* expect her to perform. In the first case, the client is likely to seek help because she is not as happy as she thinks she could be. In the second case, the person is not functioning according to the way others want her to perform.

The latter case often poses a problem in goal setting because the goals of the referral source may be different from the client's goals. Where mutual expectations are shared between client and referral source, desired change is more likely to occur. That is, clients who set goals for themselves instead of trying to reach goals set by others are likely to be more successful in attaining them. In either case, however, it is crucial that desired behaviors be specified and mutually agreed on by counselor and client for the counselor to be effective in helping the client.

The process of formulating goals not only specifies "where we are going" but also provides standards by which the counselor can demonstrate her effectiveness in getting there. Subgoals and objectives which are specifically defined can be used to measure the client's progress from week to week. Measurable goals provide direction in counseling and prevent the counselor from claiming effectiveness without demonstrating it (Hackney, 1973).

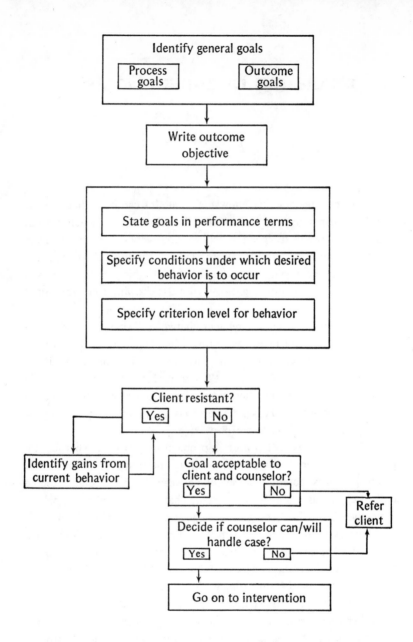

Figure 21. Summary of Formulating Treatment Goals

IDENTIFY PROCESS AND OUTCOME GOALS

Counseling goals can be categorized into two types: process and outcome. **Process goals** refer to therapeutic conditions and are *chiefly the counselor's responsibility*. On the other hand, **outcome goals** refer to specific behavioral changes for which the client is seeking help. Outcome goals are *shared goals which both the client and counselor agree on.*

Example Exercise

In the following situation, identify possible counseling goals and then categorize them according to process and outcome goals.

The client is a 19-year-old girl who said she came for counseling because she needed advice on how to help a friend. She said her friend is married but is flirting with a lot of guys, and she fears that either her friend and/or her friend's husband will get hurt. As the interview proceeded, however, the client indicated that she has never had a date and has conflicting feelings about it. On the one hand, she'd like to go out, but on the other, she's afraid she wouldn't know what to say or do. In groups of people, she never initiates a conversation with males although she responds if they ask her specific questions. She views herself as unattractive and overweight, and she says she doesn't know if she ever wants to get married since she's seen so many bad marriages. Although the client talked readily for awhile, she then became reticent and only talked in answer to specific questions.

Answers

Some possible goals are:
1. improve her self-esteem
2. improve her social skills
3. reduce her fear around males
4. resolve her conflicting feelings (the approach-avoidance conflict concerning males)
5. initiate dating behavior
6. build a relationship in which she feels free to express herself

The first five are outcome goals and the last one is a process goal. That is, the first five relate to behaviors the client should exhibit following counseling, and the last refers to conditions the counselor should provide during counseling.

WRITE OUTCOME OBJECTIVES

After general goals are determined, the counselor's task is to help the client identify specific outcome objectives for treatment, i.e., *what the client should be doing, at what level,* and *under what conditions,* when treatment is completed. Each of these aspects of outcome objectives is treated in greater detail in the following pages.

State Goals in Performance Terms

After goals are stated generally, it is helpful to translate these into specific behaviors which are measurable. That is, the counselor must ask *what* behaviors the client will be performing to demonstrate he has reached his goal.

In cases where behaviors are to be decreased or extinguished, desirable behaviors to replace these should be identified. For example, a father complains that his eight-year-old son starts pounding on the floor when someone comes to the door. The father states the goal as getting Jack to stop pounding on the floor when someone comes to the door. However, the counselor should ask the father to specify what Jack *should be* doing at that time (e.g., playing quietly with his sister, reading a magazine).

In the counseling situation, the specified terminal behaviors describe what the client will be doing as a result of counseling. Vague descriptions of the terminal behavior (e.g., motivated, functioning effectively) would not be acceptable since there would be no way to measure them reliably. For example, if the client's goal is to have a conversation with another person, the objectives might be stated in terms of what the client will be saying or activities he and his friend may participate in together (going to the movie or bowling alley, etc.).

Establishing behavioral objectives plays an important role in tailoring counseling techniques to a particular client. Without specifically stated client objectives that people can see or hear, individualizing counseling for the particular client becomes very difficult. Unfortunately, the ambiguity of counseling goals has long influenced traditional therapies to continue the same type of counseling for all clients. Determining the most appropriate intervention to reach a specific objective places more responsibility on the counselor, for it is the counselor who tries to "fit the client" rather than expecting all clients to fit one type of counseling (Thoresen, 1972).

Example Exercise

Translate the general goals listed earlier into specific operational objectives:

1. improve her self-esteem
2. improve her social skills
3. reduce her fear around males
4. reduce her conflicting feelings (the approach-avoidance conflict concerning males)
5. initiate dating
6. build a relationship in which she feels free to express herself

Answers

1. The client will make fewer negative self-statements and more positive statements about herself.
2. First in a role-playing situation and later in a real-life situation, the client will be able to initiate a conversation with males, carry on a conversation, and terminate a conversation.
3. The client will initiate _____ conversations with _____ males next week.
4. This goal is closely related to Goals 2 and 3 and will likely be resolved when they are reached.
5. The client will have _____ dates during the next _____ week/s.
6. The counselor will show understanding of the client's feelings. This objective will be reached if at least 50 percent of the counselor's responses are at Level 3 or above on the Carkhuff (1969) scales.

Specify Conditions Under Which Desired Behavior Is To Occur

Once the counselor and client have agreed on the goal, the next step is to specify the conditions under which the goal behavior will occur. The conditions of the desired behavior will often be situation specific. That is, it may be easier for a child to talk with his brother than to a boy who sits in front of him. Consequently, the goal may be first to talk with his brother, then to his peer. Likewise, it may be easier for a student to take a test alone than with a group of people. In each case, the set of conditions may serve as sequential steps or objectives to the desired behavior.

The conditions under which the behavior is to occur also make it clear where the behavior is to take place. For instance, a teacher may wish a child to say "hello" or "good morning" to her, but she would be displeased to have a student phone her at 5:00 a.m. to wish her "good morning." Likewise, she doesn't want to place students into a compliance situation by attempting a chorus response, "Good morning, Miss . . . ." The teacher in this instance might prefer that a child say "good morning" or "hello" to her as he enters the classroom in the morning.

Similarly, suppose that a child wishes to play with others. This seems to be a worthwhile behavior, but more specific information such as the setting in which the behavior is to take place is needed.

Whom do you want to play with?

Where do you want to play?

Quite obviously, if the child wishes to play with specific peers in the neighborhood, it would be helpful if this behavior occurred in a place where it could be monitored. That is, if possible, the setting selected for the goal behavior should be one in which the behavior can be observed and recorded.

Specify Criterion Level for Behavior

Once the goal has been specified in performance terms and the setting in which the behavior is to occur has been identified, an acceptable level of performance must be established. This criterion specifies *how well* and *how often* the behavior is to be performed. For example, to comply with parental requests is not a useful indicator of successful performance of the desired behavior. However, if the goal is restated as "complying with parental requests 80 percent of the time up to 10 requests," then the counselor, client, and others will know when the goal has been reached. This helps to insure that observers (e.g., parent, client, etc.) will *agree* whether the objective has been met.

In determining the criterion level of success, it is essential to specify how the client is behaving relative to the goal behaviors:

How often does the goal behavior occur?

How often does the undesirable behavior occur?

These questions help to establish the baserate of the behavior (see Chapter 4 for a review of baserate). The baserate provides a standard by which to measure the client's progress toward her goal and to determine the amount of learning needed by the client to achieve the desired outcome. The level of performance for the first step or objective should be low enough to insure success and consequent rewards. As a practical rule of thumb, it is better to set the criterion too low than too high. If the criterion is too high, the desirable behavior often will not occur. If the criterion is set too low, the counselor may have wasted a trial (Tharp and Wetzel, 1969), but this is less harmful than the failure of the behavior to occur.

The question of criterion generally becomes, "Can the individual perform the behavior?" If he can, successive steps or objectives are designed to lead toward the final terminal objectives. To illustrate, when a person learns to drive a car, there are a number of successive operations to be performed (turning on the ignition and lights, shifting gears) before he can drive. Likewise, a child who wants to develop interpersonal relationships may need to first learn how to stand close to individuals; secondly, initiate a conversation; thirdly, maintain a conversation; and finally, ask someone to do something. Successive approximations through the use of intermediate objectives maintain the client's motivation to achieve terminal behaviors or objectives.

DEAL WITH CLIENT RESISTANCE

Goal setting with the client is not always an easy task. Some clients are very resistant to setting goals. This may be manifested several ways. Some clients simply change the subject; others will deal only with generalities such as wanting peace of mind; still others may only want to talk about the behavior of other persons which disturbs them, rather than their own behavior.

When clients resist, it is important to determine why they're resisting and what current behavior they are trying to protect. For instance, a student may want to get along better with his teacher, but he doesn't like giving up the attention he gets from his peers when he misbehaves. Likewise, the alcoholic may be aware of the negative consequences of her drinking, but she wants to hang on to its pleasurable effects. In this case, it is the counselor's task to help identify the reasons for resistance, i.e., the reinforcing properties of the current behavior and then determine if substitute reinforcers can be given for desirable behavior. For instance, in the case of drug abusers, the counselor may work with the client on ways to have "natural highs."

DETERMINE IF GOALS ARE ACCEPTABLE
TO CLIENT AND COUNSELOR

If the client is not resistant or if the resistance has been dealt with, the goal(s) should be agreed on by both counselor and client. Although the client should actively participate with the counselor in formulating treatment goals, there are some times when the counselor may not agree with the client's goals. When the client commits acts that are illegal (stealing) or detrimental to himself (taking pills), society or others, the counselor must consider existing legal and societal sanctions. When the counselor disagrees with the client's goals, he should discuss the issues involved. The counselor in this case might say:

Are you aware that this is illegal?

I can't support a goal which is harmful to others.

In some cases, the client may want to set self-defeating goals. For instance, a child who is having difficulty with peer relationships might choose to ignore this until he gets into the next grade. Also, clients may choose to avoid unpleasant situations or select inappropriate behaviors such as being able to beat up every kid in his class. Sanctioning such goals reinforces a client's avoidance of the problem or reinforces the selection of inappropriate means of handling a problem situation. To discourage avoidance, the counselor might say, "You've said you're unhappy about the situation now. What can be done now? What goal can we set for this week?"

Sometimes clients may make poor goal choices. For example, a bright student may choose to attend a trade school only because his best friend is enrolled there. Although the counselor recognizes the boy's right to make his own decision, she may feel that the boy's reason for attending the trade school is unjustified. These kinds of situations should be discussed by the counselor and client. If they cannot reach agreement on the goal, the counselor should assist the client in obtaining professional assistance elsewhere.

DECIDE IF COUNSELOR WILL/CAN HANDLE CASE

Once the counselor and client have decided on an acceptable goal, the counselor might decide whether he has the necessary skills to handle the case and if he is willing to do so. It is important to make that decision only after an appropriate goal has been specified. Counselors may often steer a client toward a goal they are capable of treating, i.e., rather than selecting a goal that is likely to alleviate the client's problem, the counselor establishes a goal which fits within his own set of techniques. Refusal to design an intervention which focuses on the presenting problem allows the counselor to avoid learning important skills necessary for helping people with their problems.

There are several things the counselor can do to decide whether she has the necessary skills to help the client reach his goal. First, the counselor should familiarize herself with techniques that have proven beneficial in alleviating a specific problem. Also, she should become familiar with interventions relevant to the problem behavior. Then, she can check out her skills in these areas through responding to programmed texts, attending selected workshops where supervision is provided, and checking with other counselors on how to handle specific cases. If the counselor feels competent to handle the case, the intervention should be related to specific goals of the client. If, on the other hand, the counselor feels inadequate to handle the case, the client should be referred elsewhere.

CHECKLIST FOR FORMULATING TREATMENT GOALS
Check yes in the spaces below as the procedure is completed. Then go on to the next step.

Completed?

1. *Identify general goals.*   _____

   yes   no

   a. Identify process goals.   ___   ___
   b. Identify outcome goals.   ___   ___

2. *Write outcome objectives.*   _____
   a. State goals in performance
       terms.   ___   ___
   b. Specify conditions under which
       desired behavior is to occur.   ___   ___
   c. Specify criterion level for
       behavior.   ___   ___

3. *Client resistant?*   ___   ___
   If yes,

a. Identify gains from current
behavior.   ___   ___

If no,

a. Goal acceptable to client
and counselor?   ___   ___

b. Counselor can/will handle the
case?   ___   ___

4. *Go on to intervention.*   _____

PROGRAMMED EXAMPLES

Choose one or more phrases that accurately complete the statements
and follow individual instructions for other questions.

1. An objective should be stated in performance terms. Of the fol-
    lowing objectives, which are so stated?
    a.   Be able to interact more effectively with peers.
    b.   Decrease acting-out behavior in the classroom.
    c.   Increase number of assignments completed and turned in.
    d.   Decrease aggression.

    If you chose (c), you are correct. This goal states the desirable
    behavior to be emitted. Responses (a), (b), and (d) are not specific
    enough that two or more persons could easily agree when they're
    achieved. In addition, responses (b) and (d) do not specify the
    desirable behaviors to replace the undesirable ones.

2. Given the following objectives, indicate which ones specify the
    setting or conditions:
    a.   In the next History class, the client will volunteer four com-
         ments.
    b.   The student will arrive on time each week.
    c.   The client will initiate at least three conversations per day.
    d.   The client will study psychology in the library for 45 minutes
         each day for the next two weeks.

    If you answered (a) and (d), you are right. "In the next History
    class . . .." and "In the library . . .." express where the desired
    behavior will occur. Objective (b) does not state where the student
    will arrive or what is meant by "on time." Likewise, in Objective

(c), *to whom* and *where* the client will initiate three conversations are not specified. Unless conditions for the terminal behavior are specified there is no way to know whether the behavior has occurred.

3. Statements of performance objectives include three pieces of information:
   a. conditions, time, and location.
   b. performance, condition, and criterion.
   c. performance, time, and criterion.
   d. performance, condition, and percentage.
   B is the only correct answer. While the other responses contain some elements of good performance objectives, they do not contain everything. Unless the event or behavior to be achieved is known, when or where the performance will occur is stated, and how well or how much must be performed, precise measurement cannot be achieved.

4. Given the three basic criteria for an adequate performance objective, indicate which objectives meet all the criteria:
   a. Jim will report five positive self-thoughts or more per day by May.
   b. The student will arrive on time for class.
   c. Given a coached client, the trainee will demonstrate attending behaviors during at least 10 minutes of a 15-minute interview.
   d. The student will demonstrate improvement in math.
   If you answered (a) and (c), you are correct. Each of these objectives contains statements of performance, conditions, and criterion. While response (b) contains the performance (student arrival) and conditions (to class), it fails to specify the criterion (how many times). Response (d) fails to specify *how* the student will demonstrate improvement in math and *how much* improvement must be made.

5. To facilitate the specification of conditions under which the desired behavior is to occur, the counselor might say:
   "You'd like to have more friends or to be invited to play with

others more often.

a. "Part of this is going to depend on how you behave with others."

b. "Why are they leaving you out now?"

c. "It really is a bad feeling to be left out by the other children, isn't it?"

d. "Can you name some people you especially want to include you and some times when you want to be included?"

D is the best response because it asks for information about persons and times relevant to the goal. Response (a) is a judgmental statement which doesn't specify goal conditions; neither do responses (b) and (c). B is a lead for more information and (c) is a reflection of feelings.

6. An example of setting an acceptable level or criterion for goal performance is

a. making good grades.

b. improving grades.

c. making all A's and B's on the report card for second grading period.

d. performing up to ability level for the remainder of the school year.

C is the correct answer because it specifies the criterion level for success and states the goal in performance terms. Responses (a) and (d) are not stated in performance terms because phrases like "good grades" and "working up to ability level" may be interpreted differently by different people.

7. There are some times when the counselor may disagree with goals which the client sets for himself. Which of the following goals might be unacceptable to a counselor and why?

a. Increase the number of assignments completed and turned in.

b. Show I'm not a sissy by beating up some kids in my class.

c. Make friends with younger kids and ignore my classmates.

d. Decrease the number of temper tantrums I have.

You are correct if you answered (b) and (c). Responses (a) and (d) are both worthwhile and acceptable goals. However, (b) is questionable because it involves hurting someone else or perhaps may be self-defeating because the child is unable to beat up other children in the class. Response (c) is also likely self-defeating because rejection by classmates makes school very unpleasant. Child friendships with younger children after school may help, but this solution avoids the larger problem.

CRITERION TEST

Choose one or more phrases that accurately complete the statements.

1. Given the three basic criteria for an adequate performance objective, indicate which objectives meet all the criteria:
   a. Mary will initiate a conversation with her husband three times each day.
   b. The student will listen to the teacher five times each day.
   c. The client will arrive for counseling.
   d. The husband and wife will spend time together.

2. Which of the following objectives are stated in performance terms?
   a. The student will show his appreciation.
   b. The student will be less anxious.
   c. The client will show improvement.
   d. The client will initiate conversations.

3. An acceptable statement of criteria would be
   a. completing an average of 80 percent of assigned work for a four-week period.
   b. improving grades.
   c. reducing anxiety 80 percent of time.
   d. listening to others 60 percent of the time.

4. Indicate which response includes the three criteria for a performance objective:
   a. goal, percentage, condition
   b. performance, time, location
   c. performance, condition, time
   d. performance, condition, criterion

5. Indicate which client goals might be unacceptable to the counselor:
   a. avoiding an unpleasant interpersonal situation
   b. decreasing the number of fights
   c. initiating conversation
   d. arriving to school on time

6. Indicate which objectives specify a setting or conditions:
   a. The student will be able to interact more effectively with others.
   b. The student will arrive to class on time.
   c. The client will report three positive self-thoughts.
   d. The client will initiate two conversations.

CHAPTER 5
CRITERION TEST ANSWERS
1. a
2. d
3. a
4. d
5. a
6. b

6 Determining the Appropriate Intervention

After the counseling goal has been established, a counseling strategy must be decided. That is, after one or more target behaviors have been selected, the counselor must decide what she is going to do with the client to bring about the stated goals. More importantly, she must determine a logical rationale for selecting and using a particular technique. London (1972) argues that the critical question about systematic treatment is the relevance of the treatment to the person's manifest problem and to the rest of his life. In the most comprehensive sense, the relevant question to be answered is: "What treatment, by whom, is most effective for the individual with what specific problem, and under which set of circumstances?" (Paul, 1967). See Figure 22 for steps in determining appropriate intervention.

Given any specific counseling theory, a person can build a rationale for working with almost any problem within that theory. For instance, the client-centered therapist can readily give and support a rationale for dealing with most problems, consistently using a client-centered approach. On the other hand, the behavior therapist, the rational-emotive therapist, and the analyst can do likewise. However, the counseling experience must meet the client's goal and not simply reflect the counselor's own theoretical biases (Hackney and Nye, 1973). For instance, some approaches are differentially effective, depending on the presenting problem. Phobias have been treated most effectively and quickly through desensitization, and there is little or no evidence of symptom substitution. On the other hand, subjects with free-floating anxiety respond better to a rational-emotive approach (Lazarus, 1971).

Desirable results can sometimes be derived from a number of treatments brought to bear on a problem. For example, a client who is fearful of interacting with others might need relaxation training first to reduce this fear. After overcoming the fear, he also will need to be

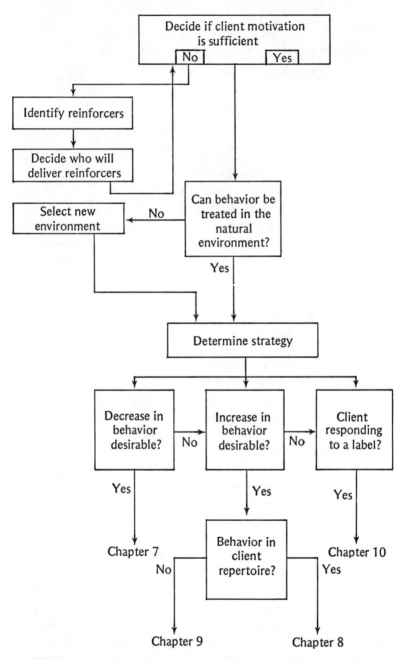

Figure 22. Summary of Determining the Appropriate Intervention

taught the necessary social skills for interacting with others in a given situation.

As a minimum requirement for deciding upon the intervention, the counselor must make a thorough analysis of the context in which the behavior occurs. That is, he must have asked and gotten answers to the following questions before determining an appropriate intervention:

1. What is the problem and how often does it occur or how intense is it?
2. What are the consequences of the problem behavior to the client and to others in his environment (e.g., teachers, friends, parents, etc.)?
3. What resources does the client have in his environment to promote change?
4. What effects would a change in his behavior have on the client and others?

DETERMINE IF CLIENT HAS SUFFICIENT MOTIVATION

Before deciding on a counseling intervention, the counselor *first* must determine if the client has sufficient motivation to work toward attaining the outcome objective (Winborn, Hinds, and Stewart, 1971). Unless the client is sufficiently motivated to continue the counseling process, little success is likely to be realized.

There are a number of reasons for insufficient client motivation. First, adequate reinforcers are not always available, either for the client or the consultee (e.g., parent, teacher, employer). And, sometimes when they are available, they aren't dispensed for various reasons. For instance, a principal may frown upon a teacher who wishes to use a reward system in her class. Or, a husband may discourage a wife from losing weight because he receives more attention for his "cutting remarks" than any benefit derived from his wife's loss of weight.

The secret in providing client motivation is to make the client target behavior reinforcing to the person who can give reinforcers. If the wife were to lose weight and improve her appearance, her husband may be more likely to offer positive comments. Likewise, he may encourage her progress if she is able to do more around the house or participate in more activities (swimming, tennis) with him.

DETERMINE IF TREATMENT
CAN OCCUR IN NATURAL ENVIRONMENT

In many cases, the client's behavior cannot be reinforced in the natural environment (home, school, etc.). Parents may possess reinforcers and may even agree to deliver them on contingency, but their marital relationships or other problems prevent them from doing so. In homes where alcoholism, drug addiction, or marital discord is prevalent, the client may receive contradictory or inconsistent cues from persons in his environment. For example, a child may be told by his father not to go outside while the mother tells him it is all right. This pattern of inconsistency is undesirable. It may result in the child's serving as the scapegoat for the marital difficulties. In this case, placement of the child in a new environment may be necessary.

Often, it is appropriate for the counselor to work with both the client and her family. For example, many communities have Re-Ed or alternative schools where children receive help and where the child's placement is contingent upon the family's receiving marital counseling and/or parent training. If this isn't possible, the counselor might enlist the cooperation of social agencies, such as welfare offices, drug and alcohol rehabilitation programs, or half-way houses, to provide useful services. Knowledge of specific agencies and their services would be helpful to the counselor.

DETERMINE STRATEGY

In providing guidelines for determining an appropriate treatment, there is an inherent danger of the implication that only one particular approach can work with a particular type of problem. While this is not the case, certain interventions *have* proven more effective than others in ameliorating certain classes of behavior problems. There is some overlap, however, in interventions which are effective in changing behavior problems. Although each strategy is discussed separately in this chapter, in actual practice, more than one intervention will likely be used in helping a client (Gottman and Leiblum, 1974). For example, systematic desensitization may be employed to reduce examination anxiety, but a study-skills program and training in assertive responses for talking with teachers and classmates may be warranted as well. Likewise, a counseling goal may be to decrease a child's fighting behavior, but it is also important to determine which desirable behaviors (studying, talking to others) will take the place of fighting. The intervention package may include a variety of approaches including response decrement, response increment, response acquisition, and cognitive restructuring.

Decide If Decrease in Behavior Is Desirable

Some behaviors occur in excess in either their frequency, intensity, duration, or inappropriateness and consequently need to be reduced. Examples of such behaviors at the operant level include stealing, fighting, arguing, and lying; excessive respondent behaviors include fears and anxieties. In addition, some clients may make excessive use of appropriate behavior. That is, they know what to do and say in certain situations, but they do it so much they are obnoxious to others, e.g., the person who is constantly asking for help in class or the client who apologizes excessively for cancelling an appointment.

After identifying the excessive behavior, the counselor must ask if the conditions following the excessive behavior are helping to maintain it. If so, it is necessary to teach others (friends, teachers, parents, etc.) to ignore it (extinction). The result should be a decline in the frequency of maladaptive behavior over time unless the target response (fighting, crying to get spouse's attention) is reinforcing.

Before using extinction, however, the counselor must answer the following questions to his satisfaction.

1. Can the behavior be tolerated temporarily?
2. Can an increase in behavior be tolerated?
3. Is the undesirable behavior likely to be imitated?
4. Can reinforcers be identified?

Unless the counselor, teacher, parent, etc. can consistently ignore the client's undesirable behavior, a different reductive procedure should be considered. Such a procedure might be removal of the client from the reinforcing situation (classroom, ward, etc.) or withdrawing the reinforcers from the client (alcohol, tokens, points).

When the behavior is under the control of conditions which elicit it (e.g., fear or anxiety reactions), systematic desensitization can be used to reduce anxious thoughts and open the way for more adaptive behavior. Before starting systematic desensitization, however, the counselor must ask if the anxiety is rational or if the client is avoiding a situation because he lacks the requisite skills to cope with it. If either of these conditions exists, desensitization is inappropriate. Otherwise, the client is taught relaxation responses to use while visualizing an anxiety-provoking situation. Due to the incompatibility of anxiety and relaxation, the client's anxiety decreases.

Decide If Increase in Behavior Is Desirable

Behaviors which already occur in the client's repertoire, but which are deficient, call for techniques that will strengthen them. Some examples of behaviors which may need to be strengthened are smiling, attending to the lesson, and interacting with others. Clients who manifest behavioral deficits frequently report negative subjective attitudes including anxiety, depression, or lack of self-confidence.

To strengthen behavior which is already in the client's repertoire, reinforcers in the natural environment (e.g., attention, approval, and praise) should be used initially. These reinforcers are easy to deliver, and behaviors which are under the control of the natural environment are more likely to generalize or maintain. In instances where praise or approval cannot control the individual's behavior, however, activity or material reinforcers can be used. Material or activity reinforcers may be necessary for young children or juvenile delinquents if social reinforcers have little relevance.

Determine If Behavior Is in Repertoire

When the client cannot perform the desired behavior (interacting appropriately with others, completing an assignment) because the behavior is not in his repertoire, these behaviors should be taught. To select the most appropriate procedure to teach new behaviors, the counselor should ask if the environment contains any models who exhibit the desired behavior. If so, it is not always necessary to actively teach new behavior patterns. Rather, the learning can be accomplished symbolically through observation of others. From observing the model show both the behavior and the consequences of that behavior, the client may inhibit or disinhibit previously learned responses as well as learn new ones.

If modeling proves to be unsuccessful or if the behavior to be learned is too complex, the counselor might utilize shaping procedures. Here, the desired total response is broken down into a series of steps which are necessary for mastery of the final response. Each smaller response is reinforced until it is under the client's control. Gradually, more accurate approximations of the final response are required before reinforcement is delivered. This continues until the entire response is learned. For example, in teaching a child to interact with others, reinforcement may initially be given for the child standing near others, then initiating conversation, getting information, and finally for providing information. Or, a person who is fearful of getting a job may be reinforced initially for role playing a job interview, then for completing a job application, then for calling about a job, and finally for going to an actual interview.

A third procedure which is helpful in learning new behaviors is role playing. Role playing or behavior rehearsal may be employed in a variety of therapeutic contexts—groups, home, or laboratory. It provides a chance for the client to practice and anticipate new responses with the opportunity for self-correction and feedback. Oftentimes, when clients manifest difficulties in social interaction, the main problem may not be so much a function of how to say something but rather what to say or do. Simple written information about what one might say or do in various situations may be helpful initially. Then behavioral rehearsal can provide a safe medium by which to practice the new behavior.

Determine If Client Is Responding To a Label

A person's internal responses affect his behavior, i.e., what he tells himself influences his feelings and behavior. Unrealistic anticipation of negative events produces debilitating anxiety which is difficult to cope with. Clients who have such an anticipation of negative events need to be taught more adaptive ways to think about things, rather than be taught to increase or decrease existing behaviors or taught new overt behaviors. Their emotional reactions may be viewed as responses to the way they label situations and not necessarily to the situations themselves. Thus, although their emotional reaction may be appropriate to the label they attach to a situation, the label itself may be basically inaccurate. For example, a person may feel upset in a situation he has mistakenly labeled awful or catastrophic, but it is the label and not his reaction that is inappropriate.

The individual who is behaving inappropriately often does so because his thoughts are irrational. For example, he may tell himself that other people should be different, that he should be loved by everybody, etc., and because this isn't the case, he feels angry or anxious. The anger and anxiety then keep him from constructively working on the situation itself. The problem is more likely to arise, then, from how a person interprets others' behavior than from their actual behavior.

The counselor's task is to help the client change his irrational thoughts to more rational ones. For instance, the client thinks, "Johnny doesn't like me. He should and because he doesn't, it's a catastrophe." The client is taught to restructure her thought to, "Johnny acts as though he doesn't like me. That disappoints me and I wonder what I can do about it." The latter thought elicits less anxiety than the former, allowing the client to more constructively think of alternatives.

Clients who mislabel situations often suffer from depression and anxiety. As stated earlier, anxiety can be reduced through systematic desensitization, but there is some evidence that systematic desensitization is more appropriate for situation-specific anxiety. On the other hand, learning not to respond to labels (cognitive restructuring) is most appropriate for generalized anxiety.

CHECKLIST FOR THE APPROPRIATE INTERVENTION

Check yes in the spaces below as the procedure is completed. Then go on to the next step.

Completed?

1. *Decide if client motivation is sufficient.*   _____

2. *Determine whether behavior can be treated in natural environment.*   _____

3. *Determine strategy.*   _____

	yes	no
a. Behavior decrease desired?	____	____
b. Behavior increase desired?	____	____
c. New skills need to be taught?	____	____
d. Client responding to a label?	____	____

PROGRAMMED EXAMPLES

Choose one or more phrases that accurately complete the statements and follow individual instructions for other questions.

114

1. What questions must the counselor ask before determining an appropriate intervention?
   a. What are the immediate and long-term consequences of the problem behavior to the client and his environment?
   b. What are the elements related to the problem?
   c. What resources does the client have in his environment to prompt change?
   d. What does the client think about the problem?

   You're right if you answered (a) and (c). It's important to know what is maintaining the behavior (a) as well as what resources the client can bring to bear on the problem(c). The second alternative (b) is inappropriate since the client has already determined the problem. The last alternative (d) provides little information.

2. Extinction is often appropriate when
   a. the client is making irrational statements.
   b. the rate of overt behavior is excessive.
   c. behavior does not occur in client's repertoire.
   d. duration and frequency of behavior are deficient.

   You're correct if you checked (b). Behaviors such as fighting and crying often are excessive and need to be decreased. The other alternatives warrant other interventions.

3. Before considering systematic desensitization for anxious behavior, the counselor must ask if
   a. the behavior can be tolerated.
   b. the problem behavior should be decreased.
   c. the problem behavior should be increased.
   d. the client is avoiding a particular situation because he lacks the requisite skills.

   If you answered (d), you are correct. Systematic desensitization is appropriate if the client is anxious. However, if the client lacks the necessary skills, then a skills-training package would likely be the appropriate intervention. We assume that the anxious behavior should be decreased (b) and that the client does not want to increase it (c) or tolerate it (a).

4. Positive reinforcement strategies are appropriate when

115

a. the client's behaviors are deficient.
b. the client lacks the necessary behaviors in his repertoire.
c. the client has obsessive thoughts.
d. the client feels depressed.

If you checked (a), you are correct. Behaviors which already occur in the client's repertoire but which are deficient call for strategies that will strengthen them. The other alternatives are not directly related to increasing appropriate behavior.

5. If the client's environment cannot be altered, the counselor might consider
a. contacting an appropriate service agency for assistance.
b. treating the client's behavior in another environment.
c. terminating the case.
d. repeating the treatment.

If you answered (a) and (b), you are correct. If the environment is responsible for the undesirable behavior and those in the environment are unwilling or unable to assist the client, then a new environment for treatment should be specified and an appropriate agency might be contacted to remediate the maladaptive environment. Terminating the case (c) or repeating the treatment (d) will do little to remove the problem.

6. If there are no models or the behavior to be learned is too complex, the appropriate intervention would likely be
a. zen therapy.
b. role playing.
c. shaping.
d. systematic desensitization.

You're correct if you checked (c). The complex behavior is broken into smaller steos. Each response is reinforced until it is under the client's control until the entire pattern is learned. Other procedures are ineffective in teaching complex behaviors.

7. Restructuring internal response patterns is effective when
a. the client doesn't like his old behavior.
b. the client's irrational or self-defeating thought patterns are

affecting overt behaviors.

c. the client is resistant to change.

d. the client lacks the necessary behaviors in his repertoire.

If you checked (b), you are correct. When the client is saying inappropriate or self-defeating things to himself and it is causing maladaptive overt behavior, cognitive restructuring is warranted. If the client lacks necessary behaviors in his repertoire (d), teaching these behaviors is the treatment of choice. Cognitive restructuring may or may not be effective when the client doesn't like his old behavior (a) and resistance (c) would be no easier to deal with from this approach than any other.

8. The counselor must make the following major determination before utilizing extinction procedures:

a. Is mild punishment appropriate?

b. Can the increase in behavior be tolerated temporarily, or is the behavior likely to be imitated?

c. Is the desirable behavior incompatible with the undesirable behavior?

d. Is extinction powerful enough to reduce the undesirable behavior?

If you answered (b), you are correct. Although (c) and (d) are appropriate questions, the critical issue is whether the individual's behavior can be tolerated briefly or whether others are likely to imitate it if extinction procedures are implemented.

9. If there is a risk of client failure, the most appropriate procedure might be:

a. cognitive restructuring.

b. in vivo desensitization.

c. group therapy.

d. role playing.

You're on target if you answered (d). Role playing provides the client an opportunity to practice new responses in an environment less threatening than the natural setting. The other techniques (a, b, and c) either do not teach new overt behaviors (a and b) or do not provide a simulated session to practice the new behavior (c).

Choose one or more phrases that accurately complete the statements.

1. When the rate of an overt behavior is too great, the counselor might first use
   a. cognitive restructuring.
   b. role playing.
   c. extinction.
   d. shaping.

2. To determine an appropriate intervention, the counselor must ask the following question(s):
   a. When should the intervention begin?
   b. Is the problem important to the counselor?
   c. What are the immediate and long-term consequences of the problem to the client and his environment?
   d. What resources does the client have in his environment to facilitate change?

3. When the client has the necessary behaviors in his repertoire but they occur at a low rate, the counselor might use
   a. role playing.
   b. cognitive restructuring.
   c. systematic desensitization.
   d. positive reinforcement.

4. Systematic desensitization is most effective when
   a. the client's anxiety is situation specific.
   b. the client's behavior is controlled by its consequences.
   c. the client is avoiding a situation because he lacks the requisite skills.
   d. the client has a poor self-image.

5. When there is a risk of failure or it isn't possible to use modeling or shaping, the most appropriate intervention would likely be
   a. relaxation.
   b. role playing.
   c. insight therapy.

d. systematic desensitization.

6. Extinction procedures are most appropriate when
    a. the problem behavior cannot be tolerated.
    b. the problem behavior can be observed.
    c. the problem behavior will not likely be imitated.
    d. the appropriate reinforcers for desirable behaviors cannot be identified.

7. When the client's environment fails to reinforce the desirable behavior, the counselor might consider
    a. treating the client's behavior in another environment.
    b. verifying the problem.
    c. terminating the case.
    d. contacting the appropriate service agency for assistance.

8. When the client's irrational or self-defeating thought patterns are affecting his overt behavior, the most appropriate intervention would likely be
    a. skills training.
    b. shaping.
    c. cognitive restructuring.
    d. role playing.

9. If there are no models available or the behavior to be learned is too complex, the most appropriate intervention would likely be
    a. shaping.
    b. role playing.
    c. cognitive restructuring.
    d. systematic desensitization.

CHAPTER 6
CRITERION TEST ANSWERS

1. c	6. c
2. c and d	7. a and d
3. d	8. c
4. a	9. a
5. b	

7 Decreasing Behavior

IF DECREASE IN OVERT BEHAVIOR IS DESIRABLE, TRY EXTINCTION

If the client presents a problem behavior she wishes to reduce, the counselor has a variety of alternative procedures available to him (see Figure 23 for steps). Probably the easiest procedure to use is extinction or mild punishment, e.g., the client loses privileges or other reinforcers. An extinction procedure reduces the probability of a behavior's occurrence by withholding reinforcers that customarily have been presented. For example, if it has been determined that attention from a peer is maintaining the aggressive behavior of an elementary school child in the classroom, the peer could be encouraged to stop attending to such behavior in hopes of extinguishing it. This will only work, however, if attention is rewarding. *In short, extinction is nothing more than ignoring an undesirable behavior or failing to reinforce it; if extinction is used effectively, the undesirable behavior will gradually weaken over time and finally disappear from the client's repertoire.*

Extinction is commonly used by people at one time or another. Parents, teachers, counselors, and marriage partners use extinction without being aware of it. A husband's eyes focus intensely on a basketball game while his wife talks to him, a teacher ignores a child who is holding up his hand, and counselors may ignore inappropriate verbalizations from clients. In each of these instances, knowingly or unknowingly, behaviors are being extinguished.

If the counselor wishes to use extinction effectively, she can do this in combination with other procedures. When undesirable behavior is ignored and desirable behavior is simultaneously reinforced, undesirable behaviors decrease at a faster rate. For example, Krumboltz and Hosford (1967) were able to increase verbal participation and decrease undesirable verbalizations for five participants in a group. The coun-

121

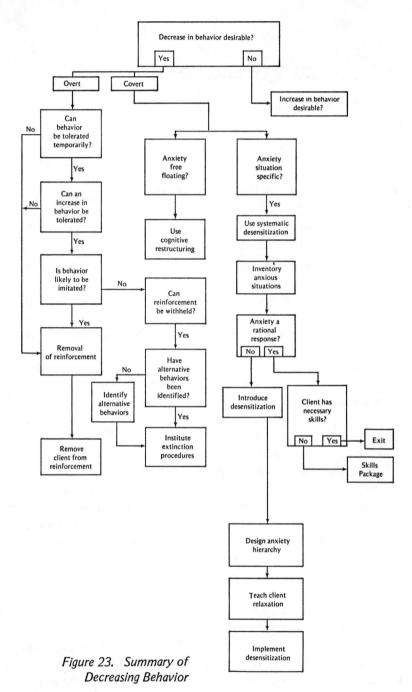

*Figure 23.   Summary of
Decreasing Behavior*

selor ignored a group member whenever he left the group or made inappropriate remarks, but he immediately reinforced verbal participation with attention and interest.

Ask a Series of Questions Prior To Using Extinction

Can the Behavior Be Tolerated Temporarily? If extinction is the chosen intervention, then the counselor must ask a series of questions to determine whether extinction can be applied with maximal effectiveness. If the counselor wishes to reduce the undesirable behavior, he must elicit the client's cooperation and determine whether the client and/or others can tolerate the present rate of behavior temporarily (Benoit and Mayer, 1974).

To make this determination, it is helpful to observe and record the actual rate that the behavior is occurring unless the behavior is too objectionable, e.g., hitting someone.

Behaviors such as fighting, drinking, or taking pills which have aversive consequences cannot be ignored. In this instance, mild punishment or some other faster-acting procedure should be combined with extinction to decrease the behavior.

Another reason why some undesirable behaviors cannot be ignored is that people around the client have difficulty tolerating the problems. For example, a teacher may prefer punishing or scolding a child for misbehavior rather than ignoring it. (Unfortunately, the misbehavior of the child may be reinforced by the teacher's attention, even if it is only scolding.) When asked if she can ignore it, the teacher might say, "If I let him get away with it, others will try to do the same." Similarly, the parent whose child has temper tantrums may find such behavior very difficult to ignore.

In other cases, persons around the client may prefer to ignore the behavior but because of the expectations of others (e.g., teachers, principal, neighbors, spouses, etc.) for punitive control, they are unable to do so. For example, a mother may attempt to ignore a child's verbal threats but cannot because the father retaliates by punishing the child and scolding the mother.

In addition, counselors must be sensitive to teachers or parents who are not able to tolerate common problems of a less severe nature. Tolerance levels differ, and the counselor must allow for these individual differences; otherwise, resistance toward extinction procedures will

123

develop. Because extinction procedures must be systematically implemented, it is not advisable for counselors to suggest extinction procedures to someone who lacks patience or who is under extreme personal pressure.

If the rate of the problem behavior in question cannot be tolerated temporarily or if other resistances exist (expectations from others), then the counselor probably should recommend that the teacher or parent reject extinction as the preferred intervention and consider some other procedure to decrease behavior.

Can an Increase in the Behavior Be Tolerated? There is a body of evidence to indicate that behavior which has been reinforced in the past will occur with greater frequency during the early stages of extinction. Thus, the client's problem behavior will actually get worse before it gets better. Temper tantrums, for example, may well soar to frightening intensities, initially mild dependency demands may culminate in a sharp kick in the shins, and negative attention-getting behavior may assume increasingly ludicrous forms (Bandura, 1969). Furthermore, certain frustration behaviors (e.g., crying, aggression) may accompany or replace the undesirable behaviors. As dominant modes of behaviors are extinguished, the client may use alternative courses of action that have proven successful on previous occasions in similar circumstances. This is no problem unless the new behaviors also are undesirable (e.g., complaining, crying). Here the counselor must extinguish both the problem behavior (talking to others during math) and the undesirable behavior which replaces it (complaining).

Teachers or parents can avoid problems associated with extinguishing a long succession of inappropriate behaviors by combining extinction procedures with rewarding competing responses. For example, a client can't be studying and crying or fighting at the same time. Consequently, the aim is to reward studying behavior.

Is the Behavior Likely To Be Imitated? Certain client problem behaviors are likely to be imitated by others who observe them. This is particularly true when others see the client as similar to themselves and when the client's problem behavior is rewarded. In cases where these behaviors are dangerous or may be imitated by others, extinction is an inappropriate procedure.

Can Reinforcement Be Withheld? It may sometimes be difficult to withhold reinforcement for the undesirable behavior. Schedules of reinforcement as well as the nature of the reinforcing consequences may obscure what is maintaining the behavior. It is difficult, for example, for parents to extinguish delinquent behavior which is maintained by peers. It also is sometimes difficult to determine which reinforcers are maintaining the behavior, particularly when the reinforcer is seldom presented. For example, an occasional smile or glance from someone may maintain acting-out behavior. On the other hand, other behaviors often cannot be separated from their reinforcing consequences. This is true of stealing, sex offenses, aggression, and the use of drugs or alcohol.

Where the reinforcer has been identified and a controlled environment exists, the counselor might enlist the cooperation of those who control the reinforcers. For example, if the teacher is having difficulty ignoring the behavior consistently, the counselor might sit in the rear of the room and signal the teacher when she is to ignore the undesirable behavior and reinforce the incompatible behavior. Subsequent praise for ignoring the behavior and a chart showing a decrease in the level of the problem may serve as a further reinforcer (Sulzer and Mayer, 1972). Likewise, arrangements can be made to praise students when they ignore the undesirable behavior. If this fails to work, the counselor might attempt to reward the entire group when the client responds in an appropriate manner. For example, the counselor might arrange with the teacher to provide a bag of candy after Mary initiates conversation with others 15 times, with each member in the group receiving a piece of candy. In this way, children are more likely to be near Mary and be more friendly toward her. Unless all reinforcers are identified and withheld for inappropriate behavior, some other reduction procedure should be considered.

If a client in a group counseling session gets a lot of attention for funny statements irrelevant to the topic, the counselor and group members can extinguish such behavior by removing reinforcement, i.e., by ignoring any irrelevant statement and attending to all appropriate statements.

Have Alternative Behaviors Been Identified? Extinction shouldn't be used alone. That is, when a behavior is removed from a client's repertoire, a desirable behavior should take its place. Consequently, a desirable behavior *incompatible* with the behavior to be extinguished should replace the bad behavior. For example, a mother may be encouraged by the counselor to ignore tantrums but attend to appropriate conversation. The teacher may attend to the child while working at his desk but ignore speaking out of turn. The counselor may attend to self-revelatory statements of the client but look away when the client talks about how "awful" all his neighbors and friends are. By providing an alternative behavior, the counselor can increase the probability that the problem behavior or accompanying frustration behavior (e.g., crying, complaining) will be extinguished. In this case, it is impossible to take something away without replacing it.

In the following excerpt from an interview, the counselor is attempting to reward positive behaviors and extinguish chronic complaints:

Client: Well, then, I had a headache and couldn't take the test. My back was hurting, too.

Counselor: (Looks in other direction and makes no response)

Client: The other day, I didn't feel so bad and got some of my work finished.

Counselor: Great! That must have made you feel good.

While the selection of alternative goal behaviors was discussed in Chapter 4, it is critical to reiterate the need to make sure that the alternative goal behavior is incompatible with the undesirable problem behavior. For example, if a student talks out loud in class (problem), the competing goal behavior might be to reinforce study behavior. However, if the payoff is for accuracy and completion of assignments, the student may continue to talk out once his work is completed. Here, the counselor should examine the number of assignments or amount of reinforcement given to help insure that the goal behavior is incompatible with the problem behavior.

INSTITUTE EXTINCTION PROCEDURES

Remove Reinforcement for Undesirable Behavior; Reinforce Desirable Behavior

Once each of the above questions has been satisfactorily resolved, the counselor is ready to institute extinction procedures. Here, the counselor encourages all those who are potential reinforcers of inappropriate behavior to work toward withholding the payoff following the undesirable behavior. Thus, this effort involves stopping an event that occurs

126

after (or along with) a response. It does not apply to stopping an event that occurs before the problem behavior. For example, if the teacher tells the child to study and the rate of study behavior decreases, she has not used extinction. The teacher's telling the child occurs before studying so it is not a reinforcer. Extinction does not occur when a prior event leads to an increase in the response. If a mother tells a child to stop complaining and he stops, the mother's request is a prior event and cannot be considered an example of extinction. However, if the mother ignores the child's complaints and complaining decreases or stops, extinction has occurred; the reinforcing event *following* complaining has been withheld.

In the same manner, the counselor may wish to extinguish an undesirable client behavior during the interview. The counselor can differentially reinforce specific client interview behaviors by not attending to undesirable behavior and attending to desirable ones. He can selectively attend with eye contact, head nods, or facial expressions when the client is describing the problem in behavioral terms. When the client is vague, the counselor can ignore this and ask for more specific information.

In the following interview, notice the client behavior to be extinguished:

Client: Well, sometimes I talk with people.
Counselor: Right. Can you give me examples when this happens?
Client: I don't know.
Counselor: (Looks in the other direction and says nothing)
Client: Mary Alice spoke to me the other day, but I couldn't talk to her.
Counselor: (Nods) That's interesting. Can you tell me what happened in this situation?

In the preceding example, the counselor attempts to extinguish off-task statements which are unrelated to the question by ignoring them, and he reinforces related statements.

Example Exercise

In the exercises below, identify the target behavior which is being extinguished. (If no behavior is being extinguished, please indicate so.)

1. Mary would always ask her dad a question when he was reading the paper. Her father occasionally responded, but always with a

127

comment not pertinent to what she had said. Mary would then go over and shake the baby's crib. Father would yell at Mary to stop it. After awhile, Mary stopped asking her father questions but continued to shake the baby's crib.

2. Mrs. Jones spent most of her time disciplining her students. Only when her students were studying quietly would she not say anything to them. At the end of the grading period, Mrs. Jones was alarmed to find that class achievement had gradually decreased over time.

3. Laura would cry each time she was put to bed. On most occasions, her parents would ignore it. However, occasionally, they would get her out of bed so she would stop crying. Nevertheless, crying persisted.

4. Jack would often call others names. Occasionally, someone would threaten to hit Jack if he called him another name. The name calling stopped temporarily.

5. Mrs. Harris, a teacher, would always say critical things about school policies to Mr. Moore, the counselor. Whenever she would criticize school policies, Mr. Moore looked down at his food. When she changed the subject and began talking about positive behaviors of her children, Mr. Moore would nod his head and ask her questions about them.

6. Mrs. Aubrey began most of her counseling sessions by telling her counselor all the reasons why she couldn't change things in her life. During this time the counselor turned and looked through his filing cabinet. When she stopped complaining and blaming, he faced her and responded to what she said.

Answers

1. Mary's questions
2. Studying quietly and students' achievements
3. No behavior is being extinguished
4. No behavior is being extinguished
5. Negative statements about school policies
6. Complaining and blaming

Two points worthy of repetition here are the importance of consistently withholding reinforcement of the undesirable response (off-task statements) and reinforcement for desirable behavior (on-task statements). *Occasional* reinforcers for undesirable behavior will only serve to maintain the undesirable behavior. Keeping note cards may be helpful to the counselor and others in reminding them of specific behaviors to ignore and reinforce. Thus, extinction efforts can become more efficient.

Figure 24 illustrates the gradual reduction of off-task statements over sessions. It shows consistency in procedures used for extinguishing undesirable behavior. In the sixth session, the counselor inadvertently began attending to a story the client was telling him. While the story was interesting, it had nothing to do with the client's problem; the counselor became aware of this after listening to a tape of the session. Consequently, in sessions seven and eight, he ignored the client's off-task statements, which resulted in their decrease. It should be noted also that attention to the client's on-task behavior increased except for the sixth session when attention was being given to off-task statements.

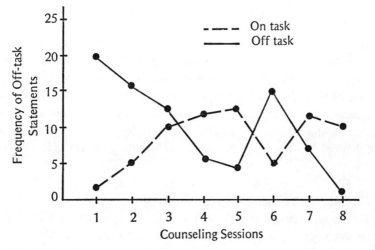

Figure 24. Frequency of Off-Task Behavior over Counseling Sessions

Example Exercise

In Figure 25 (page 130), identify the behavior that is being extinguished. Explain why.

Answer

This graph shows that the counselor has extinguished the client's posi-

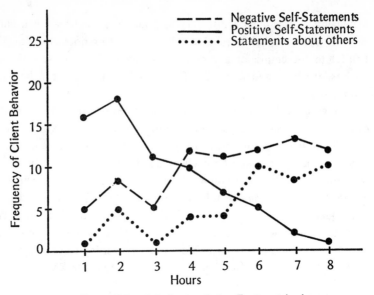

Figure 25.   A Behavior Being Extinguished

tive self-statements. We know this because there is a gradual reduction over time, indicating that the counselor provided no intermittent reinforcement (attention) for positive statements. Also, the counselor appears to be giving little attention to the client's discussion of others. However, during the sixth and eighth hours, statements about others were reinforced, causing an increased level for them. Extinction of a behavior is contingent on the continued nonreinforcement of it.

IF EXTINCTION DOESN'T WORK, USE REMOVAL FROM REINFORCEMENT: TIME OUT

The removal from reinforcement is a technique widely used by counselors and teachers to encourage students to forego undesirable behavior. The removal from the reinforcer differs from extinction in that the latter simply involves discontinuing the reinforcer that ordinarily follows a given misbehavior; whereas, in the former, punishing consequences are applied through the loss of special privileges. For example, a child's fighting behavior may be maintained by peers who laugh or cheer when it happens. If the counselor and teacher decided to use extinction procedures as a means of weakening this misbehavior, they would simply ignore the child's fighting tactics and would encourage

130

the peer group to do likewise. Thus, the reinforcer that maintains the behavior would have been removed.

Ask Questions Before Using Time Out

If removing the reinforcer does not work, removing the child from the reinforcing situation may be warranted. This procedure is called **time out**. Before using it, however, several questions should be answered.

1. *Is this behavior harmful to the client or others?*

In the preceding example, fighting may result in someone's getting hurt. Other behaviors which may be harmful are playing in the street, stealing, and taking drugs or alcohol. If these types of behaviors occur, the cheapest way to deal with them is to remove the reinforcers (alcohol, drugs, etc.) from the person rather than removing the person from the environment (bar, pool hall, etc.). In this way, the client is removed from the discriminative stimulus that is eliciting the undesirable behavior. However, cooperation must be established with significant others in the client's environment (bartender, friends, etc.) who will agree not to provide the reinforcer.

2. *Can the problem behavior be ignored?*

As discussed earlier, when behaviors are dangerous to self or others, they cannot be ignored. However, as earlier indicated, some teachers, parents, etc. are better able to tolerate certain behaviors than others. In cases where tolerance is low, the counselor should probably suggest to the teacher or parent that she attempt to remove the child from the situation rather than to continue to reinforce his problem behavior (teasing, talking out, etc.) even if it is not dangerous to others.

3. *Can the client be immediately removed to a neutral situation which is not rewarding?*

Time out is most appropriately done in an institutional setting (home, school, hospital). Obviously, it is difficult to monitor behaviors occurring outside such a setting. How does someone remove a child who is fighting in the neighborhood, or an alcoholic who is drinking in a bar? Time out must be administered in a way that will not produce fear and avoidant tendencies which could undermine the effects of the aversive control program. It must be done under tightly controlled conditions.

The teacher, parent, etc. must have a small time-out area which is free of distracting or attractive activities. If removal from the group is rewarding instead of punishing, then it will not be effective in modifying the student's behavior. If the student is able to talk with friends who pass by in the hall or to look at his friends in the classroom and laugh, then the time out becomes a rewarding experience and his misbehavior pays off for him. Likewise, if a child is sent to his bedroom by his mother and is able to read or play there, then time out becomes an escape from an unpleasant situation. Ideally, the client should be placed in a dull, unstimulating room or corner of the room with a chair and a light. Many teachers complain that they cannot use time out since they have no special isolation rooms, but actually, a special room is not always necessary. Many teachers have used screens effectively to isolate students. The screen is placed at the back of the room in a position such that the student can no longer be seen by his peers but can be seen by his teacher. Some teachers have placed the student between the wall and filing cabinets. With children, a space 2 x 3 feet is adequate.

4. *Is the individual being removed from a reinforcing situation?*

For time out to be effective, the individual must be removed from a situation that is *reinforcing*. Obviously, if a student is removed from a classroom where he is failing and the teacher is yelling at him, time out will only serve as an escape from an unpleasant situation. In fact, a child may do things to consistently remove himself from the situation. His disruptive behavior may increase substantially in situations (tests, oral reports) where he is afraid or doesn't have the skills to succeed. However, if the child has the opportunity to be *rewarded for appropriate behavior upon leaving the time-out area*, then time out will become more effective in reducing undesirable behavior. This often can be accomplished in the classroom by having reinforcing activities and objects immediately available for appropriate behavior. Poor results from the time-out procedure often are attributable to relatively low magnitudes of payoff for correct responding.

If each of the four questions has been resolved, the counselor is ready to suggest implementation of time out; otherwise, the counselor should encourage the teacher or parent to remove a reinforcer from the individual rather than place him in the time-out area.

Institute Time-Out Procedure

First, the teacher or parent who implements time-out procedures should be firm but matter-of-fact, as though the child experienced a logical or natural consequence for his misbehavior. The teacher, parent, or attendant must avoid scolding at this time since this may only reinforce the undesirable behavior. For example, the teacher might say, "You were hitting Billy with a ruler rather than studying," *and no more*. Here the child knows why he is being removed and what he should have been doing. The probabilities of the child's leaving quietly are enhanced if the consequences of misbehavior have been agreed on previously.

Secondly, the teacher, parent, or attendant might use verbal and/or nonverbal signals before initiating time out. For example, the teacher might say, "Stop" when Johnny is hitting Billy with a ruler. If Johnny notices this and the behavior (hitting with the ruler) is occurring at a low magnitude, it may be enough to suppress the behavior.

Thirdly, if possible, the counselor should encourage the teacher or parent to monitor the individual's behavior while in the time-out area. *The individual should be displaying desirable behavior before he is allowed to return to the situation.* Allowing the child to leave the time-out area when he is crying or screaming only reinforces this behavior. The individual should be kept in time out five to ten minutes and allowed to return when he is behaving. Longer periods of time prevent the individual from learning more adaptive responses in the environment.

Example Exercise

In the following example, determine whether time out is an appropriate procedure:

Eric would always complete his work before the other children. When he was finished, he would get out of his seat and talk to others. The teacher would tell him to "get in his seat and get busy." Although Eric would go to his seat, he would continue to talk to others. When this occurred, the teacher would jerk Eric from his seat and walk him to an area behind the filing cabinet.

Answer

Although Eric's behavior is undesirable, it is likely that the teacher and peers could ignore this. Eric is receiving no reinforcement for completing his work. The teacher might give him more work and let him earn the privilege to talk to others in a play area when he is finished. *When the client's behavior is dangerous to self or others and the situation she is in is reinforcing, withdrawal from the reinforcing environment or time out is appropriate*

Unlike extinction, time out decreases the rate of problem behavior rapidly. As Benoit and Mayer (1974) suggest, this can be both an advantage and a disadvantage. It is a disadvantage because some teachers find it so reinforcing that they use it for any problem behavior rather than trying extinction. Counselors should help teachers and parents to make the distinction. *Time out is a more aversive contingency than extinction. Removal from the classroom can cause the student to miss classroom instruction, and it consequently should be considered only when extinction is inappropriate.*

Example Exercise

Read the following dialogue and answer the questions.

Counselor: It seems from the observations that Ron continues to bite Mary. I think we should try to decrease this behavior. Did you read the handout on time out?

Mother: Yes, maybe that's a good idea. When I spank him, it doesn't help.

Counselor: First, we need a good place in the house to isolate him. How about his bedroom?

Mother: Yes, that would be a good place.

Counselor: Okay, you might jot down procedures we are going to use so you can present them to Ron and discuss them with your husband. First, you must tell him you want him to stop it. Next, tell him you have a plan which will work.

Mother: He won't listen.

Counselor: Wait until you have his attention and then tell him you want him to stop. Tell him you will warn him by saying, "Stop" but if he continues to bite his sister, it will cost him five minutes in his room. Take him to the room and show him how to sit there and how you will signal him when it's time to leave. Show him the egg timer and how you will set it.

Mother: When should he leave the room?

Counselor: Set the timer for five minutes and let him leave when it goes off.

Mother: When he continues to bite his sister, what should I do?

Counselor: You should say, "You were biting your sister. That will cost you five minutes in your room." Don't scold him. Then take him firmly by the hand to his room.

1. Did the counselor discuss whether the time-out area was a neutral site? Why?
2. Were provisions made to make the child aware of why he is being removed to a time-out area?
3. Did the counselor include a warning signal to the child?

Answers

1. No, his room was selected because it was isolated. There may have been games or toys which he could have enjoyed; thus, the time-out area might have been reinforcing. It would have been preferable to have a neutral site. However, it is quite likely that simply the exclusion from the original area tends to be a punishing event, whether or not reinforcing activities exist in his bedroom.
2. Yes, the counselor discussed how the mother and father might present the program to the child.
3. Yes, he said to say "Stop," and if the child continued, he would be taken to his room.

USE RESPONSE COST IF OTHER PROCEDURES FAIL

When the client cannot be removed from the reinforcement to a neutral area or when the undesirable behavior cannot be ignored by others, removing reinforcers from the individual or response cost appears to be the next best alternative. **Response cost** represents a form of punishment in which previously acquired reinforcers (e.g., food, alcohol, approval, activities) are forfeited *contingent* upon an undesirable response. Rather than ignoring the undesirable behavior (extinction) or removing the individual from the situation where he can earn reinforcement (time out), response cost asks the client to give up something such as a privilege. Consider again the child whose fighting is maintained by facial expressions of his classmates. In this case, the teacher is unable to reinforce peers for ignoring his behavior. Likewise, when a behavior is dangerous to others, extinction is not advised. However, the teacher may remove recess privileges for one day when fighting occurs. The effectiveness of this type of punishment will depend, in part, on how much the student values the loss of a privilege (going out to recess).

Determine Strong Reinforcers

In suggesting a response-cost procedure, the counselor should ask the following question:

Does the loss of a positive reinforcer exert greater control in suppressing the target response than does the reinforcer in maintaining the target response?

In the case of the boy whose fighting is a problem, we are pitting the loss of privileges (recess) against the reinforcers maintaining his behavior (frightened expressions of his peers). Removal of dinner privileges must exert greater control in suppressing fighting with a brother than the laughter of his sister in maintaining the fighting behavior. The critical factor here is to determine if the reinforcers potentially lost are indeed valued. (See Identifying Reinforcers.) They must be genuine reinforcers in the sense that individuals will work to earn them.

If it is impossible to identify reinforcers which can exert greater control on the individual's behavior than those reinforcers maintaining the undesirable behavior, then mild punishment procedures are preferred. Otherwise, removal of reinforcement or response-cost procedures are preferable.

Set Up Reasonable Earnings-Cost Program

There are several guidelines for counselors to follow in implementing removal of reinforcement procedures. First, the overall earnings-cost program should not contain items that can be replaced easily. It is not easy to replace a recess period, especially when there is a two-hour block of time before the next recess. However, the loss of 10 minutes of free time when the individual has three hours of free time to use does not appear costly. This is why logical consequences are preferable to arbitrary consequences. Rather than arbitrarily assigning fines (e.g., not being able to attend party or pep rally, shortened recess or lunch time), the counselor and teacher might use logical consequences, e.g., "If you don't complete your assignment, it will be a part of your homework" or "If you spill your food, you must clean it up." The "costs" or consequences applied in this way are realistic and don't bankrupt the individual or put him in the hole. When the ratio between

136

the amount earned and amount lost results in an overall deficit, e.g., giving up more tokens than are received, the incentive for working for a reinforcement decreases and the system may break down.

Secondly, response cost requires a clear explication of the relationship between each undesirable response and the appropriately assigned penalty. For example, the counselor might say, "You didn't reschedule your appointment when you cancelled so there's no time open today." Or, the teacher might say, "You have written on your desk so you must clean it" or "You used obscene language so you must apologize." Like other procedures, response cost must be used in conjunction with positive behavior which can replace the undesirable behaviors. For example, the teacher may say, "Remember, if you complete your assignments, you may go outside; otherwise, you must stay in and finish them." Here, the teacher is reminding the child of both the positive and negative consequences of his behavior. When the client is reminded of the consequence, the effectiveness of response cost as a deterrent is maximized.

Regardless of the situation, however, it is important for the counselor to use response cost sparingly. If a student is denied a good grade for misbehavior, he is likely to give up. However, if the student has acquired a certain number of points toward a grade or other back-up reinforcer, then losing a small number of points still gives him an opportunity to retain enough points to maintain his desired average. Or, if a client is denied a counseling session because she has not completed the agreed upon "homework," she may become discouraged and drop out of counseling. On the other hand, if a strong relationship has been built and the client is experiencing progress, she is more likely to return, bringing along the homework.

Example Exercise

Given the following client problems, identify a natural consequence for each.

1. Bill took Jim's baseball glove and lost it.
2. Jack got drunk and missed three days of work.
3. Max got in a fight and broke Fred's glasses.
4. Willard missed his appointment for the job interview.
5. Marilyn told Sherry she looked sloppy.

Answers

1. Bill buys Jim a new glove.
2. Jack loses three days pay.
3. Max pays for Fred's glasses.
4. Willard doesn't get the job.
5. Marilyn doesn't get invited to Sherry's birthday party.

CHOOSE PROCEDURE TO DECREASE COVERT BEHAVIOR

All of the behaviors described up to this point have been overt or easily recognizable. Yet many problems of functioning arise from an excess involving covert or internal behavior, i.e., thoughts, feelings, beliefs, and opinions. Examples of excessive covert behaviors are fear, anxiety, and depression; these behaviors cannot be reduced effectively by techniques used to decrease overt behavior.

If the behavior to be decreased is covert, then the counselor must determine other strategies which are more appropriate. In this instance, only the client can observe the relationship between his thoughts and feelings and environmental events. Many of these covert behaviors represent incapacitating anxiety. Poor social relationships, academic failure, and feelings of unworthiness are often the result of being anxious.

Inventory Anxious Situations

To decide which procedure is needed to relieve covert problems such as anxiety, the counselor and client must explore the specific situations associated with the client's anxiety. In addition, it is helpful for the counselor to inquire how long the client has had his fear and the types of situations in which it seems to be better or worse. While there is not a standard set of interview questions, the counselor might refer to a previously described subsystem of the model (identify concerns, Chapter 3) to assist her in gathering information.

The following transcript illustrates how the counselor might begin to identify the client's anxiety. (If covert desensitization must be implemented, this type of interview can be used to construct a hierarchy from the client's sometimes vague complaints.)

Counselor: You seem to have trouble in making conversation.

Client: Yes, I just seem to freeze.

Counselor: What do you mean by freeze?

Client: I just get uptight.

Counselor: Silence

Client: I just can't say anything.

Counselor: Does this occur all the time?

Client: No, only when I am at school.

Counselor: Tell me more.

Client: Well, when I see this group of girls, I can't seem to get in the conversation.

Counselor: Does this happen when you're with other people?

Client: No, I can generally talk with others.

Counselor: Why can you talk with others and not with this group?

Client: Well, I am afraid they will tell me they've got other things to do.

Counselor: It seems like you're afraid they'll reject you.

Client: Yes, they never seem to do anything with anyone outside their own little group.

Counselor: Have you ever been afraid that others will reject you?

Client: Not really.

Counselor: Why, then, are you afraid that this group will reject you?

Client: They're really neat. They're the most popular group at school.

Counselor: When was the last time you had this feeling?

If the counselor is having difficulty identifying the anxious area, he might ask the client to complete a fear survey schedule (Wolpe and Lang, 1964). This is a five-point rating scale which asks the client to rate the amount of fear caused by each of the things and events listed in the questionnaire from "not at all" to "very much" (see Table 7).

Determine If Anxiety Is a Rational Response

Once tension areas and the situations in which they occur have been identified, the counselor and the client must determine whether the tension is a rational response to a realistic circumstance. Often the mere presence of disruptive anxiety is not justification alone for using desensitization. If a child is having difficulty playing with others because he imagines they don't like him, then desensitization training would be entirely appropriate. However, if others make fun of the child and call him obscene names, then desensitization training without an additional

139

Table 7. Fear Survey Schedule (FSS-III)*

The items in this questionnaire refer to things and experiences that may cause fear or other unpleasant feelings. Write the number of each item in the column that describes how much you are disturbed by it nowadays.

	Not at all	A little	A fair amount	Much	Very much

1. Noise of vacuum cleaners
2. Open wounds
3. Being alone
4. Being in a strange place
5. Loud voices
6. Dead people
7. Speaking in public
8. Crossing streets
9. People who seem insane
10. Falling
11. Automobiles
12. Being teased
13. Dentists
14. Thunder
15. Sirens
16. Failure
17. Entering a room where other people are already seated
18. High places on land
19. People with deformities
20. Worms
21. Imaginary creatures
22. Receiving injections
23. Strangers
24. Bats
25. Journeys
    a - Train
    b - Bus
    c - Car
26. Feeling angry
27. People in authority
28. Flying insects
29. Seeing other people injected
30. Sudden noises
31. Dull weather
32. Crowds

	Not at all	A little	A fair amount	Much	Very much

33. Large open spaces
34. Cats
35. One person bullying another
36. Tough looking people
37. Birds
38. Sight of deep water
39. Being watched working
40. Dead animals
41. Weapons
42. Dirt
43. Crawling insects
44. Sight of fighting
45. Ugly people
46. Fire
47. Sick people
48. Dogs
49. Being criticized
50. Strange shapes
51. Being in an elevator
52. Witnessing surgical operations
53. Angry people
54. Mice
55. Blood
    a - Human
    b - Animal
56. Parting from friends
57. Enclosed places
58. Prospect of a surgical operation
59. Feeling rejected by others
60. Airplanes
61. Medical odors
62. Feeling disapproved of
63. Harmless snakes
64. Cemeteries
65. Being ignored
66. Darkness
67. Premature heart beats (missing a beat)
68. (a) Nude men
    (b) Nude women
69. Lightning

Table 7.   Fear Survey Schedule (FSS-III)* (continued)

	Not at all	A little	A fair amount	Much	Very Much
70. Doctors					
71. Making mistakes					
72. Looking foolish					

*Reprinted with permission. Wolpe, J., and Lang, P. J. A fear survey schedule for use in behavior therapy. *Behaviour Research and Therapy*, 1964, pp. 228-232.

intervention to resolve this problem is likely to be of little help. That is, the anxiety may be rational and warrant a behavior or environmental change as well as desensitization. Likewise, if a patient fears he has a terminal illness when a physical examination reveals he has severe heart palpitations, then the reaction of the client appears to be a rational one.

If Client Lacks Skills, Choose Training Package

Before starting systematic desensitization, it should be determined whether the client is avoiding a particular situation because he has excessive anxiety or because he lacks the requisite skills to cope with the situation. For example, in the case of the child who was afraid to play with others, it would be necessary to determine whether the child possesses the necessary skills to play with others, i.e., if he knows how to initiate a conversation, get and provide information, and leave a situation. In addition, the child may need specific skills to play particular games, such as jump rope and kickball.

Likewise, if a student is fearful of taking tests but the counselor discovers that she has no place to study at home, the test anxiety must be construed as a behavioral deficit in which the client is anxious because she lacks the necessary information. In this case, the counselor and client must go through a problem-solving process to determine how they might rearrange the client's environment. Similarly, the client who shows excessive fear of assuming a new job may be fearful either because he has inadequate job skills or because he's afraid of the "new" situation. If a client doesn't possess the requisite skills, the counselor should proceed to skills training; otherwise, she should proceed with the desensitization process.

Decide If Behavior
Is General or Situation Specific

It is important to determine whether covert behavior such as anxiety is generalized or situation specific before deciding on an intervention to decrease it. For example, clients who experience generalized or free-floating anxiety are more likely to profit from a program of cognitive restructuring, while systematic desensitization seems to be the preferred treatment for clients who have situation-specific anxiety.

Choose Cognitive Restructuring for Free-Floating Anxiety If the client experiences generalized anxiety rather than is anxious in response to a specific event, it is often because she has developed a pattern of irrational thinking. That is, she responds more to the label or thought related to the situation than to the situation itself. Consequently, cognitive restructuring seems to be the preferred treatment. See Chapter 10 for information on implementing this approach.

Choose Systematic Desensitization for Situation-Specific Anxiety While clients who experience anxiety in many situations, i.e., free-floating anxiety, benefit most by cognitive restructuring, desensitization appears to be more effective when anxiety is situation specific. There is an increasing literature (Lazarus, 1971) which suggests that systematic desensitization is effective in treating monosymptomatic phobias but less effective with free-floating anxieties. That is, if the client is anxious in the presence of certain people, desensitization would be an appropriate intervention. However, if the client appears to be anxious around people in general, other approaches may be necessary, as noted earlier.

PLAN AND IMPLEMENT
SYSTEMATIC DESENSITIZATION

Systematic desensitization is primarily a counterconditioning process frequently used to help individuals reduce tension. "Tense" responses may include irregular breathing, tension headaches, high-pitched voice, increased voice volume, rapid speech, failure to sit still, and insomnia.

The use of systematic desensitization presupposes that tension is subject to voluntary control through the systematic relaxation of skeletal muscles. When skeletal muscles are relaxed, the internal muscles of the stomach, intestines, heart, etc. also are more likely to be relaxed. Thus, if a counselor can help the client learn to be relaxed in situations which usually elicit anxiety, the learned association between that situation and the anxiety response gradually weakens and is extinguished (Hosford and de Visser, 1974).

Introduce Desensitization

Once the counselor has satisfactorily determined that the client's fear is not rational or due to a lack of necessary skills, the counselor is ready to introduce the desensitization process. While there are numerous ways to do this, the counselor might say:

It seems that there are a number of situations in which you become tense. What I would like to do is help you adjust to these situations. First, we need to help you learn to cope with the less stressful situations. Once you have learned to cope with these, we can work on those which cause you more stress. One of the things you can learn to do is relax. If we can teach you how to relax in these situations, it should make you feel less tense. This process is like anything else that you first try; it becomes easier as you practice it. (Give an appropriate example such as playing in a basketball game, driving a car, asking for your first date, etc.). Once you learn to do these things, it becomes easier and easier.

After the introduction is given, ask the client if he has any questions or discuss certain situations where he first learned something and how it became easier with time.

Design Anxiety Hierarchy

Use Relevant Dimensions and Behavioral Terms Once the desensitization procedure is introduced to the counselor's and client's satisfaction, they then begin to rank situations from least to most anxiety provoking. The dimensions which are relevant in ranking items in the hierarchy are time, distance away from stressful events, number of persons involved, and what the client or others are doing in that situation.

The anxiety hierarchy may include as many as 30 situations with others added if necessary. However, it is not unusual for those hierarchies which represent a very specific fear (e.g., taking a test) to contain more items. These items should be as concrete as possible so that the client will be able to imagine the situation (Goldfried and Davison, 1976). Each relevant dimension of an item should be stated in behavioral terms, i.e., behaviors whose occurrence two or more people can agree on. For example, "giving a lecture" would not be as desirable as "approaching the lectern, placing the notes on top of it, and looking out at the audience."

Example Exercise

Given the following items, identify those which include relevant dimensions stated behaviorally
1. Going to the dentist.
2. You're walking out the back door to get on the bus.
3. You are afraid of making a mistake when your boss is present.
4. The morning of the trip, you are folding your socks and underwear into your suitcase.
5. You are in the room waiting for a call.

Answers

Items 2 and 4 include relevant dimensions stated in behavioral terms. Item 1 doesn't explain how or when the person is leaving for the dentist. Likewise, in item 3 the kind of feared mistake is not identified. In item 5 the room is unclear (bedroom, living room) and the expected caller is not identified. *Items must contain relevant dimensions and be stated in behavioral terms.*

Rank Situations, Filling Gaps One of the most common techniques for establishing a hierarchy of anxiety-provoking situations is to give the client a set of 3 x 5 cards with the anxiety-provoking situations listed on them. Next, the client may rank the cards from least to most anxiety provoking. The counselor might vary this by asking the client to place an anxiety value from 0 (least) to 100 (most anxious) on each item.

The counselor can begin by reading each card aloud and having the client rate it as high, medium, or low, depending upon how much anxiety it provokes. Once this division is made, the counselor can ask the client to assign a numerical rating to each item, whereby the low-anxiety items are rated between 0 and 33, the moderate ones 34 to 66, and the highest ones 67 to 100 (Goldfried and Davison, 1976). By assigning these numbers, the counselor and client can often discover gaps between items that should be filled. Gaps can often be filled by

145

including items that reduce the stress of the event, introduce fearless models, or increase the length of time or distance from the anxiety-provoking event. For example:

Original item, rated 50:
Getting on the bus to go to school on Monday when peers are at the bus stop.

Original item, rated 60:
Bus turns the corner on Monday when peers are at the bus stop.

Inserted item, rated 35:
Getting on the bus to go to school on Tuesday when peers are not at the bus stop.

The client may fill out additional cards if necessary, each containing a description of a situation which produces a certain level of anxiety in him. *As a general rule, new items should be generated where gaps exceed more than 10 units.* In the preceding example, the counselor should introduce a new item since there is more than a 10-unit gap between getting on the bus to go to school on Tuesday (rated 35) and getting on the bus to go to school on Monday (rated 50). Perhaps the counselor could reduce both the time and distance by introducing an item such as "waiting at the bus stop in front of your house on Monday morning." If the client rated this item between 35 and 50, it would reduce the gap.

The exact nature of the hierarchy will vary depending on the client's particular fear and perception of the situation. For example, someone who fears that others are "talking behind his back" may describe a number of situations where this occurs, each differing in the level of fear arousal.

Where the client has a specific fear, the description of the increasing anxiety-provoking situations may differ on the spatio-temporal dimension. For example, someone who is anxious about taking a math test might list situations which lead from signing up for the class to seeing his grade on the exam. An example follows. Anxiety ratings are given in parentheses.

1. Signing up for a math class. (5)
2. Going to first class, hearing assignments, and finding out when the exams will be given. (10)
3. Getting notes for a class you missed. (12)
4. Engaging in a weekly review session. (20)

5. Discussing the exam with a bright achievement-oriented student who says it will be a tough test. (30)
6. Reviewing old exams and seeing how much you know. (32)
7. Studying the evening before the exam. (35)
8. Seeing how late it is and how much material you still have to study. (40)
9. Conducting a last-minute review to cram in the things you don't know as well as you would like to. (50)
10. Coming into the room on exam day. (60)
11. Getting the exam and writing your name on it. (65)
12. Skimming the exam and running across items the answers to which are not immediately evident. (70)
13. Instructor interrupts your train of thought to correct errors in typing. (80)
14. Teacher throws out an ambiguous item that you were sure you knew the answer to. (82)
15. Finding yourself stuck on a question and seeing everyone else busy working. (85)
16. Noticing your bright achievement-oriented friend hand in his paper 30 minutes after the exam began. (88)
17. Realizing that only five minutes remain on the exam and that you still have several items left to do. (90)
18. Talking to fellow students after the exam and finding out that they answered the questions differently. (95)
19. Coming into class the next day to get your grade on the exam. (100)

Hierarchies may vary also in terms of the number of people present in a particular situation as well as a combination of this and the time and distance away from anxiety-provoking objects. For example, consider a client who is afraid of speaking in front of groups. The choice of items might reflect the facial expressions of certain people in the audience, people who are leaving, and the time of day and location Only after careful observation and interviewing can the counselor and client determine the most relevant items in the hierarchy.

In a previous example, the counselor and client had identified that the client was fearful of talking to a group of girls. In identifying which situations or times the client is most fearful, the counselor might say the following.

Counselor: When do you first feel anxious?

Client: When I first get off the bus.

Counselor: What is happening when you first get off the bus?

Client: They are usually standing near the corner when I get off the bus.

Counselor: Do you get this uptight feeling when you are on the bus coming to school?

Client: Yes, on Mondays and Wednesdays, I do.

Counselor: Why then?

Client: Well, those are the only days we stop at the corner.

Counselor: What happens the other days?

Client: Well, we go to the back of the building to pick up the band.

Here, the counselor is beginning to discover the time and the situation when the client becomes anxious. In this case, the counselor will want to explore anxiety-provoking situations and feelings leading up to getting on the bus.

When the client has specified the hierarchy, the counselor and client list each step and add intermediary steps if necessary. It is important to make the items at the upper end of the hierarchy realistic. For example, it is unlikely that the group of girls will approach the client to talk with her; rather, the girl will likely have to approach the group to initiate conversation. The final hierarchy should represent a gradation of anxiety-provoking situations, each of which the client can easily imagine.

Teach Client Relaxation

Next, the client is taught some kind of relaxation procedure. This proce-dure should represent a modified version of a technique developed by Jacobson (1938) which consists of alternately tensing and relaxing specific body muscles. The client, thus, first learns to discriminate be-tween being relaxed and being tense and then to relax more deeply (Hosford and de Visser, 1974). The assumption here is that tension inhibits one's effectiveness and if he can learn to control this tension, then he can become more effective.

The counselor should provide a rationale for the training. There should be no set speech in presenting the rationale because clients differ in intelligence; the level of explanation and choice of words must be suited to the client's particular needs. First, the counselor should communicate to the client that he is going to teach him to relax. Secondly, he might explain that he is going to teach him to alternately tense and relax opposing sets of muscles. All muscle groups should be held tense for a period of five seconds and then released completely. At this point, the muscle group being tensed should be completely relaxed. It is also helpful throughout training to discuss with the client changes the client is experiencing in his body. For example, the counselor might say, "See the difference between tensing and relaxing your muscles," or "Notice how that muscle feels . . . . Do you see how much more relaxed you are?"

The training should take place in a quiet, attractive room. It is best to select a room away from ringing telephones, typewriters, or other disturbing noises. Lighting should be dimmed; direct lighting from desk lamps should be shaded. The floor, a soft reclining chair which supports the client's legs and arms, a couch, or soft chair may be used for the relaxation training.

The following script (Froehle and Lauver, 1971) can be used as a guide for relaxation training.

Script for Relaxation Training*

First of all, let me suggest that you find a place on the floor where you can stretch out full length without touching anyone else or any object other than the floor surface (Long Pause). After you have found this place, stretch yourself out lying on your back with your arms at the sides of your body. Your elbows should be slightly extended, your feet apart, and if you have a pillow or something else to roll-up and place under your neck, fine (*Long Pause*).

When you get comfortable, close your eyes and try to tune out all sensations that are coming into you from outside of you except my voice. Breathe deep, in and out (*Pause*) in and out. Concentrate on the different areas of your body, noting the sensations that they are causing you to receive. Study your hands, your lower arms, your upper arms; how do your neck and face feel? Your shoulders and upper back? Now concentrate on your chest, your stomach, and your lower back. Finally, what kinds of feelings do you have in your hips, your thighs, your

*Reprinted with permission. Froehle, T., and Lauver, P. Counseling techniques: Selected readings. Indiana University, 1971.

lower legs and your feet? (*Pause*).

Now you are ready to begin relaxing by doing some exercises. In these exercises, you will work with the main muscles of the body. I will have you tense or tighten each one tighter and tighter, and then I will ask you to relax and to let them go. Doing this over and over again works the tension out of the muscles and nerves and at the same time trains them to relax automatically. A general feeling of being refreshed should come from these exercises and, hopefully, they will "facilitate your functioning" in other situations.

Now with your eyes closed so that you become less aware of objects and movements around you and in this way prevent any surface tensions from developing, breathe in deeply and feel yourself becoming heavier (*Pause*). Take in a long, deep breath and let it out very slowly .... Feel how heavy and relaxed you have become (*Pause*).

Fine (*Pause*). Now let us begin with relaxation of the arms .... As you relax like that, clench your right fist, clench your right fist tighter and tighter and study the tension as you do so. Keep it clenched and feel the tension in your right fist and forearm .... (*Pause*) and now relax. Let the fingers of your right hand become loose and observe the contrast in your feeling (*Pause*). Now let yourself go and try to become more relaxed all over (*Pause*). Once more clench your right fist really tight, hold it, and notice the tension again (*Pause*). Now let go and just relax (*Pause*). Let your fingers straighten out and notice the difference once more (*Pause*).

Now let's repeat that with your left fist. Clench your left fist while the rest of your body relaxes. Clench that fist tighter, and feel the tension (Pause), and now relax (*Pause*). Again enjoy the contrast (*Pause*). Repeat that once more. Clench the left fist tight and tense (*Pause*). Now do the opposite of tension, relax and feel the difference (*Pause*). Continue relaxing like that for awhile (*Pause*). Clench both fists tighter and tighter. Both fists tense, forearms tense. Study the sensation (*Pause*) and then relax. Straighten out your fingers and feel that relaxation. Continue relaxing your hands and forearms more and more (*Long Pause*).

Now bend your elbows and tense your biceps. Tense them harder and study the tension (*Pause*). That's fine. Now straighten out your arms and let them relax (*Pause*). Feel that difference again and let the relaxation develop (*Pause*). Once more, tense your biceps, hold the

150

tension and observe it carefully (*Pause*). Now straighten your arms and relax and enjoy the warm heavy feeling in your arms (*Pause*). Be sure to pay close attention to your feelings when you tense up and when you relax and always try to notice the difference.

Now straighten your arms, straighten them so that you feel the most tension in the triceps, the muscles along the back of your arms. Stretch your arms and feel that tension. Now relax (*Pause*). Your arms should feel comfortably heavy as you allow them to relax (*Pause*). Let's do that again. Straighten your arms once more, so that you feel the tension in the triceps muscles. Stretch them way out and feel that tension, and now relax (*Pause*). Now let's concentrate on pure relaxation in the arms without any tension. Get your arms comfortable and relax further; without any tension (*Pause*). Get your arms comfortable and relax further and further (*Pause*). Continue relaxing even further. Even when your arms seem fully relaxed, try to go that extra bit further. Try to achieve deeper and deeper levels of relaxation (*Long Pause*).

The next step in progressive relaxation is the facial area and the neck, the shoulders and upper back. This should take you from four to five minutes. Let all your muscles go loose and heavy. Just settle down quietly and comfortably.

Now let's work on your facial area. Wrinkle up your forehead (*Pause*). Wrinkle it tighter and tighter (*Pause*). And now, stop wrinkling your forehead, relax, smooth it out and just relax (*Pause*). Picture the forehead and scalp becoming smoother as the relaxation increases (*Pause*). Now let's do that again. Frown, crease your brows real tight and study the tension (*Pause*). Now let go of the tension again. Smooth out the forehead once more (*Pause*). Now close your eyes tighter and tighter. Feel the tension (*Pause*). And now relax your eyes (*Pause*). Keep your eyes closed gently and comfortably and notice the relaxation. Now let's do that again. Close your eyes tighter and tighter and feel the tension (*Pause*). And now relax your eyes keeping them closed gently and comfortably and notice the difference. Notice the relaxation. Now clench your jaws, bite your teeth together. Study the tension throughout the jaws. Fine. Now relax your jaws, now let your lips part slightly, (*Pause*) and appreciate the relaxation (*Pause*). Now press your tongue hard against the roof of your mouth; press it harder and harder and look for the tension (*Pause*). All right, now let your tongue return to a comfortable and relaxed position (*Pause*). Now press your lips together tighter and tighter (*Pause*). And now release and relax the lips. Note the contrast between the tension state and the relaxation state. Relax more fully and feel the relaxation all over your face, all over your forehead and scalp, eyes, jaws, lips, tongue, and throat (*Pause*). You should be sensing deeper and deeper relaxation (*Pause*). Fine, now attend to your neck muscles. Press your head back as far as it can go, and feel the tension in your neck (*Pause*). Roll it to the right and feel the tension shift (*Pause*). Now roll it to the left (*Pause*). Straighten your head and bring it forward. Press your chin against your chest (*Pause*). Let your head return to a comfortable position and again study the relaxation. Let the relaxation develop (*Pause*). OK, now, shrug your shoulders and try to touch your ears with your shoulder. Hold the tension (*Pause*). Drop your shoulders and feel the relaxation. Shrug your shoulders again, and move them around. Bring your shoulders up, push them forward (*Pause*) and then back (*Pause*) and forward again and hold them there (*Pause*). Feel the tension in your shoulders and your upper back (*Pause*). Now drop your shoulders and once more relax. Let the relaxation spread deep into your shoulders and into your back muscles. Relax your neck and throat and your jaws and other facial areas as pure relaxation takes over and grows deeper and deeper (*Pause*), ever deeper and deeper.

The next step is the relaxation of the chest, the stomach, and the lower back. This should take about four to five minutes. OK, first of all relax your entire body as you have learned to do up to this time. Feel that comfortable heaviness that accompanies relaxation. Breathe easily and freely in and out (*Pause*). As you breathe out, just feel that relaxation. Now breathe in and feel your lungs. Inhale deeply and hold your breath. Study the tension (*Pause*). Now exhale. Let the walls of your chest grow loose and push the air out automatically. Continue relaxing, breathing freely and gently. Good (*Pause*). Feel the relaxation and enjoy it (*Pause*). With the rest of your body as relaxed as possible, fill your lungs again. Breathe in deeply and hold it again (*Pause*). That's fine now breathe out and appreciate the relief (*Pause*). Just breathe normally now and continue relaxing your chest. Let the relaxation spread to your back, to your shoulders, to your neck and arms (*Pause*). Merely let go and enjoy the relaxation.

Now let's pay attention to your abdominal muscles, your stomach area. Tighten your stomach muscles, make your abdomen hard.

Notice the tension (*Pause*), and then relax. Let the muscles loosen and notice the contrast (*Pause*). Once more, press hard with the stomach muscles, hold the tension and study it (*Pause*), and now relax. Notice the general well-being that comes with relaxing your stomach (*Pause*). Draw your stomach in (*Pause*), way in. Pull the muscles right in and feel the tension (*Pause*). Now relax, let your stomach out and enjoy the relief. Continue breathing normally and easily and feel the gently massaging action all over the chest and stomach (*Pause*). Now pull your stomach in again and hold the tension (*Pause*). Now push out and tense like that. Hold the tension (*Pause*). Once more pull in and feel the tension (*Pause*). Now relax your stomach fully. Let the tension dissolve as the relaxation grows deeper (*Pause*). Each time you breathe out notice the rythmic relaxation both in your lungs and in your stomach. Notice how your chest and stomach relax more and more. Try to let go all contractions anywhere in your body (*Long Pause*).

Now direct your attention to your lower back. Arch up your back, make your lower back quite hollow and feel the tension along your spine (*Pause*). Now settle down comfortably again relaxing the lower back (*Pause*). Again arch your back and feel the tensions as you do so. Try to keep the rest of your body as relaxed as possible. Try to localize the tension throughout the lower back area. Good, now relax your back once more (*Pause*). Relax your lower back (*Pause*), relax your upper back (*Pause*), spread the relaxation to your stomach, chest, shoulders, arms, and facial areas. Relax these parts further and further and ever deeper.

The next step in our relaxation is the relaxation of the hips, thighs, and calves followed by complete body relaxation. Let go of all tensions and relax. First, we'll flex the buttocks and thighs. Flex your thighs by pressing down on your heels as hard as you can (*Pause*). Relax and note the difference (*Pause*). Straighten your knees and flex your thigh muscles and again, hold the tension (*Pause*). And now your hips and thighs. Allow the relaxation to spread on its own (*Pause*). Good. Now let's work on your feet and calves (*Pause*). This time bend your feet toward your face so that you feel tension along your shins. Bring your toes right up (*Pause*). OK, release and again relax. Let yourself relax further all over (*Pause*). Relax your feet, ankles, calves, and shins. Relax your knees, thighs, buttocks, and hips. Feel the heaviness of your lower body as you relax still further.

Now spread the relaxation through your stomach, your waist, and your lower back. Let go more and more *(Pause)*. Feel that relaxation all over *(Long Pause)*. Let it move to your upper back, chest, shoulders, and arms, and right to the tips of your fingers *(Pause)*. Keep relaxing more and more deeply *(Pause)*. Make sure that no tension has crept into your throat. Relax your neck and your jaws and all your facial muscles. Keep relaxing your whole body like that for awhile. Let yourself go *(Pause)*. Now you can become twice as relaxed as you are merely by taking in a really deep breath and slowly exhaling. With your eyes closed so that you become less aware of movements and objects around you and thus prevent any surface tension from developing, breathe in deeply and feel yourself becoming more and more relaxed as you slowly exhale, and become more and more relaxed. Now you should be feeling totally relaxed. If you can, let yourself relax this way for a few minutes and, if you wish, just let yourself slip off to sleep. You will awake feeling very much refreshed and full of new energy. If you cannot go to sleep at this time just remain totally relaxed for a few minutes and then bring yourself back to a fully awakened state by counting slowly backward from 5 to 1. At the count of three start to stretch, open your eyes and awaken fully. At the count of one, face a brighter world *(Long, Long Pause)*.

Implement Desensitization

The last step is the implementation of the desensitization procedure itself. The desensitization session begins with the client spending three to five minutes relaxing himself. The counselor usually asks the client to raise his finger when he is anxious. Relaxation is incompatible with anxiety; therefore, when the client is in a relaxed state, he is asked to visualize the item in the hierarchy that is least anxiety provoking. If the client signals anxiety (lifting a finger or hand), the scene is withdrawn and relaxation is reinstated. The item is repeatedly presented until it no longer elicits an anxiety response. As the client learns to remain relaxed in the presence of imagined situations, steps in the hierarchy are introduced in sequence until the client is to imagine the most anxiety-provoking situation without experiencing anxiety. When the client keeps experiencing anxiety, the counselor can present the control scene (a pleasant situation the client has described, e.g., lying on a warm beach). The control item is presented for approximately 15 seconds after which the counselor proceeds with the desensitization procedure.

Each scene of the hierarchy is presented three to four times with a maximum exposure time of five seconds for the first presentation and a gradual increase of up to 10 seconds for subsequent presentations. The hierarchy items are presented in ascending order, starting with the least feared item, and relaxation periods are provided between each scene. An example of a desensitization session with a school-phobic child appears below. The counselor says:

> Imagine your mother calling you in the morning and she says, "You had better get up or you will be late for school." (Pause 5 seconds.) Stop imagining that scene . . . . Now you are getting dressed. (Pause 10-15 seconds.) Stop imagining that scene and think of your fist—let go—let the tension out gradually. (Pause 10 seconds.) You are eating breakfast and your mother says, "Your bus will be here in about 5 minutes . . . ." (Pause 15 seconds.)

After the last scene is presented, the counselor usually asks the client to relax. He might say:

> O.K. Relax . . . . Stay this way until I count to 10. When I reach 10, open your eyes and relax. (Pause . . . .) One . . . feeling at ease . . . two . . . very relaxed . . . three . . . very calm . . . four . . . and five . . . .

The counselor should present each scene until the client has gone through several consecutive successes. If, on the other hand, the client has two consecutive failures (experiences anxiety), the counselor should return to the last scene with which he was successful and proceed through the hierarchy. If this fails, a successful scene should be presented so the client ends the session with a positive experience. Occasionally, the counselor might ask the client if a specific scene disturbed him. That scene should be presented again. If the client indicates he was disturbed by it again or could not imagine it, the counselor should end the session and discuss this and any other difficulties the client might be having. If, for example, the client is having difficulty visualizing the scene, the counselor might discuss those aspects of the scene he can see. In this instance, the counselor and client might reconstruct the scene so it is more vivid to the client. Finally, following systematic desensitization, some form of in-vivo desensitization should be employed where the client sequentially practices encountering and coping with scenes in the hierarchy in real life.

CHECKLIST FOR DECREASING BEHAVIOR

Fill in the blanks. Check items yes or no and move to successive steps.

Problem behaviors to be decreased:

1.

2.

3.

ALTERNATIVE INTERVENTIONS:

A. OVERT BEHAVIOR

	Yes	No
1. *Extinction*		
a. Can the behavior be tolerated?	____	____
b. Can an increase in behavior be tolerated?	____	____
c. Can reinforcement be withheld?	____	____
d. Have alternative behaviors been identified?	____	____

If all the above answers are yes, use extinction. If there are some no answers, go on to Alternative 2.

	Yes	No
2. *Time Out*		
a. Is this behavior harmful to the client or others?	____	____
b. Is this a behavior which can't be ignored?	____	____
c. Can the client be immediately removed to a neutral situation which isn't rewarding?	____	____
d. Is the individual being removed from a reinforcing situation?	____	____

If all the above answers are yes, use time out. If there are some no answers, go on to Alternative 3.

	Yes	No
3. *Removal of Reinforcement or Response Cost*		
a. Is the loss of a positive reinforcer more potent in stopping this "bad behavior" than the reinforcer which is maintaining it?	____	____

b. Can natural consequences be used in determining positive reinforcers to remove? _____ _____
c. Are the behaviors overt? _____ _____
If all the above answers are yes, use removal of reinforcement. If
the answer to (a) is no, use mild punishment. If the answer to (c) is
no, go on to systematic desensitization or cognitive restructuring.

B. COVERT BEHAVIOR

4. *Systematic Desensitization*   Yes   No
   a. Is the client anxious? _____ _____
   b. Is the anxiety an irrational response? _____ _____
   c. Is the anxiety situation specific? _____ _____
   d. Does the client have requisite skills to
      cope with the problem situation? _____ _____
   If the above answers are yes, use systematic desensitization. If the
   answers to (a), (b), and (d) are yes, and to (c) is no, cognitive restructuring may be warranted. If the answer to (d) is no, skills
   training may be needed.

5. *Cognitive Restructuring*
   (See Checklist in Chapter 10).

PROGRAMMED EXAMPLES
Choose one or more phrases that accurately complete the statements
and follow individual instructions for other problems.

1. Clients who experience free-floating anxiety often benefit from
   cognitive restructuring while clients who are anxious in specific
   situations often benefit most from
   a. insight counseling.
   b. systematic desensitization.
   c. relationship counseling.
   d. eclectic counseling.
   If you answered (b), you are on target. Systematic desensitization
   seems to be more effective when the anxiety is situational. The
   other approaches, while appropriate, have been less effective in
   alleviating situational anxiety.

157

2. Systematic desensitization can effectively reduce tension by helping the client to
   a. take responsibility for his own actions.
   b. relax in situations which produce anxiety.
   c. assert himself in social situations.
   d. relax.
   If you answered (b), you are correct. Simply relaxing (d) is not enough; it must occur in the presence of the anxiety-provoking object (b). Once tension has been reduced then the client can learn assertive skills (c) and to take responsibility for his actions (a).

3. While there are several steps in implementing the desensitization process, the first step is for the counselor and client to
   a. rank order the anxiety-provoking situations.
   b. specify one anxious situation.
   c. employ relaxation techniques.
   d. inventory the anxiety-provoking situations.
   If you answered (d), you're correct. The counselor and client must first identify all anxiety-producing situations. The client may be anxious in more than one situation (b). Once anxious situations have been inventoried, relaxation may be taught (c) and anxiety-provoking situations may be rank ordered (a).

4. Before the counselor implements systematic desensitization, he must determine whether
   a. the anxiety is a rational response.
   b. the client lacks the necessary skills.
   c. the client is interacting well with others.
   d. the client can build an anxiety hierarchy.
   If you answered (a) and (b), you are correct. It may be that the anxiety response is real. No one would desensitize someone to walk in front of traffic. Also, the client may lack the necessary skills to enter a situation, e.g., someone who is test anxious may lack the necessary skills to pass the test. If the client is fearful of interacting well with others, then (c) is relevant. These questions must be answered before the hierarchy is developed (d).

5. Once the anxiety-provoking situations have been identified from

the interviews and/or fear survey schedule, the client should
a.   implement in-vivo desensitization.
b.   implement systematic desensitization.
c.   learn new social skills.
d.   design an anxiety hierarchy.
If you answered (d), you are correct. Each anxiety-provoking situation should be placed on an index card. Cards then can be ordered from least to most anxiety provoking. In some cases, the client can assign a numerical value from one (least) to 100 (most) anxiety provoking. Situations must be rank ordered before the client is desensitized (b) or is asked to approach the anxiety-provoking object (a). If training is necessary, it should follow desensitization (c).

6.   Once the hierarchy has been developed, the counselor should teach the client how to
a.   relax.
b.   identify anxious situations when they occur.
c.   raise one finger when he is anxious.
d.   cope with anxiety-provoking situations.
You're on target if you responded with (a). The client must first learn to discriminate between being relaxed and being tense. The instructional process will vary depending upon the sophistication of the client. Anxious situations should have been identified (b) and the client should learn how to relax before desensitization is implemented (c) and (d).

7.   In introducing relaxation, the counselor should explain to the client that he is going to
a.   teach him to alternately tense and relax opposing sets of muscles.
b.   teach him how to cope with his anxiety.
c.   teach him how to avoid anxious situations.
d.   teach him to count backwards from 100 when he feels anxious.
You're correct if you answered (a). The client must understand that he will be tensing and relaxing opposing sets of muscles. He must learn that relaxation is a gradual process. Relaxation is only

one step in teaching the client to cope with his anxiety (b). The other two items (c) and (d) are unrelated to the relaxation process.

8. In the final phase when desensitization is implemented, the client learns that
   a. relaxation occurs after anxiety.
   b. relaxation is incompatible with anxiety.
   c. relaxation occurs before anxiety.
   d. relaxation is an unlearned response.
   If you answered (b), you're right. When the client is in a relaxed state, he can't be anxious. Thus, he is asked to visualize each item in the hierarchy when he is in a relaxed state. Relaxation must occur in the presence of the anxiety-provoking object, not before (c) or after (a) it. Relaxation is a learned rather than unlearned (d) response.

9. During desensitization, when the client feels anxious, he is asked to
   a. lift his finger.
   b. leave the room.
   c. visualize himself on an off-sea island.
   d. relax.
   If you answered (a), you are correct. The client must signal to the counselor when he is anxious. Once this occurs, the anxiety-provoking scene is withdrawn and relaxation procedures are reinstated. The other items fail to make the counselor aware of the client's anxiety.

10. When the client signals that he is experiencing anxiety two consecutive times, the counselor should ask him to relax and
    a. return immediately to the control scene.
    b. return to the last scene in which he felt relaxed.
    c. list additional scenes where he feels anxious.
    d. count backwards from 100.
    If you answered (b), you're right. The counselor should ask the client to return to the last scene in which he felt relaxed. If the client still feels anxious, then it is best to return to the control scene (a). Listing additional scenes (c) or counting backwards from

100 (d) will likely be unproductive.

11. Following systematic desensitization, the counselor should encourage the client to
    a. encounter each scene in the hierarchy in real life.
    b. construct new anxiety hierarchies.
    c. terminate counseling.
    d. indicate whether he is still anxious.
    You're correct if you answered (a). Only if the client can approach the anxiety-provoking object can the intervention be considered successful. New hierarchies (b) or termination of counseling (c) should not occur until the client has successfully approached the anxiety-provoking object. This is the best measure of the client's anxiety (d).

12. Given the following items in a desensitization hierarchy of a client who fears public speaking, identify any gap(s) which may exist and write a new item containing a relevant dimension.
    a. You are practicing your speech in your bedroom the night before the speech. (rated 40)
    b. A friend calls you that night to ask you if you have your speech memorized. (rated 50)
    c. You are leaving the house for school the next day. (rated 55)
    d. You park your car in front of the speech building. (rated 70)
    A gap (more than 10 units) exists between (c) leaving the house and (d) parking the car in front of the speech building. Suggested items to introduce might include:
    You stop to pick up a member in your speech class. (rated 60)
    He asks you if he can read your speech. (rated 65)

13. List those dimensions which are relevant in ranking items in the hierarchy.
    a.

    b.

    c.

    d.

You're correct, if you answered (a) time, (b) distance away from the anxiety-provoking object, (c) number of people present, and (d) what those people or the client does in that situation. For example, a person fearful of a party situation may become more fearful as the time of the party draws nearer (a). Secondly, the individual may be more anxious depending upon the number of people who will be at the party (c). Thirdly, as he gets nearer these people, he may be more anxious (b). Finally, his anxiety may be raised, depending on what he says to them or what they say to him (d).

14. List five questions that must be resolved before instituting extinction procedures.

a.

b.

c.

d.

e.

a. Can the behavior be tolerated?
b. Can an increase in behavior be tolerated?
c. Is behavior likely to be imitated?
d. Can reinforcement be withheld?
e. Have alternative behaviors been identified?

15. Given the following examples, indicate which one best exemplifies the use of extinction.
   a. A counselor keeps nodding his head as the client describes his problem.
   b. A child gradually stops asking questions while his father continues to read the paper.

c. A teacher calls on a child who holds up his hand.

d. A teacher sends a child from an area where he fights, but the child continues to fight.

From the information provided, only (b) would be correct. Only when a behavior is being ignored and it gradually stops can we say the behavior has been extinguished. In the other examples, behavior probably is being reinforced (a) and (c) or punished (d).

16. From the graph (Figure 26), identify the behavior that is being extinguished. Explain why.

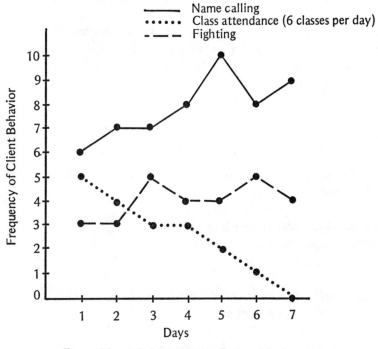

Figure 26. A Behavior Being Extinguished
(Question 16)

In the above graph, the client's class attendance has been extinguished. We know this because there is a gradual reduction over time, indicating that the teacher provided no intermittent reinforcement (attention) to attendance. The frequency of fighting and name calling show no gradual decline and the behaviors fail to stop.

17. Given the following situations, indicate which best exemplifies the use of natural consequences.
    a. A child hit another child and was suspended from school.
    b. A child studied a long time for a test but failed it.
    c. A client arrived 20 minutes late for a counseling sesson, but the counselor said nothing.
    d. A mother failed to complete her weekly observations, and the counselor would not allow her to participate in the parent group.

    If you answered (d), you are right. The mother lost a privilege related to her behavior (not bringing her assignments). In the other examples, the consequences for the behavior appear to be arbitrary or unrelated.

CRITERION TEST

Choose one or more phrases that accurately complete the statements and follow individual instructions for other questions.

1. Systematic desensitization appears to be most effective with clients who
   a. experience free-floating anxiety.
   b. experience anxiety in specific situations.
   c. experience irrational thinking.
   d. lack necessary skills.

2. Clients who are desensitized can
   a. solve their own problems.
   b. relax.
   c. relax in situations which produce anxiety.
   d. make rational statements.

3. If anxiety is rational and the client lacks the necessary skills, then
   a. systematic desensitization is an appropriate intervention.
   b. cognitive restructuring is an appropriate intervention.
   c. shaping is an inappropriate intervention.
   d. extinction is an appropriate intervention.

4. The first step in implementing desensitization is to
   a. discuss relaxation.
   b. specify two anxiety-provoking situations.
   c. rank order the anxiety-provoking situations.
   d. inventory the anxiety-provoking situations.

5. Once anxiety provoking situations have been identified, the client should
   a. rank each situation from least to most anxiety provoking.
   b. discuss relaxation training.
   c. brainstorm other problem areas.
   d. explain desensitization.

6. The principle of relaxation is based upon
   a. breathing deeply.
   b. observing and recording your pulse rate.
   c. alternately tensing and relaxing opposing sets of muscles.
   d. avoiding anxious situations.

7. Desensitization is based upon the principle that
   a. relaxation is an unlearned response.
   b. clients often want help with their problems.
   c. relaxation is incompatible with anxiety.
   d. relaxation is free floating.

8. When the client reports he is anxious on two consecutive occasions during desensitization, the counselor should ask him to relax and
   a. terminate the session.
   b. return to the last scene in which he was relaxed.
   c. discuss the desensitization with him.
   d. have the client stand and take a deep breath.

9. When the client lifts his finger in desensitization, it usually means
   a. he is anxious.
   b. he wishes to terminate the session.
   c. he is relaxed.
   d. he is ready to go on to the next scene.

10. When the client has completed desensitization, he should be
    a. taught how to relax.
    b. taught how to assert himself.
    c. encouraged to re-enact the hierarchy in real life.
    d. encouraged to develop new hierarchies.

11. Given the following items in a desensitization hierarchy of a client who fears taking tests, identify any gap(s) which may exist and write a new item containing a relevant dimension.
    a. You are studying the night before the test. (45)
    b. The alarm goes off the morning of the test. (50)
    c. You leave the house for school (day of test). (60)
    d. You arrive at school but can't find a parking place. (75)

12. List relevant dimensions for designing a desensitization hierarchy.

    a.

    b.

    c.

    d.

13. List five questions which must be resolved before instituting extinction procedures.

    a.

    b.

    c.

    d.

    e.

166

14. Given the following examples, indicate which one best exemplifies the use of extinction.
    a. The child's attendance increases when the counselor greets him at the door.
    b. A man quits looking for a job when he gets no response from his applications.
    c. A man quits his job when his boss tells him he is irresponsible.
    d. A woman continues to drink while attending AA meetings.

15. From the graph (Figure 27), identify the behavior that is being extinguished. Explain why.

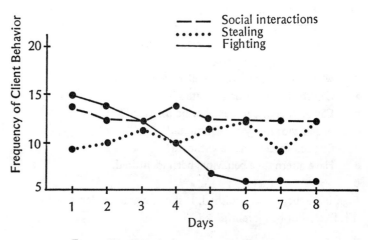

Figure 27. *A Behavior Being Extinguished*
(Criterion Question 15)

16. Given the following situations, indicate which best exemplifies the use of natural consequences.
    a. A child who stole $20 had to replace it.
    b. A boy who stole $20 was sent to a detention center.
    c. A boy who was caught fighting was expelled from school.
    d. A man who was 10 minutes late for his counseling session was excused.

167

CHAPTER 7
CRITERION TEST ANSWERS
1. b
2. c
3. c
4. d
5. a
6. c
7. c
8. b
9. a
10. c
11. Between items (c) and (d) there is a gap of 15.
    New item: You turn the corner and see the sign "University of Louisville Main Campus."
12. a. time from anxiety-provoking event
    b. distance from anxiety-provoking event
    c. number of people present
    d. what those people or the client does in the scene
13. a. Can the behavior be tolerated?
    b. Can an increase in behavior be tolerated?
    c. Is behavior likely to be imitated?
    d. Can reinforcement be withheld?
    e. Have alternative behaviors been identified?
14. b
15. Fighting is being extinguished. It shows a gradual decrease because it is likely not being reinforced.
16. a

8 Increasing Behavior

DETERMINE IF BEHAVIOR IS IN CLIENT'S REPERTOIRE

Before the counselor uses response increment procedures, she must determine whether the desirable behaviors for the client are available in his repertoire. For example, a teacher may refer a child to the counselor because "he talks to others and doesn't finish his assignments." If the child is spending at least occasional moments sitting quietly and working and if he finishes a portion of his assignments, he obviously has the desired behavior in his repertoire. These behaviors can be increased. On the other hand, if the child never completes any of his work and spends all his time in activities incompatible with working, this behavior (sitting quietly and working) may not be in his repertoire. Obviously, then, this behavior must first be acquired before it can be increased (see Chapter 9, Teaching New Behaviors).

To increase behaviors already in the client's repertoire, a simple reinforcement procedure may be effective (see Figure 28 for steps in increasing behavior). Where the behaviors do not exist, they may be acquired through strategies such as shaping and modeling.

USE POSITIVE REINFORCEMENT TO INCREASE DESIRABLE BEHAVIOR

Introduce Reinforcement Procedures

Even though teachers, parents, or others who refer clients want ideas on how to change behavior, they may be skeptical of or resistant to some of the recommendations they receive. Oftentimes, they already have tried things, such as seeking advice from friends or family, or have implemented some of their own ideas. If these procedures have failed and the counselor recommends similar procedures, these also are likely

169

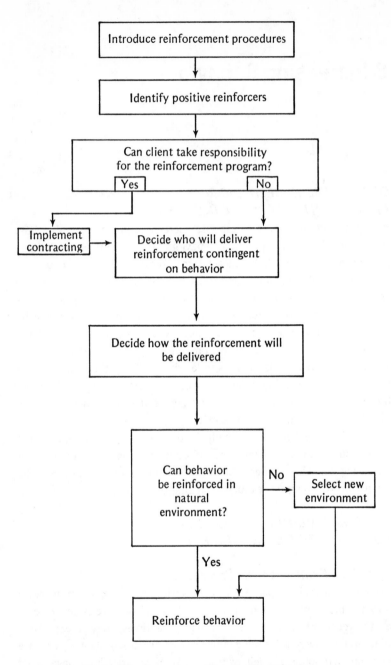

Figure 28. Summary of Increasing Behavior

to fail. If possible, alternative suggestions should be given. Otherwise, the counselor should show why the previous procedure did not work and emphasize the difference in her recommended procedure. For example:

Counselor: What do they seem to be doing?
Teacher: Well, they never bring their materials to class.
Counselor: Pause
Teacher: I've told them if they all brought their materials, I would give them a treat after school.
Counselor: What happened?
Teacher: Some of them still didn't bring their supplies.
Counselor: Ever think about giving a treat immediately to those who bring their supplies and ignore those who don't?

It is important here not to suggest that the client, parent, or teacher may have produced the undesirable state of affairs in the first place. This kind of insinuation only creates resistance in the teacher or parent, so it is better to avoid a discussion of the causes of the behavior.

In some cases, the client or consultee (e.g., parent or teacher) may wish to implement reinforcement procedures but is constrained by other people and things in his own environment (Tharp and Wetzel, 1969). For example, a teacher may be reluctant to reward a child's behavior with tokens because other teachers may disapprove. Likewise, a father may be upset because a mother is attending to her child's behavior rather than to him. In this case, the counselor must ask the client or consultee to perform behaviors within his role position which will not be punished. The reinforcement procedures should be explained to the satisfaction of others in the environment (father, other teachers), and they should be encouraged to cooperate in the program. In this way, the client and consultee (parent or teacher) are more likely to be rewarded for their behavior.

Identify Positive Reinforcers

In implementing reinforcement procedures, it is essential to first identify reinforcers in the client's environment which are sufficient to cause the client to perform the desired behavior. The crucial procedure is the manipulation of the reinforcing stimuli to extinguish undesirable behavior and increase desirable behavior. Often, one finds there are classes of reinforcers (e.g., food, smiles, etc.) which are effective for many individuals, and there are reinforcers that are unique to the individual. For example, for one person, ice skating may be reinforcing, while for another, roller skating is the most enjoyable behavior. *The counselor must identify reinforcers which are stronger than those which the client is receiving for his present undesirable behavior.* For example, it may be more reinforcing for a client to have his friends laugh at him for his inappropriate remarks than to receive the teacher's praise for desirable academic behaviors. Similarly, it should be no shock to parents or school officials that being expelled from school is more reinforcing for some students than many of the activities the school offers.

Use Interviews and Forms Determining effective reinforcers is a difficult process, but the best starting point is to ask the client what he enjoys:

What are some of the things you like to do?

When do you feel good about yourself?

Whom do you like to be with the most?

To determine reinforcers for young children, the counselor might ask them to name three wishes or to tell things they would like to take on a long trip to another planet. These questions take very little time to ask and often provide useful information. The counselor can determine by the child or client's enthusiasm whether the activity is reinforcing. Additional questions are provided by Tharp and Wetzel (1969). See Table 8.

Table 8. Mediator Reinforcement Blank*

Name _____

Date _____

School _____

1. My favorite grown-up (adult) is _____

   What do you like to do with him? _____

   _____

2. The best reward anybody can give me is _____

3. My favorite school subject is _____

4. When I grow up I want to be _____

5. Two things I like to do best are _____

_____

_____

6. My favorite adult at school is _____

7. When I do something well, my mother will _____

_____

8. I feel terrific when _____

_____

9. The way I get money is _____

_____

10. When I have money I like to _____

_____

11. When I'm in trouble my father _____

_____

12. Something I really want is _____

_____

13. If I had a chance, I sure would like to _____

_____

14. The person I like most to do something for me is _____
How? _____

15. The thing I like to do best with my brother or sister is _____

_____

16. The thing I do that bothers my teacher the most is _____

_____

17. The weekend activity or entertainment I enjoy most is _____

_____

18. If I did better at school I wish my teacher would _____

_____

19. I will do almost anything to get _____

_____

Table 8. Mediator Reinforcement Blank* (continued)

20. It sure makes me mad when I can't ————————————

————————————————————————————

21. When I am in trouble, my mother ————————————

————————————————————————————

22. My favorite friend in Louisville is ————————————
23. The thing I like to do most with him or her is ————————

————————————————————————————

24. The only person I will take advice from is————————————
25. Not counting my parents, a person I will do almost anything for
    is ————————————————————————————
26. I hate for my teacher to ————————————————

————————————————————————————

*Reprinted with permission. Tharp, R. G., and Wetzel, R. J. Behavior modification in the natural environment. New York: Academic Press, 1969.

These questions are redundant so that the counselor can cross check the client's report. The number of times a client reports an event as being reinforcing also can serve as a clue to the potency of the reinforcer. Once the interview is completed, the counselor summarizes the results and asks the client to rank them in order of importance to him. The counselor may exclude some reinforcers because they are unavailable. For example, a child may want a mini-bike which the parents cannot afford. In other cases, the reinforcing activity cannot be arranged, e.g., a day off from school will likely be contrary to school policy (see characteristics of effective reinforcers later in this chapter).

Another approach which is especially effective is the "reinforcement menu." Here, the counselor provides the client with a list of items that he may choose from when he has performed a desired behavior. One example of a reinforcement menu is the Reinforcement Survey Schedule (Cautela and Kastenbaum, 1967; see Table 9). Events are listed in categories and the client can be asked to rate each event. Counselors can modify this scale or select specific items depending upon the age of the client and the type of situation he is in, i.e., reinforcers may differ for school and home settings.

Table 9.   Reinforcement Survey Schedule *

The items in this questionnaire refer to things and experiences that may give joy or other pleasurable feelings. Check each item in the column that describes how much pleasure it gives you nowadays.

	Not at all	A little	A fair amount	Much	Very much
Section I					
1. Eating					
a. Ice cream	—	—	—	—	—
b. Candy	—	—	—	—	—
c. Fruit	—	—	—	—	—
d. Pastry	—	—	—	—	—
e. Nuts	—	—	—	—	—
f. Cookies	—	—	—	—	—
2. Beverages					
a. Water	—	—	—	—	—
b. Milk	—	—	—	—	—
c. Soft drink	—	—	—	—	—
d. Tea	—	—	—	—	—
e. Coffee	—	—	—	—	—
3. Alcoholic beverages					
a. Beer	—	—	—	—	—
b. Wine	—	—	—	—	—
c. Hard liquor	—	—	—	—	—
4. Beautiful women	—	—	—	—	—
5. Handsome men	—	—	—	—	—
6. Solving problems					
a. Crossword puzzles	—	—	—	—	—
b. Mathematical problems	—	—	—	—	—
c. Figuring out how something works	—	—	—	—	—
7. Listening to music					
a. Classical	—	—	—	—	—
b. Western/country	—	—	—	—	—
c. Jazz	—	—	—	—	—
d. Show tunes	—	—	—	—	—
e. Ryhthm & blues	—	—	—	—	—

Table 9. Reinforcement Survey Schedule* (continued)

	Not at all	A little	A fair amount	Much	Very much
f. Rock & roll	—	—	—	—	—
g. Folk	—	—	—	—	—
h. Popular	—	—	—	—	—
8. Nude men	—	—	—	—	—
9. Nude women	—	—	—	—	—
10. Animals					
a. Dogs	—	—	—	—	—
b. Cats	—	—	—	—	—
c. Horses	—	—	—	—	—
d. Birds	—	—	—	—	—

Section II

	Not at all	A little	A fair amount	Much	Very much
11. Watching sports					
a. Football	—	—	—	—	—
b. Baseball	—	—	—	—	—
c. Basketball	—	—	—	—	—
d. Track	—	—	—	—	—
e. Golf	—	—	—	—	—
f. Swimming	—	—	—	—	—
g. Running	—	—	—	—	—
h. Tennis	—	—	—	—	—
i. Pool	—	—	—	—	—
j. Other	—	—	—	—	—
12. Reading					
a. Adventure	—	—	—	—	—
b. Mystery	—	—	—	—	—
c. Famous people	—	—	—	—	—
d. Poetry	—	—	—	—	—
e. Travel	—	—	—	—	—
f. True confessions	—	—	—	—	—
g. Politics & history	—	—	—	—	—
h. How to-do-it	—	—	—	—	—
i. Humor	—	—	—	—	—
j. Comic books	—	—	—	—	—
k. Love stories	—	—	—	—	—
l. Spiritual	—	—	—	—	—
m. Sexy	—	—	—	—	—
n. Sports	—	—	—	—	—
o. Medicine	—	—	—	—	—

	Not at all	A little	A fair amount	Much	Very much
p. Science	—	—	—	—	—
q. Newspapers	—	—	—	—	—
13. Looking at interesting buildings	—	—	—	—	—
14. Looking at beautiful scenery	—	—	—	—	—
15. T.V., movies or radio	—	—	—	—	—
16. Like to sing	—	—	—	—	—
a. Alone	—	—	—	—	—
b. With others	—	—	—	—	—
17. Like to dance					
a. Ballroom	—	—	—	—	—
b. Discotheque	—	—	—	—	—
c. Ballet or interpretive	—	—	—	—	—
d. Square dancing	—	—	—	—	—
e. Folk dancing	—	—	—	—	—
18. Performing on a musical instrument	—	—	—	—	—
19. Playing sports					
a. Football	—	—	—	—	—
b. Baseball	—	—	—	—	—
c. Basketball	—	—	—	—	—
d. Track & field	—	—	—	—	—
e. Golf	—	—	—	—	—
f. Swimming	—	—	—	—	—
g. Running	—	—	—	—	—
h. Tennis	—	—	—	—	—
i. Pool	—	—	—	—	—
j. Boxing	—	—	—	—	—
k. Judo or karate	—	—	—	—	—
l. Fishing	—	—	—	—	—
m. Skin-diving	—	—	—	—	—
n. Auto or cycle racing	—	—	—	—	—
o. Hunting	—	—	—	—	—
p. Skiing	—	—	—	—	—
20. Shopping					
a. Clothes	—	—	—	—	—
b. Furniture	—	—	—	—	—
c. Auto parts & supply	—	—	—	—	—
d. Appliances	—	—	—	—	—
e. Food	—	—	—	—	—
f. New car	—	—	—	—	—
g. New place to live	—	—	—	—	—
h. Sports equipment	—	—	—	—	—

Table 9.   Reinforcement Survey Schedule (continued)*

		Not at all	A little	A fair amount	Much	Very much
21.	Gardening	—	—	—	—	—
22.	Playing cards	—	—	—	—	—
23.	Hiking or walking	—	—	—	—	—
24.	Completing a difficult job	—	—	—	—	—
25.	Camping	—	—	—	—	—
26.	Sleeping	—	—	—	—	—
27.	Taking a bath	—	—	—	—	—
28.	Taking a shower	—	—	—	—	—
29.	Being right	—	—	—	—	—
	a. Guessing what somebody is going to do	—	—	—	—	—
	b. In an argument	—	—	—	—	—
	c. About your work	—	—	—	—	—
	d. On a bet	—	—	—	—	—
30.	Being praised					
	a. About your appearance	—	—	—	—	—
	b. About your work	—	—	—	—	—
	c. About your hobbies	—	—	—	—	—
	d. About your physical strength	—	—	—	—	—
	e. About your athletic ability	—	—	—	—	—
	f. About your mind	—	—	—	—	—
	g. About your personality	—	—	—	—	—
	h. About your moral strength	—	—	—	—	—
	i. About your understanding of others	—	—	—	—	—
31.	Having people seek you out for company	—	—	—	—	—
32.	Flirting	—	—	—	—	—
33.	Having somebody flirt with you	—	—	—	—	—
34.	Talking with people who like you	—	—	—	—	—
35.	Making somebody happy	—	—	—	—	—
36.	Babies	—	—	—	—	—
37.	Children	—	—	—	—	—
38.	Old men	—	—	—	—	—
39.	Old women	—	—	—	—	—
40.	Having people ask your advice	—	—	—	—	—
41.	Watching other people	—	—	—	—	—
42.	Somebody smiling at you	—	—	—	—	—
43.	Making love	—	—	—	—	—

178

		Not at all	A little	A fair amount	Much	Very much
44.	Happy people	___	___	___	___	___
45.	Being close to an attractive man	___	___	___	___	___
46.	Being close to an attractive woman	___	___	___	___	___
47.	Talking about the opposite sex	___	___	___	___	___
48.	Talking to friends	___	___	___	___	___
49.	Being perfect	___	___	___	___	___
50.	Winning a bet	___	___	___	___	___
51.	Being in church or temple	___	___	___	___	___
52.	Saying prayers	___	___	___	___	___
53.	Having somebody pray for you	___	___	___	___	___
54.	Peace and quiet	___	___	___	___	___

Section III—Situations I Would Like To Be In

How much would you enjoy being in each of the following situations?
1. You have just completed a difficult job. Your superior comes by and praises you highly for "a job well done." He also makes it clear that such good work is going to be rewarded very soon.
not at all ( ) a little ( ) a fair amount ( ) much ( ) very much ( )
2. You are at a lively party. Somebody walks across the room to you, smiles in a friendly way, and says, "I'm glad to meet you. I've heard so many good things about you. Do you have a moment to talk?"
not at all ( ) a little ( ) a fair amount ( ) much ( ) very much ( )
3. You have just led your team to victory. An old friend comes over and says, "You played a terrific game. Let me treat you to dinner and drinks."
not at all ( ) a little ( ) a fair amount ( ) much ( ) very much ( )
4. You are walking along a mountain pathway with your dog by your side. You notice attractive lakes, streams, flowers, and trees. You think to yourself, "It's great to be alive on a day like this, and to have the opportunity to wander alone out in the countryside."
not at all ( ) a little ( ) a fair amount ( ) much ( ) very much ( )
5. You are sitting by the fireplace with your loved one. Music is playing softly on the phonograph. Your loved one gives you a tender glance and you respond with a kiss. You think to yourself how wonderful it is to care for someone and have somebody care for you.
not at all ( ) a little ( ) a fair amount ( ) much ( ) very much ( )
6. As you are leaving your place of worship, a woman turns to you and says, "I want you to know how much we appreciate all that

Table 9. Reinforcement Survey Schedule* (continued)

you did for us in our time of trouble and misery. Everything is wonderful now. I'll always remember you in my prayers."
not at all ( ) a little ( ) a fair amount ( ) much ( ) very much ( )

Now place a check next to the number of the situation that appeals to you most.

Section IV

List things you do or think about more than:

5	10	15	20 times a day?
_____	_____	_____	_____
_____	_____	_____	_____
_____	_____	_____	_____
_____	_____	_____	_____
_____	_____	_____	_____
_____	_____	_____	_____
_____	_____	_____	_____

*Reprinted with permission of author and publisher from: Cautela, J. R., and Kastenbaum, R. A Reinforcement Survey Schedule for use in therapy, training, and research. *Psychological Reports*, 1967, 20, 1115-1130.

Examples of reinforcement menus for varying grade levels are presented in Tables 10 and 11.

Table 10. Reinforcement Menu: Ages 5–12

1. Pick out a game to play.
2. Wear the principal's tie for a day.
3. Listen to stories on the record player with ear phones.
4. Record a story on the tape recorder.
5. Teach a lesson to the class.
6. Get a drink any time without permission.
7. Clean the erasers and blackboard.
8. Talk to your best friend for 10 minutes.
9. Leave class 10 minutes early.
10. Take a trip to a football game.

Table 11. Reinforcement Menu: Ages 15–16 (History Class)

1. Doing extra credit problems to raise grade.
2. Listening to "Greatest Moments in History" with earphones.
3. Designing a scrapbook of World War II.
4. Writing a letter to a local Congressman.
5. Playing charades.
6. Visiting a natural history museum.
7. Producing a science fiction movie.
8. Designing a radio show of "You Are There."
9. Viewing a film of the Potsdam Conference.
10. Leaving class 10 minutes early.

Use Formal Observation Another way the counselor can determine what is reinforcing for the client is to observe him carefully in his natural environment. The counselor can record what the client does in his free time, the activities he participates in, the food he eats, etc. With each client, reinforcing activities must be selected on the basis of formal observation, i.e., how often or how long he engages in an activity. Systematic observation is preferred over the counselor's or teacher's presumption of what is reinforcing (Sulzer and Mayer, 1972).

Example Exercise

Mrs. Smithburn, the counselor, wished to measure positive thinking in her client. Following the fourth session, she decided to praise the client each time she made a positive self-statement. By looking at Figure 29, (see p. 182) can we assume that Mrs. Smithburn's praise had a reinforcing effect on the frequency of the client's use of positive self-statements?

Answer

Yes, it did. An event is only reinforcing when it increases the level of target behavior (e.g., positive self-statements) which precedes it. Only by observation of the client's response can we determine the reinforcing or nonreinforcing characteristics of a given stimulus.

In cases where the client hasn't been exposed to an activity or the counselor or teacher is unsure of its value to the client, the counselor might allow the client to sample it and observe his reaction. Holz,

181

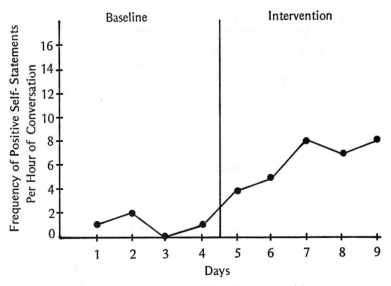

Figure 29.   Frequency of Client Positive Self-Statements

Azrin, and Ayllon (1963) found that children were more likely to "purchase" the privilege of watching a film if they were exposed to a portion of it than if they were not allowed to view it at all. Advertisers send free samples to potential customers with the hope that by trying it, the customer will like and purchase it. In this case, the counselor or teacher must allow the client to sample only a small portion of it; otherwise, it may lose some of its reinforcing quality.

Example Exercise

Note the following example of choosing a reinforcer. The counselor observed that Tony would spend a great deal of time with animals before science class. Occasionally, he would ask the teacher if he could clean the pens or feed the animals. Tony often had difficulty completing his assignments. Whenever he did finish his assignments, the teacher would ask him to clean the test tubes. Look at Figure 30 and decide whether cleaning the test tubes was reinforcing for Tony.

Answer

No. Cleaning the test tubes was not reinforcing. In this case, the teacher

182

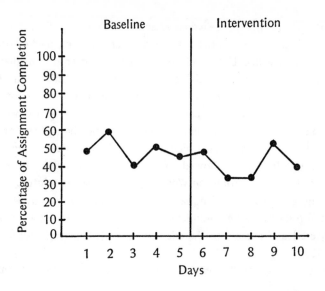

Figure 30. Frequency of Completed Assignments

or counselor might have been more observant of Tony's subtle hints to feed the animals or clean the pens and chosen this as a reinforcer for Tony. The real test would be to tell Tony that he could feed the animals when he satisfactorily completed his assignments. If this *increased* his level of assignment completion, then one could say that feeding the animals or cleaning the pens is reinforcing. Because a counselor is a trained observer, he can be extremely helpful to teachers or parents in identifying those behaviors in which the client typically engages.

Choose Strong Reinforcer

Evaluate Reinforcers According To Characteristics Once the counselor has discovered a number of stimulus events which can be used as reinforcers, she must determine those reinforcers that can be easily implemented in treatment. Gelfand and Hartmann (1975) describe several characteristics of an effective reinforcer.

1. *The reinforcer can be delivered immediately following the occurrence of the desired behavior.*
    Reinforcers which occur infrequently and only occur at fixed

time intervals cannot be delivered after the desired behavior. Baseball games, T.V. programs, Christmas presents, and skating parties occur only at certain times. Unless reinforcers can be delivered immediately following the occurrence of the desired behavior, the client may feel the counselor has broken her agreement because she failed to reinforce his desirable performance. Secondly, because of the long interval between the occurrence of the desirable behavior and the delivery of the reinforcement, it is unclear which behavior is being reinforced. For example, a child who is allowed to go to the skating rink on Friday night for cleaning his room on Wednesday may also be reinforced for not cleaning his room on Thursday. If the counselor or parent must delay reinforcement, he should use back-up reinforcers (e.g., points, tokens, etc.) and explain to the client what he is being reinforced for (see p. 192).

2. *The delivery of the reinforcer is under the control of the treatment agent.*

Unless the reinforcer is under the control of the treatment agent, it will lose its effectiveness because the client can obtain it otherwise. If a parent gives the child candy any time she wants it, then it will not serve as an adequate reinforcer. In this case, the counselor might encourage the child's parents to limit her access to the candy while the treatment program is in effect. It is advisable to select reinforcers which the client does not have normal access to (e.g., promotions, raises, grades, etc.)

3. *Reinforcers with which clients will not become quickly satiated are most effective.*

If the client becomes satiated or tired of the reinforcer, the rate or level of desired client behavior will likely decrease. Satiation can also be detected by client comments, such as "I'm bored" or "That doesn't interest me." Such comments suggest that the activity no longer has a reinforcing effect.

There are several things a counselor can do to resist satiation. First, the counselor can make several reinforcers available so that if the client gets tired of one reinforcer, another can be used. Using reinforcement menus and questionnaires provides a variety of reinforcers and thereby helps avoid satiation (see pp. 180-181.)

Secondly, the amount of time available for earning reinforcers can be brief. That is, rather than implementing a procedure for an entire day, the counselor might restrict the length of time when the client can earn a reinforcer. For example, a parent may wish to reinforce cooperative play by her child after school. Or, a parent or teacher may wish to reinforce word recognition at certain times during the day. Rather than reinforcing throughout the entire day, then, the counselor might attempt to keep the sessions at 15 or 20 minutes, thereby limiting the amount of time for receiving reinforcement and allowing the counselor to change any procedures as necessary.

Thirdly, the use of conditioned reinforcers such as money or approval are resistant to satiation. A **conditioned reinforcer** is an event which is paired with another reinforcing event. Thus, a smile or a pat on the shoulder becomes reinforcing because it is paired with other reinforcers (e.g., food, good grades, promotion, etc.).

4. *The reinforcer is compatible with the treatment program.*

Food or cigarettes would not be appropriate reinforcers for a client who is trying to lose weight or stop smoking. Likewise, an aggressive play activity should not be used for a child who frequently fights with others. In each of these cases, then, the reinforcer is competing with the client behavior to be changed.

5. *The reinforcer is inexpensive.*

An effective reinforcer is one that is not costly and can be easily transported in large supplies. Parents are generally not able to purchase expensive toys such as mini-bikes or trains. Likewise, these reinforcers cannot be given in small units. If a costly reinforcer is to be used, then, the counselor should use points, checks, or tokens which eventually can be exchanged for the back-up reinforcer (e.g., trip, prize, award).

Example Exercise

In the following examples, indicate whether the reinforcer meets each of the criteria for effectiveness.

1. Jack is having difficulty studying. The counselor suggested a program in which for each 10 minutes Jack stayed at his desk studying, he would earn 30 minutes to watch T.V.
2. Mary is having difficulty meeting new people. For each three persons she introduces herself to, she can go to a movie of her choice.
3. Joe is criticized for being so negative with others in the group. For each positive statement he makes to others, he receives positive

feedback from others in the group and a point toward leading the group.

4. Mike's parents agreed to let him go swimming on Fridays if he had washed the dishes each night.

Answers

	Reinforcer Delivered Immediately	Reinforcer Under Control of Treatment Agent	Reinforcer Resistant To Satiation	Reinforcer Compatible With Treatment Program	Reinforcer Is Inexpensive
1. Jack	✓		✓		✓
2. Mary			✓	✓	✓
3. Joe	✓	✓	✓	✓	✓
4. Mike		✓		✓	✓

1. While TV may be a powerful reinforcer for studying, the ratio of the reinforcer (TV) to the target behavior (studying) is 3 to 1. It is conceivable that Jack would be spending most of his time watching television rather than studying. Perhaps for each 10 minutes Jack studies he could earn five minutes watching TV. Likewise, it is unclear as to whether the reinforcer is under the control of the counselor. If Jack's parents allowed him to watch television any time he chose, then the reinforcer would likely be ineffective.

2. Going to a movie can be an effective reinforcer but often one which cannot be delivered immediately. Likewise, it is not a reinforcer under the direct control of the counselor. Perhaps, if the counselor were to check on Mary often, he could adequately monitor her progress.

3. Positive approval from the group is a conditioned reinforcer which will likely be resistant to satiation. In addition, the consequences of Joe's positive behavior allows him to lead the group. All criteria are met.

4. Swimming is an event which cannot be delivered immediately fol-

lowing the desired behavior (washing dishes). Furthermore, the client may get satiated with it. Thus, the counselor might arrange to give checks and approval for each night Mike washes the dishes. In addition, she might identify other potential reinforcers in case Mike becomes bored with swimming.

Example Exercise

In the following situations, tell which of the procedures you would use to identify positive reinforcers for the clients: (a) questions such as three wishes, what you like, etc., (b) questionnaires to fill out, (c) reinforcement menu, and (d) observation of what the client chooses to do in his spare time.

1. Mrs. Jones, first grade teacher, referred Homer to the counselor because he does about half of his writing papers and then stops.
2. Susan's school attendance has been poor, but when she comes to school, she especially likes recess and gym periods. When asked what she likes, she has difficulty discriminating and says she likes everything.
3. Bill is a seventh grader who was referred because he's timid and doesn't approach others very often. He's a bright student. You want to find out what might be reinforcing for him.

Answers

1. Since this is a first grader, it would be inappropriate to use questionnaires or materials he has to read. Observation (d) would be a good approach to finding what Homer likes. Asking him questions (a) would also be useful.
2. Since Susan can't discriminate, she would likely select everything on a questionnaire and would have trouble deciding among reinforcers on the menu and oral questions. In her case, observation (d) of what she spends the most time with would be best.
3. Since Bill is bright and probably reads well, a questionnaire (b) would be a quick way to determine what is reinforcing for him.

Decide Who Will Deliver the Reinforcement Contingent on Behavior

Once a list of reinforcing activities has been completed, the next step is to determine who will dispense them. It should be someone who spends time with the client and whom the client values. For some clients, going to a party is a reinforcing activity, but this is often contingent upon the persons who are at the party. Brown (1975) found that student achievement increased when the student was allowed to choose someone (best friend, teacher, etc.) who would monitor his progress and award points accordingly.

The important point here is that many reinforcing activities are interpersonal, and some reinforcers require a particular individual to successfully deliver them (Tharp and Wetzel, 1969). There are only two criteria for a reinforcing individual: (1) he can deliver high-ranked reinforcers for the desired behaviors and (2) he can dispense these reinforcers on contingency. For example, if a child chooses staying up 30 minutes later each night to watch T.V. as a reinforcer, the teacher could not dispense that reinforcer. On the other hand, a boy who wishes to play basketball after school may need the coach to dispense the reinforcer. In some cases where teachers are unwilling or are unable to dispense reinforcers, the counselor must identify someone else who will monitor the client's behavior and dispense a reinforcer on contingency. For example, with a child who wouldn't speak so he could be heard, the counselor first taught him to look at her and speak loudly. Then, for each three minutes the child did this without putting his head down or whispering, he received a token which could be traded in for a game or puzzle following the 20-minute counseling session. Once the child could make eye contact with the counselor and speak up, the program was transferred to the teacher who at first had been unwilling to try anything. In any respect, once a reinforcer has been identified for the client, the next step is to identify a valued individual who can deliver the reinforcer on contingency.

Example Exercise

Given the following situations, tell when reinforcement should be delivered and by whom.

1. Zener was typically slow to start on her work when assignments were given. However, today, as soon as instructions were given, she immediately began work.
2. Frank had a tendency to skip school and had an excessive number

of absences. The only thing of importance to him at school was playing basketball, and the coach was the most significant person at school for him.
3. When Mr. Harwood came home at night, he complained excessively about work. Mrs. Harwood wanted to increase the number of positive statements he made about his day's experiences.

Answers

1. The teacher should reinforce Zener as soon as she begins work, e.g., "Zener, I really like the way you started on your assignment immediately." Or, "Zener, here's a token for starting on your work immediately."
2. The coach could deliver reinforcement to Frank each day that he comes to school. This could be done early in the day on days Frank attends.
3. Anytime Mr. Harwood says anything positive, Mrs. Harwood should reinforce this. This may be done through ignoring the negative statements and responding to the positive ones.

In each of the preceding situations, after the behavior occurs at the desired level for a period of time, reinforcement may be delayed.

The contingent delivery of a reinforcement is imperative. The reward should be one which the client can get only when he exhibits the desired behavior and should always be delivered immediately after the desired behavior occurs.

Example Exercise

In the following situations, tell why the reinforcement was unsuccessful.

1. Mrs. Guthrie was concerned that Dycie was very slow to respond when asked a question. Occasionally, she answered immediately but most of the time, she looked down and failed to answer. On one particular day, Dycie responded readily on two occasions so at the end of the day, Mrs. Guthrie said, "I want you to be my special helper this afternoon because you spoke up today." However, the next day Dycie didn't speak up anymore than before.
2. Mrs. Hardman gave her whole class 30 minutes of free time be-

cause as a group, they had behaved well. Except for two pupils, everyone had listened and completed his work. The next day, Mrs. Hardman expected good behavior from everyone, but this didn't occur.

Answers

1. The reinforcement was not given immediately and hence not given contingently. That is, Dycie exhibited the desired behavior twice but failed to do so on several other occasions. If the reward were given contingently and the behavior still stayed at the same level, the presumed reinforcer may not actually be reinforcing. Actually, we can call a reward a reinforcer only if it increases behavior.
2. Reinforcement was not made contingent upon desired behavior. The two children who didn't behave well got the same reinforcer as the children who did behave well.

Reinforcement for the occurrence of a low-frequency response is best when it can be delivered *quickly*, contingent upon the behavior. As earlier mentioned, when there is a delay between the response and the reinforcement, it is likely that the client may emit additional behaviors which are also reinforced. For instance, a teacher may say "good job" to a child who has received a grade-A paper and who has also been misbehaving. In this case, the teacher must make it clear to the child which of his behaviors (the good work) is being reinforced. If she had immediately reinforced the child for his performance, she would not have had to make this distinction.

The immediate delivery of a reinforcer is closely related to the nature of the reinforcer. A teacher, for example, may not be able to allow a child to visit an art museum immediately upon completing his work with 100 percent accuracy, but she can give him a token or point and tell him how well he is doing immediately upon his finishing the assignment. When a child has completed his work, he may put up a red flag which signals the teacher to come and check his work. Then the teacher can deliver reinforcement immediately.

Crucial timing of reinforcement delivery is just one more reason why the counselor must identify those in the client's environment, e.g., employers, friends, teachers, siblings, parents, who can dispense the reinforcer immediately following the desired behavior. In some cases, the behavior and location will dictate the immediacy of a reinforcer. Behaviors such as appropriate conduct on a school bus are difficult to monitor. That is, because of the confusion, it would be difficult for a driver to reinforce good conduct on the school bus. However, good conduct could be reinforced by the parent before the child gets on the school bus and by the playground teacher after the child gets off the bus. *Behaviors which are reinforced in a variety of settings by different people are more likely to generalize to another setting where reinforcement is withheld.*

Once a target behavior is occurring at the desired level over a period of time, the counselor can gradually encourage the teacher, parent, or friend to gradually increase the delay of the reinforcement. For example, if a child has been consistently arriving at school on time, the teacher might wait five minutes and then tell him, "You made it to school on time again. That's great." Gradually, the time interval between the arrival at school on time and the reinforcer can be increased to 10, 15, 30 minutes, etc. Eventually, the child's behavior can be praised intermittently. *Behaviors which have gradually been phased into intermittent reinforcement are more resistant to extinction.*

Decide How the Reinforcer Will Be Delivered

Approval, smiles, and other social reinforcers have almost universal value, but often do not have the potency required for changing behavior. Consequently, tangible reinforcers are often necessary. If reinforcers were put on a continuum, one end might be represented by reinforcers such as candy to be delivered immediately when the desired behavior is exhibited. Next on the continuum would be tokens which can be traded in for rewards; next would be points, stars, etc. which could be traded for tangible rewards; then activity rewards; and finally on the other side of the continuum would be praise or social reinforcers. Social reinforcers are easiest to dispense and are the least expensive but do not always have the reinforcing value material rewards do. If praise alone is enough to maintain a behavior, it should be used; if not, a token or tangible reward system should be used but paired with the social reinforcement. For example, the teacher may say, "Susan, here is a token for completing your math assignment. I'm really pleased with the way you worked today."

Do Not Select Stronger Reinforcer Than Necessary It is important that the counselor or teacher never select a stronger motivational system than necessary to change a specified behavior. That is, praise and social rewards should be used if they will work. If not, activity rewards or free time should be used. If these don't work, tangible rewards can be tried. However, if tangible rewards are used, they should be faded out and eventually replaced by activity rewards and then verbal reinforcement.

Unfortunately, a child who has been repeatedly told he is stupid and who has failed often is not likely to be "turned on" when the teacher tells him, "You're a sharp student," because the praise statement conflicts with his past experience. In this case, the child probably has identified other reinforcers, such as candy or special activities or privileges. Therefore, the counselor, teacher, parent, etc. must develop a medium of exchange which will facilitate the delivery of these reinforcers. It is often difficult to deliver food and privileges immediately upon completion of a designated amount of work. Consequently, a medium of exchange, such as tokens, points, checks, can be given immediately and then later traded in for the object, privilege, or activity. Stars, coins, tickets, or stamps often become reinforcing because these objects are frequently paired with positive things in life. However, they would have little effect on the behavior of someone who has no way to exchange them or for whom they weren't paired with verbal praise.

Establish Exchange System There are several guidelines that can be used in establishing an exchange system (Becker, Engleman, and Thomas, 1975). The first step is to specify the behaviors that earn tokens and then to develop a list of back-up reinforcers. After this, a wage should be set, i.e., the total number of tokens a student could earn per hour and how many tokens he should receive for each desired behavior he emits. Secondly, prices can be assigned to the items listed on the reinforcement menu. Pupils can help to determine the value of activities, e.g., more tokens would be required to buy those activities which students like best. A sample reinforcement menu is shown in Table 12.

It is important to follow the law of supply and demand by increasing the prices of popular items and reducing the price of slow-moving items. Gradually, more work should be required for tokens. And, if the token system is working, it is possible to charge for misbe-

Table 12. Reinforcement Menu Showing Prices in Tokens

Activities	Price in tokens
Go on a field trip to a museum	30
Spend 10 minutes in the activity center	20
Play charades	15
Make a school emblem	15
Go on a picnic	15
Go to recess 5 minutes early	10

havior. The counselor or teacher can say, "From now on, leaving the room without permission will cost you five points. You can decide how you want to use your points."

Thirdly, the counselor or teacher should select tokens which are handy and cause a minimum of interference with the child's on-going behavior. In addition, tokens or points should be easily transportable from the place where they are dispensed to the area of exchange. They should also be identifiable as property of the individual and require a minimum amount of bookkeeping on the part of the teacher or parent. For example, a credit card (Figure 31) may be punched, with each hole representing one point; points or punches would be redeemable for reinforcing activities.

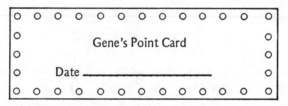

Figure 31. Sample Credit Card for Reinforcement Intervention

Credit cards can be punched by anyone in the client's environment (e.g., teacher, principal, parents). The card can be punched in the hallway, playground, and even in the neighborhood grocery if this is where the problem occurs. Other possible tokens include marks on the blackboard, plastic chips, stars, tickets, or stamps.

The final step focuses on the delivery per se. With younger children, tokens or points might be given immediately and exchanged for a treat. In this way children understand the value of the tokens. With older children, instructions may be enough. When the token is dispensed, the client should be told why he is getting it. The counselor, teacher, or parent might say, "That was neatly written," or "I am glad you made it to class on time today." In this way, the client is able to establish the connection between the reinforcing event and his behavior. It also opens the way for the counselor or teacher to pair praise with other reinforcing activities.

Example Exercise

In the following example, specify the token reinforcement procedures necessary for dealing with the problem.

Harry is somewhat withdrawn. He never gets into trouble at school, but he speaks very softly and often does not answer a question unless it is directed to him a second or third time.

Answer

First, you should have specified the behavior to earn tokens (e.g., Harry will speak in an audible tone of voice and respond to an initial question). Secondly, back-up reinforcers (e.g., playing Monopoly, cleaning the blackboard, wearing the principal's tie) should be specified for Harry. Thirdly, prices and wages must be determined for the reinforcers. Fourthly, appropriate tokens must be selected, and finally, Harry should be told why he is receiving points.

Use Contract If Client Can Set His Own Goals

Contracting is an effective agent when the parent, counselor, social worker, or teacher is trying to get the client to take more responsibility for his behavior. That is, contracting is particularly useful for clients who are aware of the negative consequences of their behavior and would like to do something about it. The contract is the client's commitment to change (Hackney and Nye, 1973).

Contracting is a form of structured bargaining that specifies clearly what is expected. The counselor is a mediator or arbitrator who facilitates mutual agreements between opposing parties about reciprocal exchanges of mutual behaviors, reinforcers, and punishers. This approach has been successfully used with marital (Stuart, 1969) and parent-youth conflicts (Stuart, 1971). Some contracts specify that the client can engage in a high-performance activity (e.g., listening to records) when he has completed a low-performance activity (e.g., mowing the yard).

The following guidelines (Homme et al., 1970) should assist the counselor in writing and negotiating a contract.

1. Contracts should be stated in a positive way. For example, rather than stating that the client will stop interrupting in class, it should state that the client will be attentive in class or spend more time on task.

2. The contract should make explicit the responsibilities of all parties, i.e., what each party will do. For example, it may state that the client will initiate five conversations with his classmates each day. Upon reaching this objective, the teacher will send a note home to Billy's mother who will allow him to stay up one half-hour later at night to watch television. In some cases, particularly with families, contracts in which each party specifies a behavior change can be used. For instance, a husband may agree to drink no more than one beer a day if the wife agrees to make no further statements about his drinking habits. Each party agrees to the role responsibilities of the contract and signs it.

3. A time line should be included in each contract. This time line should specify the amount of time within which the client can complete the contract. In the above example, the client was to initiate five conversations per day. This makes it clear when the contract has been fulfilled and signals when the reinforcer is to be delivered. The contract should also state when the agreement begins, ends, and is to be renegotiated.

4. A bonus or penalty clause may be built into the contract. For example, for each initiated conversation in addition to the five, the child may receive five minutes of television time up to one hour. Likewise, for each initiated conversation under five, the child will lose five minutes of television time. In using penalties, the counselor should be careful that the client has enough points accumulated to absorb the penalty because it becomes punishing if the counselor is taking away more points or privileges than he is giving. When a contract is initially negotiated, penalties may be left out altogether, and the consequences of violating the contract

195

would simply be loss of reinforcement. If, however, the client readily signs contracts and rarely abides by them, a penalty clause may be added.

5. Each contract should contain a provision for renegotiation. A contract should be revised when one or more of the following occur:

   a.   failure to complete two progress checks
   b.   making excuses for not fulfilling the contract
   c.   complaining

In many cases, the counselor, parent, and client may have misjudged how much work the client could complete in the given time period. In other cases, the client may wish to renegotiate to change the amount of and/or the reward. See Sample Contract in Table 13.

Table 13. Sample Contract

Date <u>Feb. 3 - Feb. 10, 1977</u>

Mary and John agree to describe two events which occurred during the day and each agrees to listen to the other.

Signed _____ Bonus _____
      John Schneppe

_____   _____
      Mary Schneppe

This contract will be reviewed one week from today.

In the final analysis, contracting provides the counselor an instrument for moving from behavioral control by the counselor, parent, etc. to control by the client. In the initial phases, the client can have a voice in determining the goals and amount of reinforcement included in the contract. Then as the client becomes more adept at designing her own program, the counselor fades his direction until the client assumes control.

Example Exercise

Write contracts for the following situations based on Homme's guidelines.

1. Eric has not been finishing his chores at home. He's supposed to take out the garbage and clean his room, but he often neglects these things and makes excuses.
2. Mike and Lucy are having marital problems. She's upset that he stops by the bar every day and doesn't get home until about 7:00 p.m. He's upset because she ignores what he has to say and fails to respond when he talks to her.

Answers

1. For each time Eric takes out the garbage and cleans his room, he will receive two points. When he has 10 points, he can trade them in for a movie. His parents will take him to the movie. If he receives two points each day this week, he will receive a 50-cent bonus.

Signed ____(Eric)____   Date _____

____(Mother)____

____(Father)____   Date to be Renegotiated _____

2. I, ____(Mike)____, agree to get home each day by 5:30 p.m. If Mike is home by that time, I, ____(Lucy)____, agree to listen and respond to what he says for 45 minutes.

Signed ____(Mike Crayford)____   Date _____

____(Lucy Crayford)____   Date to be Renegotiated _____

ENCOURAGE TRANSFER FROM NATURAL ENVIRONMENT IF NECESSARY

In many cases, the client's behavior cannot be reinforced in his natural environment. In these cases, the counselor should encourage the transfer of the client to a new environment. In homes where alcoholism, drug addiction, or marital discord is prevalent, the client's behavior should be treated in another environment. In school, if the classroom teacher is uncooperative and the classroom is out of control, a new teacher or classroom should be selected. If this is impossible, an Alternative School, Re-Ed School, or other academic setting may be necessary. This change of environment should occur, however, only after every attempt has been made to resolve the client's related problems associated with his current environment (e.g., marital discord, drug addiction, out-of-control teacher). If this isn't possible, the counselor might enlist the cooperation of social agencies, such as welfare officers, drug and alcohol rehabilitation programs or halfway houses, to provide useful services. For example, medical diagnostic teams who provide health services to indigent people often are able to serve a coordinating function by eliciting the cooperation of family and children agencies to provide parent training where needed. Knowledge of specific agencies and their functions would be helpful to the counselor.

CHECKLIST FOR INCREASING BEHAVIOR
Fill in the blanks. Check items yes or no and move to successive steps.

Behaviors To Be Increased:

1.

2.

3.

REINFORCERS:

Social	Activity	Token
1.	1.	1.
2.	2.	2.
3.	3.	*Material*
4.	4.	1.
5.	5.	2.

ALTERNATIVE INTERVENTIONS:

1. *Social Reinforcers*   Yes   No
   a. Will social reinforcers increase behavior?   ____   ____
   b. Does the client have requisite skills and does
      he exhibit the behavior sometimes?   ____   ____
   If the answers are yes, decide who will deliver the reinforcer and
   use social reinforcers. If no, go to Alternative 2.
   If yes:
   Who will deliver the reinforcer? _____

2. *Activity Reinforcers*   Yes   No
   a. Will activity reinforcers increase the behavior?   ____   ____
   If yes:
   Decide who will deliver the reinforcer _____
   Where it will be provided   _____
   When it will be delivered   _____
   If no, go on to Alternative 3.

3. *Token and Material Reinforcers*
   If Alternative 3 is chosen, the following questions must be
   answered:
   a. What token reinforcers will be used? _____

   b. What are the back-up reinforcers? _____

   c. Who will deliver the reinforcers? _____

   If Alternative 3 is selected, design a plan for fading it out and
   moving to Alternatives 2 and 1.

4. *Contracting*   Yes   No
   a. Can the client assume some responsibility for
      his behavior change program?   ____   ____
   If the answer is yes, use contracting. If the answer is no, use either
   Alternative 1, 2, or 3.

PROGRAMMED EXAMPLES
Choose one or more phrases that accurately complete the statements

and follow individual instructions for other problems.

1. Response increment procedures are most appropriate when the client
   a. does not have the necessary behavior in his repertoire.
   b. is not able to set a goal.
   c. lacks necessary skills to cope with the situation.
   d. has the necessary behavior in his repertoire.

   You are on target if you answered (d). When the client has the necessary behavior in his repertoire, then increasing the frequency of that behavior is the most appropriate intervention. When the client does not have the necessary behaviors (a) or skills (c), then an intervention must be designed to teach him those behaviors. Goals should always be set for the counseling intervention (b).

2. Mrs. Whitworth patted John on the shoulder each time he completed his work, but his rate of assignment completion did not change. This is an example of
   a. a reinforcer.
   b. an extinction procedure.
   c. a presumed reinforcer which had no effect.
   d. a time-out procedure.

   You're right if you answered (c). Here Mrs. Whitworth presumed that a pat on the back would increase John's rate of assignment completion. She might have looked for new reinforcers (a) or given him attention while he was working. Extinction (b) or a time-out procedure (d) would only be appropriate with behaviors which are incompatible with assignment completion.

3. Mrs. Maudlin would pass out candy at the end of the day if most of the class had completed their work. This is an example of
   a. positive reinforcement.
   b. noncontingent reinforcement.
   c. contingent reinforcement.
   d. a negative reinforcement.

   You are correct if you answered (b). Here some children receive candy regardless of whether they completed their work. Reinforcers are more effective in increasing the rate of a behavior when they are made contingent (c) on the desired activity. This could only be a positive reinforcement (a) if the level of work increased. A reinforcement is negative (d) when one leaves an unpleasant situation.

4. In the following situation, select the most appropriate procedure(s) for identifying a reinforcer:
Mike is a 23-year-old high school drop out who has gotten into trouble with the law. The courts referred him to a detention center where he will spend three days. There appear to be few reinforcing activities at the center.
   a. questions such as three wishes, what you like, etc.
   b. questionnaires to fill out
   c. reinforcement menu
   d. observation of what client chooses to do in his spare time
Answers (a) and (b) are the most appropriate. Since Mike will be at the detention center only three days, there are few activities from which to select (c) or time to observe (d). The counselor should probably ask him what he likes to do (a) or have him fill out a questionnaire (b). These activities would be useful for designing a treatment program for him when he leaves.

5. A reinforcement is most effective when
   a. it is delivered immediately and contingently.
   b. it is delivered immediately and noncontingently.
   c. it is delivered contingently shortly after the behavior occurs.
   d. it is delivered immediately.
If you answered (a), you are right. The reinforcer should occur immediately and only when the desired behavior occurs. If there is a delay between the response and the reinforcement, it is likely that the client may emit additional behaviors which are also reinforced.

6. Given the following situation, write a weekly contract which includes each of Homme's (1970) guidelines:
Ron fails to comply with his parents' requests. His parents' response to this is to give more directions, which sometimes amounts to 30 demands per day.

201

Suggested answer:
If Ron complies with an average of 80 percent of his parents' requests, his parents will take him to the amusement park on Sunday. In addition, his parents will not make more than 10 requests per day.

Signed _____ (Ron) _____   Date _____

_____ (Mother) _____

_____ (Father) _____   Date to be Renegotiated _____

_____ (Counselor) _____

For each additional 10 percent of complied requests, Ron can choose to do one less chore.

7. In the following situation, specify three reinforcement procedures necessary for dealing with the problem.
Joe has difficulty in completing his work. Although he doesn't cause trouble for others, he will sit in his seat and play with a tic tac toe game.
Suggested answer:
In the first procedure, you should have specified the behavior to earn tokens (e.g., Joe's attention to his assignments). Secondly, back-up reinforcers such as playing with a tic tac toe game should be specified. Thirdly, prices and wages should be determined (e.g., five minutes of tic tac toe for every 10 problems completed).

8. Given the following situation, tell when reinforcement should be delivered and by whom.
Jeff was a good athlete who would call his friends names when they made mistakes in gym class. His friends wished he'd help instead of ridiculing them.
Suggested answer:
The friends should reinforce Jeff when he doesn't call others names. They might prompt him to give help to others (what is Jack doing wrong?) and reinforce him immediately when he shows Jack or others what to do.

202

9. From the graph in Figure 32, identify the behavior that is likely being reinforced. Explain why.

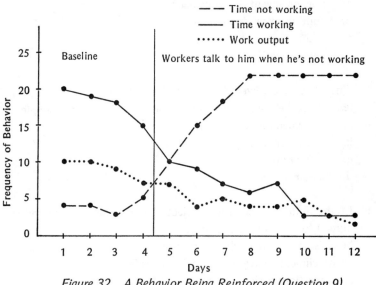

Figure 32. *A Behavior Being Reinforced (Question 9)*

Answer:
In this graph, the client's *time not working* is being reinforced. We know this because the frequency of his time off task increased only when it was followed by other workers talking to him. Concurrently, other behaviors such as amount of work and what he turned out decreased.

CRITERION TEST
Choose one or more phrases that accurately complete the statements and follow individual instructions for other questions.

1. When the client wishes to increase behaviors which exist in his repertoire, the counselor should use
   a. response increment intervention.
   b. response decrement intervention.
   c. cognitive restructuring intervention.
   d. social-skills program.

2. Mrs. Lowe would make positive comments to her husband only when he would get up to fix his breakfast. This is an example of
   a. noncontingent reinforcement.
   b. contingent reinforcement.
   c. extinction.
   d. desensitization.

3. When Mr. Moore would attend to his client's discussion of problem-related behaviors, they would increase. This is an example of
   a. presumed reinforcement.
   b. reinforcement.
   c. extinction.
   d. shaping.

4. In the following situation, select the most appropriate procedure(s) for identifying a reinforcer:
   Mary is an alcoholic who is an outpatient in a community mental health clinic. She lives by herself and has few friends.
   a. questions such as three wishes, what you like, etc.
   b. questionnaires to fill out
   c. reinforcement menu
   d. observation of what the client prefers

5. Reinforcers are most effective when
   a. they are delayed and contingent.
   b. they are delivered immediately upon contingency.
   c. they are delivered immediately and noncontingently.
   d. they are delivered on fixed intervals.

6. Given the following situation, write a daily contract which includes each of Homme's (1970) guidelines.
   Mrs. Olsen often missed weekly parent meetings with the counselor. In addition, she often failed to bring in completed data concerning the behavior of her son.

7. Specify the reinforcement procedures necessary for dealing with the problem in the following situation.
   Philip frequently argued with his brothers and sisters. Argumentative behavior included name calling, screaming, and fighting. The desired goal was cooperative behavior with his siblings.

8. Given the following situation, tell when reinforcement should be delivered and by whom.
   Tom was having difficulty in completing his math assignments. He would look out the window and doodle on his paper. When the bell would ring, he would race to the outdoor club where Mr. Roberts, his favorite teacher, talked about hunting and fishing.

9. From the graph in Figure 33, identify the behavior that is likely being reinforced. Explain why.

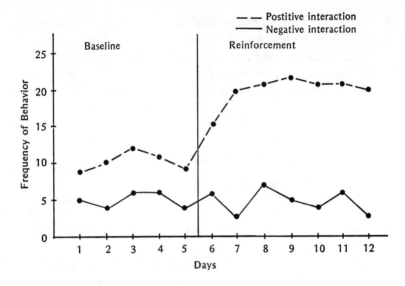

Figure 33. A Behavior Being Reinforced
(Criterion Question 9)

10. In the following example, indicate whether the reinforcer meets the criteria for effectiveness.

    Jerry was a war veteran who imagined he was going to die. For each positive self-thought (e.g., I am in good physical shape), Jerry was to record it and immediately reinforce himself with a cigarette. Jerry seemed to relax when he smoked and never seemed to tire of cigarettes.

CHAPTER 8
CRITERION TEST ANSWERS

1. a
2. b
3. b
4. b
5. b
6. Each time I attend the parent meeting I will receive a refund of $5.00. If I bring completed data concerning my son, I will receive

a $1.00 bonus.

Signed _____ (Mrs. Olsen) _____

Signed _____ (Parent Trainer) _____

Date _____

Date to be renegotiated _____

7. Argumentative behavior should be ignored by family members, and cooperative behavior should be immediately praised by them.
8. Mr. Roberts should allow Tom to attend the outdoor club meetings *only* when he has completed his math assignments.
9. Positive interaction is likely being reinforced. Its average rate has increased from baseline ($\bar{x} = 10$) to reinforcement ($\bar{x} = 20$).
10. Yes, cigarettes would be an effective reinforcer. They can be delivered contingently and immediately, are under the control of the person dispensing them, are resistant to satiation, and are relatively inexpensive.

9 Teaching New Behaviors

While response-increment strategies are effective for increasing desirable behaviors which the client exhibits sometimes, a new set of strategies is necessary for teaching behaviors which do not exist in the client's repertoire. (See Figure 34 for steps in teaching a new behavior.) In this instance, the client may not be performing the desired behavior because she lacks the necessary information or because she lacks the necessary skills to respond appropriately in that situation. A child who is not getting along with others may be told what to do (e.g., stop telling on others, share toys or books with others), but she also needs practice in implementing those behaviors.

When the desired behavior is complex, it may warrant being broken down into a series of steps which lead to the desired terminal behavior. For example, many interpersonal and academic skills require a series of subskills. A person who is socially competent must be able to enter a situation, give and receive information, and leave the situation. However, appropriate behavior differs across situations. What may be accepted in one situation may be rejected in another. That is, most behavior is situation specific and determined by the expectations or demands of that situation. For this reason, most situations need to be analyzed to determine the necessary tasks or skills to function effectively in them.

CONDUCT TASK/SKILLS ANALYSIS

Record Behaviors Needed
Counselors, teachers, and others have used several methods to define situation-specific competencies. One of the most common but unsuccessful methods is for authority figures to prescribe what they think is best for the person. A parent will often tell the child to "be nice" or

209

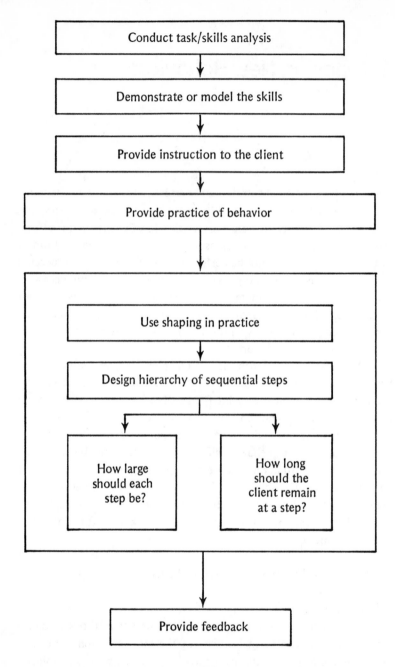

Figure 34. Summary of Teaching New Behavior

say "thank you" when someone does something nice for him. Likewise, teachers often assume that "being still" and "being quiet" are related to academic performance.

A more appropriate method, however, is a situational analysis in which the counselor systematically observes the problematic situation and records those behaviors which are necessary for the client to function effectively. If the counselor has difficulty in observing some of the necessary behaviors, he might interview others (e.g., peers, teachers) to determine the necessary skills.

Determine Hierarchy If Needed

For example, Kifer et al. (1973) interviewed parents and their children and observed a number of parent-youth conflicts. They identified five behavioral skills necessary for parents and their adolescent children to reach agreements (see Figure 35). These component behaviors were taught to parents and youth and agreements were reached in conflict situations.

This procedure is like the task analysis developed by Gagne (1967). Terminal behaviors are broken down into subtasks or skills and placed in a hierarchy from least to most complex. For example, if a client lacks the skills to interact positively with others, the hierarchy might begin with standing close to the group and end with the terminal

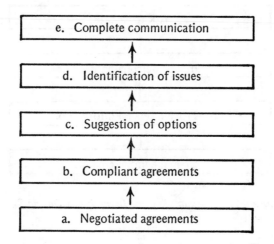

Figure 35.   Behavioral Skills for Parents and Adolescents

211

behavior of giving personal information to others (i.e., I like go-carts).

Once it is clear to the counselor what behavior is necessary to function effectively in a given situation, a client can be placed in that situation or a practice situation to determine which of the desirable behaviors he exhibits. The intervention then becomes teaching the client those behaviors he cannot perform. For example, if a client wishes to learn how to get a date, he might be placed in a simulated situation where he must call a girl on the phone and (a) initiate conversation (Hi, how was your day? Didn't I see you at Jerry's last Monday?), (b) provide general information (There is a big snow storm blowing in tonight), (c) provide personal information (I'm really into racquetball), and (d) ask her for the date (Would you like to go to a swimming party?). If the client is able to make the call and make an initial greeting, but he is unable to give general or personal information about himself or ask her for a date, these missing skills would be taught.

The assumption here is that these behaviors occur in a hierarchical fashion (from least to most complex). See the following example (Figure 36). If, however, the client were able to immediately provide personal information while unable to provide general information, then we could say that this is not a hierarchical sequence and that providing general information is not necessary before providing personal information.

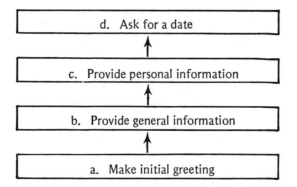

Figure 36. An Example of a Hierarchy of Dating Skills

Example Exercise

Given the following narrative description, determine a hierarchy of social skills that might be necessary for maintaining a 10-minute conversation.

Jack enjoyed interacting with others at a party. He would generally greet someone and ask, "How are you this evening?" The respondent would usually say, "Fine" and/or discuss something that happened to him that day ("Well, I got a parking ticket"). Jack always seemed to relate to their personal experiences ("Same thing happened to me last week" or "They are really cracking down on this 55 mph speed limit"). In addition, he would often disclose personal information about himself ("I can't stay too long tonight. I have an exam on Monday morning"). In addition, when a conversation seemed to end or a long pause occurred, Jack would change the topic by asking more information about something they were discussing or saying ("I would like to know more about ....").

Answer

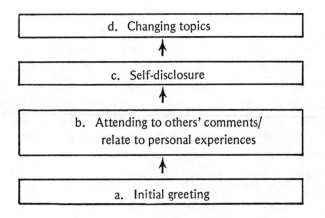

Figure 37.   An Example of a Hierarchy of Skills for Maintaining Conversation (Answer)

DEMONSTRATE OR MODEL THE SKILLS

The second step in helping the client to overcome specific performance deficits is to demonstrate or model the adaptive behavior to be learned. That is, the counselor shows the particular client what the response

213

looks like or how it sounds. Modeling has been effective in teaching clients information-seeking behavior (Krumboltz, Varenhorst, and Thoresen, 1967), career planning (Krumboltz and Schroeder , 1965), study habits (Ryan, 1966), reducing feelings of alienation (Warner and Hansen, 1970), and improving attitudes toward anti-drug use (Warner, Swisher, and Horan, 1973).

The process of modeling or demonstration often consists of the counselor providing live or symbolic models (e.g., audio tapes, video tapes) who show in sequential steps the specific behaviors necessary to solve the problem (Hosford and de Visser, 1974). Taped or filmed models have been particularly useful when the problem is basically cognitive in nature, such as information seeking or career planning (Hansen, Pound, and Warner, 1976). Since the model in this situation is being used only as a demonstration of the desired behavior, there is no opportunity for interaction between the model and the client(s). The taped model, however, may help to stimulate discussion in the desired direction. While audio and filmed models have been used mostly with cognitive problems, they may also be used with interpersonal problems.

Here, the counselor may wish to develop models for each of several counseling sessions. For example, the counselor could develop audio tapes which teach the client to (1) start a conversation, (2) maintain a conversation, (3) end a conversation, (4) listen, (5) express a compliment, (6) express appreciation, (7) express encouragement, (8) ask for help, (9) give instructions, and (10) express affection (Goldstein, 1973). Each skill could be modeled and practiced during a session if the client's skill level allowed. In this way, each modeling sequence could represent a closer approximation of a final behavior.

Use Guidelines To Design Modeling Program

In designing modeling tapes or using live models, there are several guidelines that will help achieve the model's desired objective.

1. *Modeling procedures seem to be most effective when there is a rather clear delineation of the client problem.*

The problem must be identified clearly enough so that clients know precisely what behavior the person is actually modeling. If the modeling sequence is too vague, there is little likelihood that any learning will take place. For example, rather than trying to model "awareness" to the client, the counselor should operationalize this, e.g., by identifying and labeling emotions. Or, if the counselor wishes to teach the client conversational skills, she might break conversation down into expressing and responding. These two areas might be broken down further into subskill areas, such as expressing and responding to anger, affection, etc.

It is beneficial to operationalize the skill to be learned. That is, the skill should be one that can be "seen and heard." After operationalizing the skill, the counselor can instruct the client on what the model will be saying or doing and what he should look for. The following typescript provides a model of self-disclosure. Notice how John provides information about himself to maintain the conversation.

John: Hi, are you in this biology class?

Phil: Yeah, why?

John: I just wondered if you knew what time it started.

Phil: I believe 10:30.

John: I'm really uptight about this class. I made a D in general science last year and I hear this class is a lot harder (self-disclosing information).

Phil: I don't know. I haven't heard much about it.

John: I wish someone else were teaching it. I hear Brown is a tough grader (self-disclosing information).

Phil: Yeah, he did flunk somebody last time.

John: I've got some notes from a guy who took this last year. You can borrow them if you like.

2. *Models who hold the client's attention are imperative.*

Simply exposing clients to modeled responses does not in itself guarantee that they will attend closely to them and that they will select from the total stimulus complex the most relevant events. A client will fail to acquire matching behavior if he does not attend to, recognize, and/or differentiate the distinctive features of the model's responses.

A number of attention-controlling conditions will be influential in determining which modeling behaviors will be observed and which will be ignored. First, situations should be chosen to optimize immediate recognition, understanding, and interest by the viewer. Research has shown that familiar and relevant experiences are more likely to hold attention and facilitate learning (Bandura, 1969). Also, models are generally most effective when they are of the same sex as the client and similar in appearance, age, etc. Model behaviors should focus on the

215

client problem. If the client is having difficulty entering a social situation, a person who is accepted in that situation and who is similar to the client might be asked to model or demonstrate how to get involved. The counselor might say, "I would like you to show Gene what to do when he wants to have a conversation with others." A model who verbalizes his own initial uncertainty (e.g., I'm not sure but here is one way to try it) and subsequent problem-solving or coping strategies can be helpful in eliciting the client's attention.

Another method for gaining attention from the client is to make salient those behaviors to be modeled. The counselor can instruct the model to "speak up" when he makes specific relevant responses (e.g., "How is this game played?" "How do you know when someone wins?"). Tone of voice and mannerisms also can be used to attract the client's attention. The same observation procedures discussed in Chapter 4 can be used to measure the client's attention toward the model.

3. *Another basic component of observational learning concerns the retention of modeled behaviors.*

Unless the client is able to understand and retain the essential characteristics of the model's behavior, the intervention will be to no avail. In cases in which the modeled behavior is particularly abstract, retention may be facilitated by having either the model or the counselor discuss the important features of the model's performance. For example, if a model were demonstrating socially assertive behavior to a socially conforming client who is afraid to disagree with others, the model could demonstrate a person telling others that while she understands their position, she has a different position. The model or counselor could then say: "This is an example of an assertive response: I am entitled to be myself and to say what I think, even if others disagree with me. When I tell someone my position and why I feel this way, I feel good about myself. I am being myself." By listening to the counselor or model outline the essential characteristics of an assertive response, the client is more likely to remember the general principles governing the behavior and is better prepared to apply these principles in a variety of situations (Marlett and Perry, 1975). To evaluate the client's retention, the counselor can ask the client to summarize the main features or general rules of the model's performance.

216

Example Exercise

Given the following typescript of a video-taped modeling session on responding appropriately to anger, answer the following questions.

1. What behavior(s) was being modeled in this tape?
2. Who was modeling the behavior?
3. What effects did the behavior have on others (what did they do when he behaved this way)?

Jack: I don't believe you did that. You don't have a brain in your head. Why didn't you deliver those papers on time?

Jerry: I know you're mad. It was something I couldn't help. Let's go into the next room and talk about it (appropriate response to anger).

Jack: Are you kidding? They blamed me. I may lose my job.

Jerry: (calm voice) Let's go into the next room and talk about it. I don't want to be shouted at. Come on. Let's go inside.

Jack: No! I don't want any excuses.

Jerry: I can't talk about it out here. Let's go in and talk about it calmly. It bothers me when you yell at me (appropriate response to anger).

Jerry: I'm going to keep on yelling unless something is done.

Jack: Well, maybe we can talk about it tomorrow. I'd like to take care of this matter too (appropriate response to anger).

Jack: Let's settle it now.

Jerry: Okay, let's go on in.

Jack: Okay.

Jerry: Great, maybe we can do something about this.

Answer

1. Responding to anger by going into the next room and explaining what happened (calmly)
2. Jerry
3. Jack finally decided to go into the next room.

4. *While the client may attend to the model's behavior and understand it, he still may not emulate it unless he is motivated.*

   That is, some reinforcers must be provided to encourage the client to perform the modeled behavior. When modeled behavior is not reinforced, imitation will not occur (De Rath, 1964); on the other hand, the likelihood that imitative behavior will occur increases as the probability of receiving reinforcement increases. When a client observes a model who is punished for his performance, however, he is less likely to imitate that model's behavior.

There are two ways in which the counselor can motivate the client by reinforcing the model. First, the counselor can arrange to provide reinforcers to the model for his performance. While the client does not receive reinforcement directly, he experiences it vicariously by watching the model receive it.

A second method the counselor may use to provide reinforcers to the model is to arrange the situation so the other role players will reinforce the model's behavior. For example, when the model has expressed his opinion, the other role players might say, "That's an interesting point" or "That's a thoughtful idea." By observing the model being reinforced for expressing his opinion or solving a problem, the client learns the most effective response in that situation (e.g., the behavior which is most likely to be reinforced).

IMPLEMENT CLIENT PRACTICE

Provide Instruction To the Client

Once the client attends to and understands the model's behavior, the counselor should provide instructions before the client begins practicing or trying out the new behavior. In this instance, the counselor can focus attention on the relevant and essential aspects of the model's performance. The instruction may be verbalized or written by the counselor, or it can be provided through an audio or video-tape recorder. If the client has previously learned to imitate models by following instructions, the counselor need not go through a lengthy shaping process (Gelfand and Hartmann, 1975). She might just say, "Watch how I respond to Bill's demand" (demonstrates appropriate behavior). "Now you respond to Bill's demand."

The counselor in this instance is essentially serving as a coach who prompts specific behavior for the client to try out. Instructions generally are broken down into *do* and *don't do*, and the counselor gives numerous specific examples. For instance, if the counselor is instructing the client to express his opinions, she might say: "Look directly at the other party, speak up, and express your opinion by saying 'I think . . .,

218

I feel . . ., What I believe is . . . ' Don't talk in third person such as 'Others think that . . . . ' "

The counselor might discuss when to express an opinoin (e.g., after others have had a chance to express their opinions, when someone asks you, when someone pauses) since a client may know what to say but not when to say it. By going back over the model demonstration, the counselor can pinpoint behaviors which were emitted and discuss why. This can then serve as a cue to the client on when to emit a specific behavior.

Provide Practice of the Behavior

Once the counselor has given instructions on what to say and do, the client is ready to practice the behavior. Practice is an essential part of the learning process since we learn by doing. By practicing or role playing the behavior, the client is able to try out new behaviors without the risk of failure. In addition, it allows him to anticipate difficult encounters and ways of handling them.

The first step in practicing or role playing the new behavior is to prepare the client. The client must accept the idea that practice would be an appropriate way to develop new social or problem-solving behaviors. If the client shows some resistance to this idea, the counselor can provide examples where practice has proven useful. Experience, drill rehearsal, recitation, homework, and exercises are some terms used to describe teaching tools which involve practice.

The following interaction illustrates how the counselor might prepare a client for the practice session:

Client: I just don't know what to say when I am around these people.

Counselor: It seems that you're just at a loss for words and you would like to carry on a conversation with them.

Client: Yes. I have tried to say things to them, but it just doesn't seem right.

Counselor: There seems to be a big difference in what you are saying and what you would like to say.

Client: Yes. (Pause) I really don't know what to do.

Counselor: Maybe we could practice carrying on a conversation. I'll role play some of your close friends or relatives, and we'll see how it goes. If you have trouble thinking of something to say, I'll help you. I also have some tapes of conversations that we can listen to for ideas.

219

The critical point here is that the client must feel he is not just learning a role that is artificial and unusable. Consequently, the role-playing situations should be as realistic as possible and should include verbalizations that the client feels comfortable with.

Use Shaping in Client Practice
The actual practice of new behavior often becomes a shaping process. This occurs not only because a hierarchy is employed but because the actual response itself often must be approximated. In addition, there are a number of other subskills, such as gestures, tone of voice, inflection, and eye contact, which relate directly to the client's performance. The counselor in many cases must focus on specific skills during the initial sessions and the remaining skills in the later sessions.

Design Hierarchy of Sequential Steps
The following steps should be used for the shaping process.
1. *In initiating the practice sessions, start with a situation that the client can perform with little difficulty.*

This will help him be more comfortable in the role group and at the same time, help the counselor to see how well the client can stay in the role. For example, if a person is having difficulty being included in her peer group, the counselor may want to start with an interaction in which the client can respond. Initially, the client might be asked to greet the peer group by saying, "Hi," "What's going on?" or waving her hand. Or, she might be asked to greet the least threatening member in the group. If the client is unable to do this, the counselor might ask her to engage in less threatening activities such as standing in close proximity to the group. Regardless of the activity, the counselor should begin with a nonthreatening situation.
2. *Decide on a terminal behavior you wish to practice.*

The same procedures used for selecting goal behavior (see Chapter 5) should be used in this step for specifying a terminal behavior. This also should be the final behavior to be demonstrated in the modeling sequence. In the current example, the goal may be for the client to be able to successfully leave the group. For example, the counselor might want to teach the client to "leave when there is a pause in the action," or to move away physically. There are commonly accepted nonverbal techniques which the client can use to leave the play situation.

3. *Break the behavior down into small steps which lead to the terminal behaviors.*

These steps should vary in degree of complexity and range from simple (e.g., greeting others) to the terminal behavior (e.g., leaving the situation). See Figure 38. In this case, the social interaction varies according to the level of difficulty. A second step after greeting peers might involve initiating or joining a conversation. Here, the client might say something like, "When is our next ball game?" or "How did you like that last inning?" A third step which is more difficult might involve maintaining the conversation or group interaction.

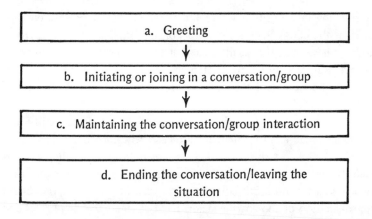

Figure 38. Summary of Task Analysis of Social Interaction

This step of maintaining a conversation requires the client to (a) ask for information ("What's your name?" "Didn't I see you at the Cardinal game last night?") and (b) supply information ("I like the Cincinnati Reds" or "Jonathan Winters is really funny"). Each of these substeps can be taught separately.

4. *When the client gets stuck and cannot think of what to say or do, the counselor can prompt him.*

The counselor can provide a sentence which fits within the context of the conversation (e.g., "Tell me some more about your experiences in the army"). It is extremely important that the prompt occur only when the client pauses or hesitates (generally about five seconds). In addition, the counselor can use hand signals to raise or lower the

221

client's voice or motion for him to come closer.

In addition, prompts should be faded as the client is able to act out the role or demonstrate the behavior. For example, rather than saying, "Tell me some more about your experiences in the army," the counselor might say, "Tell me some more . . . ." Often the counselor can begin fading prompts when the client paraphrases the counselor's prompt. For example, when the counselor says, "Tell me some more about your experiences in the army," the client might say, "I would like to know more about what you did in the army." Here the counselor should praise the client for expressing the prompt in his own words.

When the counselor is prompting the client, she should be sitting or standing in a position where the client can see her. Regardless of whether the counselor is giving verbal or nonverbal feedback (e.g., head nods, smiles, etc.), it does little good unless the client is in a position to see her. Rather than sitting or standing in back of the client, the counselor should be off to the side or in front of the client so she can be seen.

To insure that each step or situation increases in difficulty, the counselor could ask the client to rate each behavior from 1 (least difficult) to 100 (most difficult). This is similar to the procedure used in identifying levels of anxiety (See Chapter 7). It is important that each step is slightly more difficult than the preceding one and is a better approximation of the goal behavior. In cases where the client rates one situation as 45 and the next situation as 60 (exceeds 10 units), the counselor should provide intermediate steps such as "asking" or "supplying information." The counselor should always check with the client to find out if the hierarchy is in increasing levels of difficulty.

Determine How Large Each Step Should Be There is usually no specific answer to how large each step should be. If the client is making satisfactory progress, it can be assumed that the size of the step and the amount of practice at each step are appropriate. However, if the client is unable to complete a step or starts complaining, then the counselor should re-examine what he is asking the client to do or say. Possibly the step should be broken down into substeps (e.g., giving and supplying information) or a smaller step should be added (e.g., standing in close physical proximity to others). The counselor can be reasonably sure that the steps are appropriate if the practice sessions are planned with the client. For example, the counselor might say, "It seems that when George wanted to play with others, he asked them if he could hold the rope. Is that something you could do? Can you think of some other ways to get involved?" "When you moved here from Indianapolis, what did you say or do to get involved?" In some cases, the client may be able to think of less threatening ways to get involved, but regardless, it is important that the step be one that the client feels he can accomplish. If the client cannot perform the desired behavior, the counselor should go back to a behavior he can perform. If he still cannot perform the desired behavior, the counselor should check for client fatigue or satiation of the reinforcer (see page 184). It is important that the client end the session with a successful performance.

Determine Length of Each Step There usually is no one specific answer to how long a client should remain at a step. Generally, some criterion for performance is established at each step. The counselor in this case would want to make sure that the client is able to perform the behavior for a given time. If the client is able to perform a skill (e.g., greeting others, completing long-division problems), it can be assumed that the size of each step and the amount of practice at each level have been appropriately selected (Sulzer and Mayer, 1972). However, if a client's behavior begins to deteriorate, the length of time spent on the step should be re-examined.

For example, a female client who had been taught a set of conversational skills in a lab may be asked to maintain a conversation with a variety of strange people for increasing five-minute blocks of time up to 30 minutes. Figure 39 shows the client's performance measured against the changing criterion.

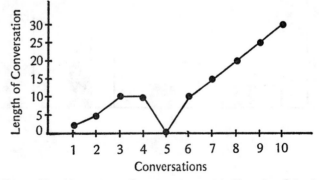

Figure 39. Maintaining Conversations with Changing Criterion

223

Figure 39 indicates that the client had difficulty meeting the initial criterion level (5 minutes) with the first stranger. In this case, the counselor should have determined how long the client could maintain a conversation (baseline) prior to the intervention. Since the client also seemed to be having difficulty between the third and sixth conversations, the step was either too big or those individuals she talked with made it difficult for her to maintain a conversation (e.g., had an appointment with someone, were nonverbal, or ill). The counselor in this case might have asked the client to maintain a conversation at the same level (10 minutes) on two or more occasions. Again, if the behavior progresses (eighth to tenth conversations), then it can be assumed that the counselor selected appropriate criteria for practice and success at each level.

Example Exercise

Look at Figure 40 and answer the questions on page 225.

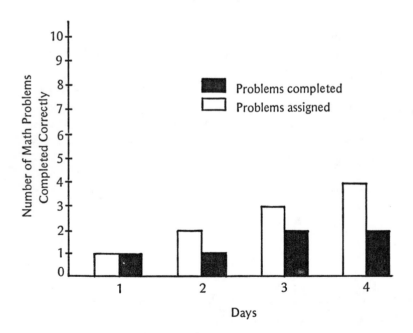

Figure 40. Monitoring Shaping Procedure

1. Describe the shaping procedure in the graph.
2. Was the length of steps appropriate?
3. Describe an alternative program.

Answers

1. One additional math problem for each succeeding day.
2. No, the criteria were too high. After the first day, the child was unable to complete the number of math problems assigned.
3. One alternative might be to assign one math problem for a four- or five-day period; then possibly complete one problem and start a second for a four- or five-day period until the child has completed the number of daily math problems you want him to complete.

In some cases, step sizes may be too small or the client is required to remain at a criterion level for too long. Clients generally show signs of disinterest (inattention to task, failure to complete assignments, etc.) when the step size is too small. If the step size is increased and the client's performance improves, then the increased step size is appropriate. *In short, it is critical that the counselor adjust the step size to the ability and performance level of the client.*

In some instances, the size of the step is so long that the client over-learns it. Too much practice can cause the client difficulty in moving from one step to the next. For example, a client, who over-practices conversing with friends may find the next step (conversing with strangers) very difficult and may rely too much on her previous practice. Thus she may have learned to talk about shared experiences with people familiar to her but lacks the additional skills necessary to maintain a conversation with a stranger (e.g., asking open-ended questions, changing topics, etc.). In this case, the counselor can encourage the client to maintain a 10-minute conversation with three people who are familiar to her, but the three people should be persons who are increasingly threatening, e.g., the first person could be nonthreatening, the second somewhat threatening, and the third very threatening. Following this, she would practice conversing with strangers who provide increasing levels of threat to her. In summary, it is critical that the counselor adjust the length of the step so that (1) the client can reach it with a minimum of practice and (2) it is long enough to maintain the client's interest.

PROVIDE FEEDBACK TO THE CLIENT

Once the client has practiced the sequence of skills, he must receive feedback on his performance. Knowledge of one's performance provides information and an incentive for improvement. Thus, information received about poor performance can be as potentially helpful for improving performance as knowledge regarding positive performance.

Some of the factors which influence the effects of feedback upon learning have been previously discussed (see sections on delivering the reinforcement in Chapter 8). In addition, there are several other factors which influence the effects of feedback.

First, feedback is usually more effective when it is solicited or agreed upon prior to practice. The counselor might say, "I'll observe you and try to give you some helpful hints." When a client denies or disagrees with feedback from the counselor (e.g., "That's not the way it sounded to me") or attempts to justify his response ("The reason I said that was . . . ."), then feedback was probably not solicited or agreed upon prior to practice. If there is resistance to feedback, the counselor should work through this (see comments on resistance in Chapter 2).

Secondly, feedback should describe rather than evaluate the client's response. For example, the counselor might play back an audio tape of what the client said and comment, "Here you say 'My mother thinks I should . . . .' Remember we agreed you would say 'I think I should . . . .' " These counselor-feedback statements avoid judgment or blame. Statements such as "That just doesn't sound right" or "I don't know why you can't do that" fail to provide helpful information to the client.

Thirdly, in some cases the counselor may wish to reinforce a client response and at the same time prompt similar responses. For example:

Client: Tell me more about your job.

Counselor: Fine. That's a good open-ended question which gets him to talk to you. Sometimes, however, a person may not want to talk about his job. Can you think of some other questions you could ask him?

Client: Sure. Tell me some more things about your child or tell me about your family.

Counselor: Good! All those questions should help to maintain the conversation.

Here, the counselor reinforced a client's open-ended statement and at the same time prompted additional questions. This should not only help to reinforce the client's use of open-ended questions in a practice session but also facilitate its generalization to other situations and people.

Example Exercise

Read the following excerpt from a counseling session and answer the questions about it. Joan (client) had agreed to use "I" statements when making a complaint.

Joan: I feel bothered that I'm not included in your activities any more.

Mary: Well, I have to spend more time with Chet now.

Joan: I know that, but I still feel left out of things.

Mary: You don't seem to realize my situation.

Joan: Maybe so, but you are always too busy for me.

Mary: Well, what do you expect me to do?

1. What behaviors should the counselor give positive feedback for?
2. What might he have said to reinforce these behaviors?
3. For what behaviors should he have given corrective feedback?
4. What might he have said?

Answers

1. The counselor should have given positive feedback for Joan's "I" messages.
2. The counselor might have reinforced the use of these behaviors by saying, "Joan, that sounded great when you said 'I feel bothered that . . . .' and/or 'I know that but I still feel . . . .' " (Here the counselor makes a short statement of praise and then describes specifically what the client said.)
3. The counselor should provide corrective feedback for "you" statements or third-party statements (". . . you are always too busy for me").
4. The counselor might have said, "On one occasion, you said, '. . . you are always too busy for me.' How might that be changed into an 'I' message?"

CHECKLIST FOR TEACHING NEW BEHAVIORS

Check yes in the spaces below as the procedure is completed. Then go on to the next step.

	Yes	No
1. *Conduct task analysis.*	___	___
a. Identify subskills.	___	___
2. *Demonstrate or model the skills.*	___	___
a. Delineate client problem.	___	___
b. Client attends to model behaviors.	___	___
c. Client retains model behaviors.	___	___
d. Client accepts model behaviors.	___	___
3. *Implement client practice.*	___	___
a. Provide instructions.	___	___
b. Practice behaviors.	___	___
4. *Shape new behaviors.*	___	___
a. Design hierarchy of sequential steps to the terminal behavior.	___	___
1. Start with situation client can perform with little difficulty.	___	___
2. Decide on terminal behavior.	___	___
3. Break terminal behavior into smaller steps.	___	___
4. Prompt desired behaviors.	___	___
5. *Provide feedback.*	___	___

PROGRAMMED EXAMPLES

Choose one or more phrases that accurately complete the statements and follow other instructions for individual questions.

1. Clients must be taught new behaviors when
   a.   they are anxious.
   b.   the desired behavior exists in their repertoire.
   c.   the desired behavior does not exist in their repertoire.

228

d.   they want better relationships with others.

You are correct if you answered (c). When the client does not have the necessary behaviors to function in a situation, the counselor or others must teach him new behaviors. Otherwise, the counselor can only increase the frequency of those behaviors which already exist (b). Anxieties (a) *may* be decreased and better relationships may be developed (d) when new behaviors are learned.

2. The first step in teaching the client new behaviors for a given situation is
    a.   observing the problematic situation and recording behaviors necessary for the client to function effectively.
    b.   deciding yourself what is necessary.
    c.   reading a textbook.
    d.   asking the client.

    The best alternative is (a). Here the counselor can determine what "well-functioning" people do in a specific situation. The other alternatives may or may not identify necessary skills to be taught.

3. The chief advantage of providing instructions to the client before the model demonstration is to
    a.   reduce the client's anxiety.
    b.   encouarge the client.
    c.   focus on relevant aspects of the model's performance.
    d.   improve the modeled demonstration.

    If you answered (c), you are right. By focusing on relevant aspects of the model's performance, the client is better able to isolate those behaviors to practice. These instructions may or may not reduce client anxiety (a) or encourage the client (b). Instructions to the client (d) would have no effect on the model's performance unless the modeling is live and the model and client receive instructions simultaneously.

4. A step (skill) may be too long if
    a.   the client becomes inattentive.
    b.   the client reaches his goal.
    c.   the client demonstrates new behaviors.
    d.   the client sets a new goal.

If you answered (a), you are correct. Usually steps are too long when the client acts disinterested or begins to complain. In this case, the step size (length of time) should be altered. If he reaches his goal (b), sets a new goal (d), or demonstrates the appropriate behaviors, (c) then, the size of the step is usually appropriate.

5. Given the following model typescript of "self-disclosure," answer these questions:
   1. What behaviors were being modeled in this tape?
   2. Who was modeling this behavior?
   3. What effects did it have on others (what did they do when he behaved this way)?

George: Has meeting at night caused poor attendance in your new class?

Jim: No, it hasn't seemed to.

George: I think the night schedule affected my students last year. After teachers work all day, they are just too tired to sit through a night class. I had eight people to drop.

Jim: Well, I had three people drop the first night.

George: Really! I had three people drop this year, too.

Jim: I'm not sure what to make of it. What do you think, George?

Suggested answers:
   1. Behaviors which reflect self-disclosure such as "I think the night . . ." and/or "I had eight people . . . ."
   2. George
   3. When George modeled "self-disclosure," Jim would describe his own class experiences: "Well I had three people . . . ." and ask George a question, "What do you think . . . ."

6. Given the following narrative description, identify the hierarchy of academic skills that might be necessary for the client's success in school.

   Bill had difficulty in school. His grades were poor, he often failed to complete assignments, and the assignments he did complete were often incorrect. In addition, Bill was often absent or tardy. In some cases, he would wander into class when it was half over.

Suggested answer:

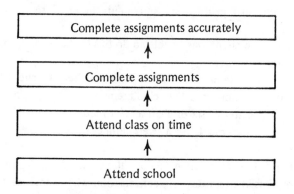

| Complete assignments accurately |
| Complete assignments |
| Attend class on time |
| Attend school |

Figure 41. A Suggested Hierarchy of Academic Skills
(Answer for Question 6)

7. Look at Figure 42 and answer the following questions.

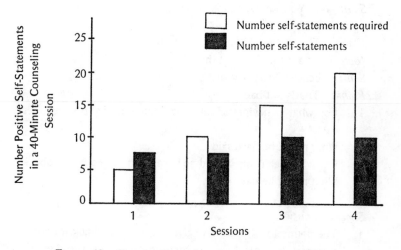

Figure 42. Shaping Procedure Being Monitored (Question 7)

1. Describe the shaping procedure in the graph.
2. Is the length of each step appropriate?
3. Is an alternative program necessary? If so, what might it be?

231

Suggested answers:

1. For each counseling session, the client was asked to make five additional positive self-statements in order to receive a reward.
2. No, the client was unable to do this in the second, third, and fourth sessions.
3. The counselor maybe could have required the client to make two additional positive self-statements per session, possibly up to as many as six or eight and/or require that the client make N self-statements for a given number of sessions.

8. In the following practice session, the client (Joe) is trying to involve himself in an ongoing conversation when someone turns his body toward him or makes eye contact with him.

    Sam: I really like racquetball.

    Frank: Yeah, it's good exercise.

    Joe: (Enters room, listening) You guys want to go down to the Anglers?

    Sam: No. You know, Frank, we ought to join that new club out on Bishop's Lane.

    Frank: That's a good idea. (Looks at Joe)

    Joe: What are the dues out there?

    Sam: I believe $80 per year.

    Frank: That's not bad.

    1. For what behaviors should the counselor give positive feedback?
    2. What might he have said?
    3. For what behaviors should he have given corrective feedback?
    4. What might he have said?

Suggested answers:

1. The counselor should have given positive feedback for appropriate statements by Joe, such as "What are the dues out there?"
2. He might have said, "Good. When Frank looked at you, that was a good time to say something on the topic."
3. The counselor should have given corrective feedback for the inappropriate statement Joe made when he entered the room.

4. "When you entered the room, you asked Sam and Frank 'Do you want to go to the Anglers?' but you got no response. Why might that have happened?" (If the client says he didn't receive eye contact or that he changed the topic, the counselor should praise him.) If he doesn't mention this, the counselor should ask him what he might have said. (Appropriate responses shall be praised.)

CRITERION TEST

Choose one or more phrases that accurately complete the statements and follow individual instructions for other questions.

1. When behaviors do not exist in the client's repertoire, the counselor should
   a. teach new behaviors to the client.
   b. teach the client to signal when he is anxious.
   c. teach the client to identify inappropriate behaviors.
   d. teach the client to set goals.

2. Before the counselor can teach the client new behaviors, he must
   a. talk with others in that situation.
   b. decide what behaviors he thinks are required in that situation.
   c. observe what others who are successful in that situation do.
   d. determine how the "experts" think a client should behave.

3. Instructions to the client before modeling
   a. reduce the client's anxiety.
   b. encouarage the client to practice new behaviors.
   c. decrease client resistance.
   d. make essentials of modeled behavior more relevant.

4. The counselor can often determine if the length of each step in the hierarchy is appropriate if
   a. the client identifies new problems.
   b. the client continues to progress and is attentive.
   c. the client arrives on time for each session.
   d. the client becomes anxious.

5. Given the following model typescript of "self praise," answer these questions.
   a. What behaviors were being modeled in this tape?
   b. Who was modeling this behavior?
   c. What effects did it have on others (what did they do when he behaved this way)?
   Gene: Hi, Joe. Want to go to the racquet club?
   Joe: Yeah. I feel a lot better when I go, and I really need to lose some weight. I've lost five pounds in the last two weeks.
   Gene: Great!
   Joe: I've been feeling good recently, and I'm able to wear clothes that I haven't had on in a year.
   Gene: When did you start working out?
   Joe: Well, I was getting tired and wasn't able to do much. I just decided about a month ago that I'd try to take off weight.

6. Given the following narrative description, identify the hierarchy of decision-making skills that might be necessary for the client.
   Rick was having difficulty deciding upon which college to attend. He was not aware of his SAT scores and his chances for succeeding at particular schools. Nor did he know about various colleges and their academic and financial requirements. In addition, he had no professional goals or knowledge of his interpersonal or professional skills.

7. Look at Figure 43 and answer the following questions.
   a. Describe the shaping procedure in the graph.
   b. Is the length of each step appropriate?
   c. Is an alternative program necessary? If so, what might it be?

8. In the following practice session, the client is trying to practice open-ended questions in a conversation. Answer the questions that follow.
   Willie: Hi, buddy. What have you been doing?
   Pat: Oh, I've been playing some tennis.
   Willie: Oh, yeah! Tell me how to make a serve.
   Pat: Well, I really would need a racquet to show you. Why don't you come over to the house, and I'll get my racquet.

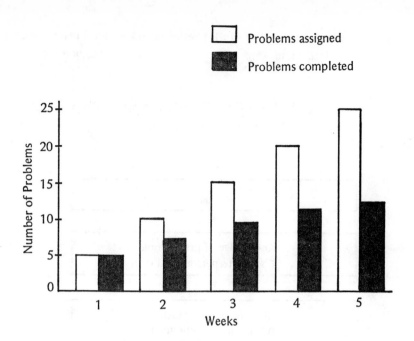

Figure 43. *Shaping Procedure Being Monitored
(Criterion Question 7)*

Willie: Where is your house?
Pat: A couple of blocks from here.
Willie: Do you still live with your mother?
Pat: Yeah.
a.   For what behaviors should the counselor give positive feed-
     back? What might he say?
b.   For what behaviors should he give corrective feedback? What
     might he say?

CHAPTER 9
CRITERION TEST ANSWERS
1. a
2. c
3. d
4. b

5. a. self praise (i.e., "I feel a lot better when I go, and I really need to lose some weight . . . ." "I've been feeling good recently . . . .").
   b. Joe
   c. Gene praised him (i.e., "Great") and asked him a question (i.e., "When did you start working out?").
6.

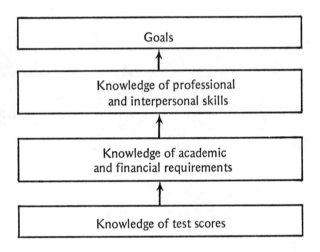

Figure 44. Suggested Hierarchy of Decision-Making Skills (Criterion Answer 6)

7. a. After the first week, five additional problems were assigned. After the first week, the student completed an additional two problems each week.
   b. No.
   c. Yes. The teacher might assign two additional problems each week. If the client completes this requirement two weeks in a row, she might assign three problems.
8. a. Praise Willie for his introduction (i.e., "Hi buddy . . . .") and question for general information (i.e., "Oh yeah! Tell me . . . .") and personal information (i.e., "Where is your house?"). The counselor might say, "Your questions were really effective in getting the information you needed."

b. The counselor should give corrective feedback for "Do you still live with your mother." This is a closed-ended question. The counselor could say, "Willie, you had one closed-ended question. How might you make that an open-ended question?"

10 Cognitive Restructuring

While systematic desensitization has proven to be effective in decreasing situation-specific anxiety, it has been less efficacious in decreasing free-floating or generalized anxiety. For clients who fall into the latter category, cognitive restructuring seems to be the preferred treatment. Many clients are generally anxious because they have internalized a set of irrational beliefs concerning self-worth, interpersonal relationships, and the way things *should* be. Because they are operating on these irrational beliefs, they have unrealistic expectations both for themselves and others and feel anxious because their expectations are never met.

REVIEW RATIONAL-EMOTIVE THERAPY

Effective therapy for these people involves restructuring their cognitive beliefs (see steps in cognitive restructuring shown in Figure 45). A specific approach designed to restructure such irrational cognitions and consequently reduce anxiety is rational-emotive therapy as described by Albert Ellis (1962). According to Ellis, emotional disturbance is almost always associated with a person's excessive caring about what others think of him and mistaken belief that he can accept and like himself only if others accept and like him. Ellis maintains that when an emotionally charged consequence (C) follows an activating event (A), individuals often mistakenly think that A caused C, i.e., that a given event caused anger, depression, or some other emotion. However, it is more likely that C is caused by B, which is the belief the individual has about the event. That is, the individual is responding to the way he is labeling the event and not to the event itself. For example, let's suppose that as you walk across the room, an individual in the room suddenly sticks out his foot and you trip, falling on the floor on your face. One person's first reaction may be extreme anger. Another person may feel little or no anger. The difference in these reactions is due to (B), the belief, or

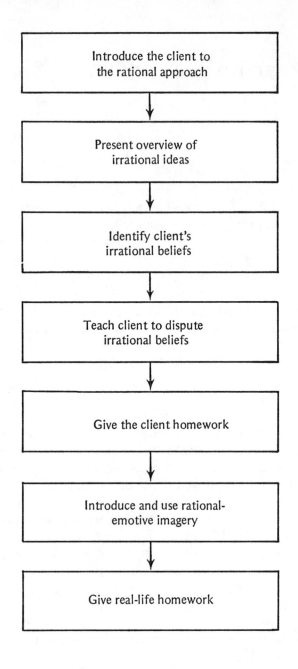

Figure 45. Summary of Cognitive Restructuring

the self-talk. The first person probably said something like, "That rude, inconsiderate clod! He has the nerve to trip me! He has no right to do such a thing to me. I know he did that purposely." On the other hand, the second person may have said something like, "Oops, I'd better start watching where I'm going. He didn't mean to trip me. It was an accident." Obviously, then, the activating event (A), being tripped, did not produce the emotions (C); rather, it was (B) the beliefs or self-talk, which was responsible. It should be noted here that self-talk may be either rational or irrational, but it is the irrational beliefs which most often result in feelings of extreme anxiety and depression.

Ellis (1962) has identified 11 irrational beliefs which are common in our society. Below are these irrational ideas, organized according to the emotions they typically produce.

Panic, self-condemnation, and self-doubt (Ellis, 1973) are produced by the following irrational ideas.

1. "The idea that it is a dire necessity to be loved or approved by virtually every significant other person in one's community (Ellis, 1962, p. 61).

2. The idea that one should be thoroughly competent, adequate, and achieving in all possible respects if one is to consider oneself worthwhile (Ellis, 1962, p. 63).

3. The idea that human unhappiness is externally caused and that people have little or no ability to control their sorrows and disturbances (Ellis, 1962, p. 72).

4. The idea that one's past history is an all-important determinant of one's present behavior and that because something once strongly affected one's life, it should indefinitely have a similar effect (Ellis, 1962, p. 82).

5. The idea that there is invariably a right, precise, and perfect solution to human problems and that it is catastrophic if this perfect solution is not found (Ellis, 1962, p. 87).

6. The idea that if something is or may be dangerous or fearsome, one should be terribly concerned about it and should keep dwelling on the possibility of its occurring (Ellis, 1962, p. 75).

7. The idea that one should be dependent on others and needs someone stronger than oneself on whom to rely (Ellis, 1962, p. 80)."

Anger, moralizing, and low frustration tolerance (Ellis, 1973) are produced by the following irrational ideas.

8. "The idea that certain people are bad, wicked, or villainous and that they should be severely blamed and punished for their villainy (Ellis, 1962, p. 66).
9. The idea that it is awful and catastrophic when things are not the way one would very much like them to be (Ellis, 1962, p. 69).
10. The idea that it is easier to avoid than to face certain life difficulties and self-responsibilities (Ellis, 1962, p. 78).
11. The idea that one should become quite upset over other people's problems and disturbances (Ellis, 1962, p. 85)."

These irrational beliefs typically lead to feelings of self-pity, pity for others, self-blame, or blame of others; none of these reactions is constructive. Rather, they create feelings that things *should* not be as they are just because we don't like them this way or make persons feel inadequate and incapable. In either case, the anxiety, depression, or inadequate feelings prevent the client from behaving in a constructive fashion to change the situation. Instead, all his energy is channeled into the anxiety, anger, or helpless feelings. The purpose of cognitive restructuring, then, is to change the client's cognitions so that his feelings will change and his consequent behavior will be constructively geared toward either changing undesirable situations or at least accepting them.

Specific how-to techniques for implementing cognitive restructuring or rational-emotive therapy as described by Ellis (1962, 1973) will be presented in the remainder of this chapter. It is arranged in a logical sequence beginning with introducing the client to the approach and continuing through the complete treatment program.

INTRODUCE THE CLIENT
TO THE RATIONAL APPROACH

After the client has identified her problem area and her feelings, the counselor can introduce the rational thinking approach by pointing out that human beings are able to think and reason and that persons typically feel the way they think. Thinking produces feelings, and the feelings in turn cause actions. Examples will be useful in helping the client to understand this. For example:

Counselor: We usually think that something which happens to us makes us feel good or bad, but it is really what we think about what happens that makes us feel good or bad. Let's suppose that your teacher tells you she wants to speak with you privately after school. If you say to yourself, "Great! I'll bet she's got some good news for me," how are you likely to feel?

Client: I'd be happy.

Counselor: Yes, but suppose you said to yourself, "Oh, no! I wonder what trouble I'm in now." How would you feel?

Client: I'd feel scared and wish I could skip out after school.

Counselor: Right. Do you see, then, that how you feel depends on what you think or tell yourself?

Client: Yes, I think so.

Counselor: Can you give me an example of that?

Client: Well, you know all the kids now use the word "bad" and it really means something is good. Well, if John said to me, "Hey, Susan, that's a bad outfit," and I thought he didn't like it, I'd feel insulted. But if I thought he liked it, I'd feel good.

Counselor: Good example! If you tell yourself it's an insult, you feel bad. If you tell yourself it's a compliment, you feel good.

PRESENT OVERVIEW OF IRRATIONAL IDEAS

After the client shows some general understanding of the connection between thinking and feeling and how different interpretations of a situation produce different emotions, he can be introduced to some of the common irrational ideas enumerated by Ellis (1962). This can be done in different ways. One way might be to ask the client to respond to a questionnaire. Since the irrational beliefs listed by Ellis are stated in an extreme form, however, many clients may answer in the negative. Consequently, the revision of these (as follows) may be answered more honestly.

1. Do you get upset when someone doesn't like what you've done or if you find out some person or persons don't like you?
2. Do you get upset with yourself when you make a mistake or when you don't do something as well as your friends or peers?
3. Do you think certain people are bad and should be punished just for being bad?
4. Do you get upset when things don't go just the way you want them to?
5. Is the main reason you get upset because someone else makes you upset by his behavior?
6. Do you spend a lot of time worrying about what *might* happen?

7. Do you try to avoid difficult situations?
8. Do you need someone stronger than yourself to ask advice from?
9. Do you believe that people can't change their behavior?
10. Do you get upset over other people's problems?
11. Do you think there is only *one* right solution for different problems? Do you get upset if you can't figure out that one right solution?

The idea here is to determine which of the irrational ideas the client tends to agree with. Following the identification of these, a discussion of why these beliefs are unreasonable can be conducted.

Another approach which can include the discussion of irrational beliefs is for the counselor to select the most typical irrational beliefs ("Everybody must love me" and "I must be perfect"), take the role of accepting one of those beliefs, and get the client to dispute it. Often, by letting the client hear someone else expound those beliefs, it becomes apparent to him how unreasonable they are. Through this, the counselor hopes that the client will realize that one's desires and demands cannot and will not always be met and that it is irrational to expect them to be met. On the other hand, it is rational to acknowledge that it would be nice for these demands to be met and unfortunate when they aren't. *It is when a person tells himself it's terrible and catastrophic when his desires are not met that emotional problems develop.*

The following is an example in which the counselor assumes a role. She is playing the role of a person who thinks everyone must love her and in so doing, hopes to demonstrate to the client how irrational this belief is.

Counselor: Some people believe that they should be loved by everyone and if someone doesn't like them, they get upset. I'm going to role play a person who believes that, and I want you to tell me what you think about it. Okay?

Client: Okay.

Counselor: Point out reasons why my belief is irrational and try to convince me I'm wrong in my belief.

Client: All right.

Counselor: I want everyone to like me and to think I'm a good person. When someone doesn't approve of something I say or do, I get upset because that means I'm a no-good person.

Client: That's ridiculous. You can't please everyone.

244

Counselor: Why not?

Client: Because people are so different. When you please some people, others won't like what you do. Anyway, you're not a no-good person just because someone doesn't like you.

Counselor: Well, I feel that way. I think that everyone should like me and say nice things to me. If they don't, I must be a bad person.

Client: People just don't go around saying nice things to everyone they meet. What if they don't say anything, either positive or negative? It sounds like you assume it's negative unless it's blatantly positive.

Counselor: But what if they don't smile and act friendly? That means they probably don't like me.

Client: That's silly. The person may be upset about something or thinking about something else. It doesn't mean you're not liked or approved of.

Counselor: Okay. That may be so. But what if the person says something disapproving to me like, "I don't like the way you dress," or something.

Client: So what? You can't expect *everyone* to like the way you dress. If you like your dress, you should be happy and realize that everyone won't agree.

Counselor: Very good. You've pointed out that I am wrong in assuming that people disapprove just because they don't smile and say nice things. You've also pointed out that it's unreasonable for me to expect everyone to approve of everything I do.

A second irrational idea—"I must be perfect"—may be explored just as in the preceding example. However, if the counselor is aware of irrational beliefs other than "I must be loved by everyone" or "I must be perfect," which the client may be operating with, these may be explored through the foregoing process.

IDENTIFY CLIENT'S IRRATIONAL BELIEFS

The next step after teaching the client how some assumptions are quite irrational is to help him identify his own irrational beliefs. The easiest way to teach this is through the ABC approach, with A referring to the *activating event*, B to the client's *beliefs* about the activating event, and C to the feelings the client has or the emotional *consequences*. The counselor may begin by asking the client to identify his feelings. Some possibilities are listed as follows:

angry	guilty	out of control
worried	hopeless	worthless
anxious	depressed	inferior
fearful	helpless	frustrated
afraid of failing	sorry for myself	bored
lonely		

After the client determines how he feels or felt at a particular time, he needs to identify the situation in which he had that unpleasant feeling. This is typically very easy for the client to do. The following is an example of the counselor leading the client to identify C (the emotional consequence) and A (the activating event).

Counselor: You mentioned that you've been feeling low this past week. What I'd like for you to do is tell me some of the unpleasant feelings you've been having.

Client: I feel angry with my son, George, and I also feel frustrated. Sometimes I just want to jump in my car and get away from the situation.

Counselor: Can you tell me what George does or what happens to make you feel angry and frustrated?

Client: He acts like he doesn't hear me when I tell him to do something. Even when he acts like he's listening, he never does what I tell him to do. It just gets me down so much that I feel irritable with everybody.

At this point, both A and C have been identified, and the next step is to determine what B (irrational belief or self-talk) is. This is more difficult to identify than A and C, partly because people are often not aware of their self-talk and automatically link C to A in a causal manner. However, it is possible to learn what the self-talk is, and the process of identifying this becomes easier with practice.

In the example begun earlier, the counselor might continue as follows:

Counselor: While people tend to think that a certain event makes them unhappy, it is usually what they tell themselves about that situation that makes them upset.

Client: Well, I'm telling myself I don't like what he does.

Counselor: That'a a rational message. There's no reason why you should like that. (It should be noted here that a person may have rational as well as irrational beliefs about a situation. It is rational for a

246

person to express unhappiness with a situation which she doesn't like; the irrational assumption is that the situation *should* be different because the individual doesn't like it as it is. One way to determine whether the client is thinking rationally or irrationally is the intensity of her feelings. *Very strong*, unpleasant emotions often signal that the person is telling herself something irrational.) Okay, you don't like it. But I think you're telling yourself some other things, too. What else are you telling yourself?

Client: Well, I'm telling myself it's ridiculous not to be able to handle a nine-year-old kid (pause), and it's disgusting that he's too lazy to do the simple things I tell him.

Counselor: Go on.

Client: When I was a kid, I did what I was told, and I didn't see it as any big imposition. I don't see why he can't . . . or doesn't do the same.

Counselor: From what you've said, it sounds to me that you're telling yourself two irrational things. First, you're saying, "I should be thoroughly competent and when my child doesn't obey, that makes me a bad parent—a failure, a louse." Secondly, I think you're telling yourself that things aren't going the way you want them to; that is, George isn't doing what he *should*, and that is terrible!

Client: Yes, I know I feel terrible when I think I'm not doing my best, and I feel like a failure as a mother. And you're right, too, that I tell George all the time he should be better and I get furious when he just acts the same way.

Counselor: Your irrational beliefs are that you have to be perfect to be worthwhile and that George *should* behave in a certain way; otherwise, this is terrible and you have to get very upset.

Some clues the counselor may employ to determine irrational client verbalizations are the use of *shoulds, awfuls,* and *overgeneralizations* (Kranzler, 1974). The shoulds include words such as *should, ought, must, have to,* and *got to.* The awfuls include words such as *awful, terrible,* etc.; the overgeneralizations include words or phrases such as *never, always, can't help it, can't tolerate it, too hard,* and self-derogations (*"I'm stupid, worthless, a louse."*).

Example Exercise

In the following example, identify the words which lead you to believe the client is thinking irrationally, and also identify the irrational assumptions which he is making.

Client: I've got to get an A out of this course. This is probably the most important course in my program, and I should get the highest grade in it. It would be terrible to do badly in this course.

Answers

The words which give clues to irrational thinking are *got to, should,* and *terrible*. The irrational assumption is that one must be thoroughly competent, adequate, and achieving in all possible respects.

It is important that clients be able to identify their self-talk or irrational beliefs before the counselor goes on to D—teaching the client to dispute irrational beliefs. An example of a client's identification of the antecedent event, feelings (consequences), and self-talk follows.

A (activating event):
At work today, three of my colleagues seemed cool toward me.
C (feelings or consequence):
I felt rejected and hurt.
B (self-talk):
1. My colleagues should always give me a lot of attention—speak to me, ask how I'm doing, and show a special interest in me.
2. Because my colleagues didn't give me special attention, I must be boring and uninteresting. They probably don't like me anymore.
3. How dare they ignore me like that!

Example Exercise

In the next example, identify the A (activating event), B (self-talk), and C (emotional consequences).

Client: I have felt rotten all week.
Counselor: Did anything in particular happen to make you feel that way?
Client: Yeah, I think it started after the talent show the other day. I sang a song, and one note came out a little sour. Then I saw people in the audience laughing.

Answer

A is the people in the audience laughing, C is the "rotten feelings," and B is: (1) I must be perfect and never make a mistake, i.e., if I make a

248

sour note when singing, I'm no good. (2) People should not laugh at me when I make a mistake. (3) If others don't approve of me, it's terrible.

TEACH CLIENT TO DISPUTE IRRATIONAL BELIEFS

The counselor's task is not only to dispute the client's irrational beliefs about a particular presenting problem, but also to teach him how to identify his irrational beliefs in various situations and how to dispute these independently. For a person to change his irrational thinking, it is necessary to dispute the nonsense he tells himself. A major part of this process is the client's giving up his commands and insistences that his desires be satisfied. These demands, according to Ellis (1973), are the root of emotional disturbance.

Question and Dispute Some Thought Categories

For one to dispute his irrational beliefs, he must be able to question his *shoulds, awfuls,* and *overgeneralizations.* For instance, why *should* other people do what I want them to do? Granted, it would make me happy and I'd feel better if they did, but there are no absolutistic reasons why others should do as I wish. It should be noted here that the irrational *shoulds* are typically *shoulds* of obligation, i.e., it is the obligation of others to please me, and are not to be confused with the *should* of probability (Since I've now moved from the Eastern to the Central time zone, it should be one hour earlier) or the should denoting a good idea (e.g., You should wear a coat on cold days) (Kranzler, 1974).

The client must be able to dispute the set of irrational statements relating to *terribles* and *awfuls.* These words denote feelings or thoughts of one's inability to take or endure a particular situation and somehow imply that the person has no responsibility for his behavior since the situation is so bad it's unbearable. The response, then, is often that of self-pity and/or anxiety and depression which impede doing what's actually possible to improve the situation. In fact, what's terrible or awful is in the eye of the beholder, and one can stand or endure most situations; otherwise, he would die.

This is not to say that no situation is undesirable or unpleasant. In fact, there are many situations which warrant changing and there are many occurrences which are unfortunate, unpleasant, inconvenient, difficult, and detrimental to one's plans or wishes. This does not denote

249

that they are catastrophic, however, and that they can't be endured. Suppose that you flunk an entrance exam and consequently can't get into a training program which is very important to you. An irrational approach would be to say, "This is awful, terrible. I'm a failure. I can't stand the disgrace of others knowing I failed, and I can't stand living unless I can be a _____." Certainly the situation would be disappointing, but when viewed through the above beliefs, it would produce such depression and anxiety that the person would have trouble even thinking of an alternative. In contrast, a rational approach would be, "This is really disappointing. I had counted on getting into this training, and I'm sorry I won't be able to be a _____. But this isn't the only profession, and I'll just have to find another program which is interesting to me."

In addition, the client must learn to dispute the set of irrational statements or beliefs involving *overgeneralizations*. As noted earlier, people who think irrationally may be prone to using such words or phrases as never, always, no one, everybody, everywhere, every minute, there's no way, can't, and impossible. Many of the self-derogating statements, such as I'm stupid, dumb, ugly, worthless, are results of overgeneralizations. In the previous example of the person flunking an entrance exam, he stated, "I'm a failure." It's true that he failed one exam, but this doesn't make a person a failure. A common irrational belief is that one's self-worth is contingent upon his performance or the way another person (or persons) treat him. It is irrational to make the jump from one person's rejection to the assumption that "I'm an unlikeable person."

Irrational thinking results in anxiety which impedes action. Consequently, the irrational thinker is often unhappy and depressed but unable to do anything about his situation. Consider the following example:

Client: My girl friend always flirts with other guys when we go out. She just tries to upset me, I think.
Counselor: Your reaction, then, is being upset and angry?
Client: Yeah, at first I'm angry. Then I feel like she must not care about me. I guess she thinks I'm ugly and boring because she flirts with nice-looking guys who talk about exciting things. Why does she do this to me?
Counselor: What have you done about it?

Client: Nothing. I just get so infuriated with her I can't stand it. Sometimes I tell myself I'm going to be a more interesting conversationalist, but then she flirts and I get so angry I just can't talk to her at all.

In the preceding transaction, the client expresses not only his inability to do anything, but also indicates that the problem is getting worse. This is because he's thinking irrationally and using his energy on anxiety. In this interchange, he doesn't mention any *shoulds* or *terribles*; yet, they are implied and can be easily identified from his verbalizations. Actually, his question, "Why does she do this to me?" is another way of saying, "She *shouldn't* do this to me!"

In the following excerpt, the counselor leads the client to dispute his *shoulds*.

Counselor: Let's look at the ABC we've talked about. A is your girl friend's flirting. C is your feeling of anger and rejection. What then is B?

Client: I'm saying she shouldn't flirt with other guys because I'm her regular boy friend.

Counselor: Why shouldn't she? Where is it written that girls shouldn't flirt with guys who aren't their regular boy friends? Who says this? What evidence do you have?

Client: I don't have any evidence, but it upsets me terribly.

Counselor: No, what upsets you is what you're telling yourself about her behavior. It's irrational to say she *shouldn't* flirt just because you don't want her to. What makes you think all your desires *have* to be met? Now, it would be nice if she didn't flirt and you'd feel better, but there's no reason she *shouldn't*, and it's not terrible if she does.

Client: That sounds good, but it's hard to change my feelings.

Counselor: Right, but you can change them if you stop telling yourself a bunch of nonsense. You're also telling yourself another irrational thing. You're saying, "I must be ugly and boring if she talks with someone other than me." What evidence do you have that you're boring or ugly? Is her inattention proof of that?

Client: Well, no, but I don't talk about things she likes very much.

Counselor: Okay. Let's consider the two possibilities. It may be true that you're boring, or this may just be in your head. Let's suppose for a minute that it *is* true. So what? Does that mean you're no good?

Client: I just wish things were different.

Counselor: Wishing isn't very helpful, is it? Will wishing make it so?

251

Client: No.

Counselor: But you may be able to do something about it if you want to. Maybe you can make a point to talk about things she's interested in.

Another approach which is helpful in dealing with the *awfuls* and *can't stand its* is to ask the client what is the worst thing that could happen. For example, the client who is afraid to ask a girl for a date because he might be rejected and feels that would be terrible might be asked, "What is the worst possible thing that could happen if she says no?" When the client thinks about and deals with the worst thing that could happen, he feels more confident that he can handle the real situation. Furthermore, the worst thing that *could* happen is often not as devastating as the person is telling himself it is, and as a rule, it is certainly not something the person can't stand.

Example Exercise

In the following interactions, identify the irrational statements and change them to rational statements.

Client I: My husband left me last week, and I just can't function anymore. He's made me a nervous wreck. The bum! He has the nerve to leave me alone with three children to support.

Client II: I'm just a nervous wreck at work. My supervisor criticized my work today, and I just feel like quitting. I can't do anything right.

Answers

Client I: Irrational self-talk:
1. I can't function anymore (overgeneralization).
2. My husband made me a nervous wreck. (No one except yourself can upset you.)
3. He should not leave me. (I'm upset that he left, but I have no evidence that he should not have.)

Client I: Rational self-talk:
I'm upset that my husband left, and I'm having trouble caring for the children alone.

Client II: Irrational self-talk:
1. Everyone should like me.
2. It's terrible that my supervisor criticized me. I must not be any good. I must be a failure if I'm criticized.

Client II: Rational self-talk:
It is unfortunate that my supervisor criticized my work. I don't like to be criticized. But I'm a fallible human being and don't always do perfect work. I can try to work on my weak areas, however.

Teach Client To Verify Perceptions

When helping a client dispute the self-talk which creates anxiety, the counselor can point out that some of this self-talk may either be true or a part of the client's distorted perception. For example, Susan expressed concern and indicated anxious feelings because her supervisor at work didn't respond when she spoke to him. One of her self-talk statements was, "He's angry with me and dislikes my work." The counselor pointed out that he, in fact, may be angry with her and dislike her work or that she may have misinterpreted the situation. In either case, the client is taught that her self-worth is not contingent upon her performance as an employee.

However, some anxiety can be avoided if clients learn to verify their perceptions. In this case, the client may have said to the supervisor, "You didn't respond when I spoke to you. Are you angry with me about something?" The supervisor may then say, "I'm sorry. I guess I was thinking about something else. I'm certainly not angry with you." Or he may, in fact, say he is angry and tell why. In either case, the client knows why the supervisor didn't speak and will have a better idea of how to handle the situation rationally.

GIVE THE CLIENT HOMEWORK

An important part of rational-emotive therapy is homework. Homework is required to give the client practice in identifying negative feelings, noting the situation surrounding these feelings, identifying the irrational self-talk, and finally disputing the irrational self-talk. The Rational Self-Help Form used at the Institute for Advanced Study in Rational Psychotherapy is reprinted in Table 14.

While the Self-Help Form can easily be used with adults, it can be simplified for younger clients. The homework form in Table 15 provides enough structure for the client to go through the ABCD procedures.

An example of a completed homework form is given in Table 16. The client is an 18-year-old female who said she was depressed because she and her boy friend of two years had broken up.

Table 14. Rational Self Help Form*

INSTRUCTIONS: Please fill out the ueC section (undesirable emotional Consequences) and the ubC section (undesirable behavioral Consequences) first.
Then fill out all the A-B-C-D-E's. PLEASE PRINT LEGIBLY. BE BRIEF!

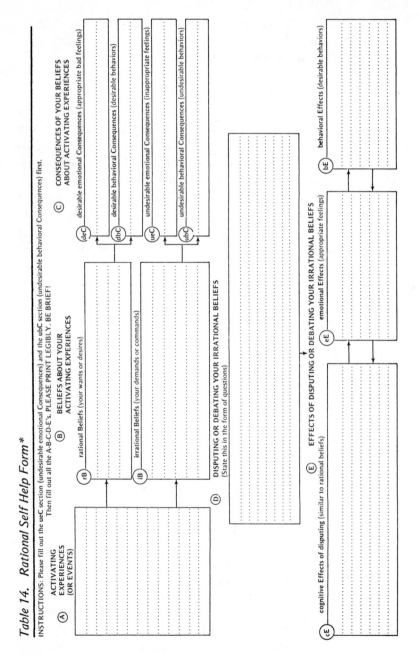

254

Table 14. Rational Self Help Form* (continued)

1. FOLLOW-UP. What new GOALS would I now like to work on? ....
....
....

What specific ACTIONS would I now like to take? ....
....

2. How soon after feeling or noting your undesirable emotional CONSEQUENCES (ueC's) or your undesirable behavioral CONSEQUENCES (ubC's) of your irrational BELIEFS (iB's) did you look for these iB's and DISPUTE them? ....
....

How vigorously did you dispute them? ....
....

If you didn't dispute them, why did you not do so? ....

255

Table 14. Rational Self Help Form *(continued)*

3. Specific HOMEWORK ASSIGNMENT(S) given you by your therapist, your group or yourself: ....

....

....

4. What did you actually do to carry out the assignment(s)? ....

....

5. How many times have you actually worked at your homework assignments during the past week? .....

....

6. How many times have you actually worked at DISPUTING your irrational BELIEFS during the past week? ....

....

7. Things you would now like to discuss with your therapist or group ....

....

....

*Reprinted with permission from Albert Ellis.
© 1976 by the Institute for Rational Living, Inc., 45 East 65th Street, New York, N.Y. 10021

*Table 15. A Simplified Homework Form
            For Rational-Emotive Therapy*

1. Unpleasant or bad feeling _____

2. What was the event about which you became upset or felt bad?

_____

3. What did you tell yourself about what happened? Beside each statement you told yourself, identify whether it is rational or irrational.

    Statements   Rat'l   Irrt'l

a. _____   _____   _____

   _____   _____   _____

b. _____   _____   _____

   _____   _____   _____

c. _____   _____   _____

   _____   _____   _____

d. _____   _____   _____

   _____   _____   _____

4. Dispute each of your irrational beliefs. Then change them to rational statements.

    a. _____

    Rat'l _____

    b. _____

    Rat'l _____

    c. _____

    Rat'l _____

    d. _____

    Rat'l _____

Table 16. *A Completed Homework Form*
For Rational-Emotive Therapy

1. Unpleasant or bad feeling: <u>depression, rejection</u>

2. What was the event about which you became upset or felt bad?
<u>My boy friend said he didn't want to see me anymore—that he</u>
<u>thought we weren't right for each other.</u>

3. What did you tell yourself about what happened? Beside each statement, identify whether it is rational or irrational.

Statement	Rat'l	Irrt'l
a. <u>I'm really disappointed that John broke up</u> <u>with me.</u>	x	
b. <u>It's not fair for him to leave me after two years.</u> <u>He shouldn't do it.</u>		x
c. <u>I'll never find anyone to love again.</u>		x
d. <u>I must be ugly and unlovable.</u>		x
e. <u>He's probably embarrassed to be seen with</u> <u>me anymore. I'm really a slob.</u>		x
f. <u>I'm probably not going to have as many dates</u> <u>until I get back into circulation again.</u>	x	

4. Dispute each of your irrational beliefs. Then change them to rational statements.

   b. <u>Why shouldn't he do it? Where is it written that he should con-</u>
<u>tinue to be my boy friend because I want him to? I have no</u>
<u>right to expect him to do just what I want.</u>

   Rational: <u>I'm disappointed that John broke up with me. I wish</u>
<u>he hadn't, but there really isn't any reason why he</u>
<u>shouldn't.</u>

   c. <u>This is irrational because it's an overgeneralization. Just be-</u>
<u>cause John has left, I can't say that I'll never find anyone else.</u>

258

In fact, there's a high probability that I will meet other people I'll care for.

Rational: I'm sorry this relationship didn't last. It's unfortunate, but I'll make a special effort to meet other people.

d. This statement is also an overgeneralization. John's rejection of me doesn't mean I'm ugly or unlovable. It may mean *he* didn't find me lovable, but that doesn't mean other people won't. And I'm certainly over-reacting by saying I must be ugly! That doesn't follow logically from John's leaving me. Furthermore, even if I am ugly, I'm still a worthwhile person.

Rational: I don't like being rejected, and I'll always see rejection as an unpleasant experience. But rejection by one person doesn't mean that everyone is going to reject me.

e. This is another overgeneralization and it doesn't logically follow from what happened.

Rational: I don't like what happened, and I don't know John's reasons. But even assuming he is embarrassed to be seen with me, that doesn't make me a slob or a no-good person. My self-worth is not contingent upon what John or anyone else thinks of me.

The purpose of the homework report is to get the client to use a rational approach in dealing with emotional upsets between counseling sessions. The client can be instructed to fill out a homework report whenever he has a strong negative emotion. It should be noted here that the client will have negative feelings even when he's thinking rationally. The difference seems to be that a person who is thinking rationally says, "I don't like this. I need to think of ways to change it." In contrast, the person who thinks irrationally usually sees himself as unable to change things, bemoans the fact that others are doing things

259

they shouldn't, and entertains ideas about his worthlessness and inability to stand what has happened or is happening to him.

INTRODUCE AND USE RATIONAL-EMOTIVE IMAGERY

The approach to this point has been to deal with specific feelings and situations and beliefs related to those feelings. Still another approach is to teach clients to change feelings through imagery. That is, the client thinks of a person or situation which is anxiety producing, identifies the irrational self-talk, and disputes it. Maultsby (1971) argues that the emotional consequences of an imagined situation are about the same as the emotional consequences of a real situation. Therefore, the person can change his feelings by disputing irrational beliefs around an imaginary situation. He further states, however, that a person should not begin rational-emotive imagery until he can do the ABC analyses well.

Rational-emotive imagery essentially allows the client to practice disputing irrational beliefs and changing emotions before he enters the real-life situation. If he can remain calm in the imagined situation and handle it well, the probability is much greater that he can do the same in real life. A crucial aspect of this process is to imagine appropriate feelings and appropriate behavior in the specified situations. An example of this follows:

Counselor: You have told me several times about how scared you feel when you have to speak in class. Today, we're going to try something a little different. I want you to close your eyes. Now I'd like for you to relax. (Here, it is possible to do a few relaxation exercises to help the client relax.) Okay, I want you to imagine that you're giving a report to your class. Can you imagine that?

Client: Even when you mention that, I get a sick feeling in my stomach.

Counselor: What are you telling yourself about talking in front of the group?

Client: Well, I'm afraid I'll make a mistake, and some people will laugh.

Counselor: Go on. Why does that upset you?

Client: And if they laugh, I'll feel like a big stupid nothing. I can't stand to be laughed at.

Counselor: Come on. Dispute those irrational statements.

Client: Okay. In the first place, they may not laugh. If they do, it doesn't mean I'm stupid or worthless. I'm allowed to make mistakes and still have good feelings about myself. And I *can* stand it. I'm not going to die if someone laughs.

Counselor: Imagine telling yourself these things as you begin to speak. How do you feel?

Client: (Pause) Well, I'm not as worried. If I botch it, I'll just deal with it when it happens. I'm usually prepared when I give reports, so I really am going to stop worrying about all the things that *could* happen.

Counselor: Let's suppose you do make a mistake. Let's say you lose your place, fumble through your papers, and stammer a little.

Client: Oh, that would be so embarrassing. Oh—I feel tense and sick again.

Counselor: Because . . . ?

Client: Because the class members will think I'm stupid.

Counselor: Why is that so upsetting?

Client: I want other people to think I do things well.

Counselor: Because . . . ?

Client: Oh, because I feel bad when others think bad things about me.

Counselor: And what are you telling yourself?

Client: That I have to please everyone and that I should never make a mistake.

Counselor: How rational is that?

Client: Okay. I know I can't please everyone, and I know I'm fallible. If I flub up, I know I'm good at other things anyway. I usually give good answers in class. I won't be the first person in the group to lose my place either. It happens to other people too.

Counselor: How are you feeling now?

Client: Much better. That sick feeling in my stomach is almost gone.

It is possible to use imaginal presentation in a manner similar to systematic desensitization. The counselor and client can make a hierarchy of increasingly anxiety-provoking situations and, beginning with the least anxiety-provoking situation, use imaginal rational restructuring to decrease the anxiety. The approaches for systematic desensitization suggested in Chapter 7, Decreasing Behavior, can be used in imaginal rational restructuring. For instance, the client can estimate her anxiety level on a range of 0 to 100, apply rational restructuring techniques, and reassess her anxiety. As the anxiety for one item decreases satisfactorily, the next item on the hierarchy can be presented. The relaxation exercises may be warranted as well.

GIVE REAL-LIFE HOMEWORK
The ultimate goal of rational-emotive therapy is to change behavior. The approach is to change behavior through changing cognitions and emotions. Consequently, after the client has mastered the ABCD approach, learned to complete homework forms, and engaged successfully in rational restructuring through imagery, it's time to use real-life homework. For instance, a client who tries to avoid situations where he might "make a mistake" (e.g., he won't share ideas at work because they may be ridiculed), may have the following homework: Share two ideas with a colleague this week. A person who is afraid of being rejected and so avoids interpersonal relationships may have homework of approaching two new people during the week. The client is instructed to use the ABCD approach in these frightening situations. This may seem a near impossible task at first, but with practice, it will become easier to do.

A major advantage of cognitive restructuring is that the client learns a system for helping him avoid emotional upsets as well as a strategy to help him analyze and remediate emotionally disturbing experiences. Once he learns the strategy, his need for or dependence on a therapist is greatly reduced.

CHECKLIST FOR COGNITIVE RESTRUCTURING
Go through the list checking yes or no.

	Yes	No
1. *Determine if cognitive restructuring is appropriate.*	___	___
a. Is the client fearful or anxious?	___	___
b. Is the client's fear and/or anxiety irrational?	___	___

If the answers to questions (a) and (b) are yes, cognitive restructuring may be appropriate. Use the following checklist, checking yes as the sequential steps of the counseling process are completed.

	Yes	No
2. *Implement cognitive restructuring.*		
a. Has the client been introduced to the rational approach?	___	___

b. Has an overview of irrational ideas been
   presented? Does the client understand
   these?   _____ _____
c. Have you identified the client's irrational
   beliefs?   _____ _____
d. Have you assigned homework reports
   for the client?   _____ _____
e. Can the client use rational-emotive imagery?   _____ _____
f. Has the client engaged in real-life homework? _____ _____
   Was he successful?   _____ _____
g. Can the client use cognitive restructuring
   techniques in situations which occur in
   everyday life?   _____ _____

PROGRAMMED EXAMPLES

Choose one or more phrases that accurately complete the statements and follow individual instructions for other questions.

1. According to Ellis, emotional disturbance is a result of
   a. a person's lack of concern for his welfare.
   b. a person's excessive caring about what others think of him.
   c. a person's lack of skill in social situations.
   d. a person's situation-specific anxiety.
   If you answered (b), you're correct. Ellis says that a person's irrational belief that he must be loved and approved of by everyone creates excessive anxiety and emotional problems. While a person may be better off if he cares about his welfare, and if he has social skills, the absence of these, (a) and (c), do not necessarily result in emotional disturbance. Anxiety (d) is more a symptom of emotional disturbance than an antecedent.

2. In the ABC approach discussed by Ellis, C is a result of
   a. A.
   b. B.
   c. both A and B.
   The answer is (b). Ellis says that C (emotional consequences) is a result of B (a person's self-talk about an event) rather than A (the particular event.)

263

3. Which of the following is *not* one of the irrational assumptions discussed by Ellis?
   a. It is necessary to be loved and approved of by virtually everyone in a person's community.
   b. A person should be thoroughly competent and successful in all endeavors.
   c. In any given situation which is disturbing, a person would be better off to explore alternative ways of changing the situation.
   d. It is better to avoid difficult situations than to face them and maybe make bad decisions.

   Answer (c) is correct. It is quite rational to explore ways of changing unpleasant situations. In fact, irrational thinking such as that in answers (a), (b), and (d) impedes constructive action.

4. Which of the following statements is not irrational?
   a. I really don't like for my son, George, to hit his little sister.
   b. George shouldn't do that!
   c. Why does George do this to me?
   d. I'm a lousy mother, obviously.

   Statement (a) is not irrational. There's no reason why a person should like annoying behaviors. What is irrational is (b) the statement that he shouldn't be annoying (Why not?) or that (d) a person is a lousy parent because her child doesn't always behave the way she wants him to (this is an overgeneralization). Statement (c) is similar to (b). Asking why George does it is another way of saying George *shouldn't* do it.

5. Which of the self-talk statements are irrational in the following situation?
   A-boy asks girl for a date and girl says, "No, I'm busy."
   C-feelings of depression and worthlessness
   a. I'll never find a girl who will go out with me.
   b. I'm really disappointed that she's busy.
   c. Who does she think she is to refuse me?
   d. I'll have to call her earlier next time.

   If you answered (a) and (c), you're correct. A is irrational because it's an overgeneralization. One refusal doesn't mean that he'll always be refused by everyone. Answer (c) implies that she should not refuse him. Why not? Where's the proof? Sentence (b) is rational because it's a statement of not liking to be refused, and answer (d) is rational because it may be possible to get a date if he calls before the girl makes other plans.

6. Identify the clues of irrational beliefs in the following client statements and tell why the beliefs are irrational.
   a. Why does he do this to me!
   b. He should act differently.
   c. I just can't stand being alone.
   d. I may do badly, and that would be terrible.
   e. I'm just stupid, that's all.
   f. I'll never find another person to love.
   g. I've got to do well in this course.

Suggested answers:
   a. The client is actually saying, "He *should* not do this to me." This is irrational, because it's a should and there's no evidence for it.
   b. The clue here also is the word *should*.
   c. *Can't stand* is an overgeneralization. In fact, a person can stand most situations. Otherwise, he would die. He may not like the situation, but he can stand it if he has to.
   d. *Terrible* is the clue word here. The client is equating catastrophe with the situation of making a mistake. It is important to recognize that all people are fallible and that one can make mistakes and still accept herself.
   e. This is an *overgeneralization*. The client is saying he's a *stupid* person because he made one mistake. Is every act of his stupid? It does not logically follow that one mistake makes a person stupid.
   f. *Never* is an overgeneralization also. It doesn't logically follow that the loss of one relationship means that all interpersonal relationships will be failures.
   g. *Got to* is an overgeneralization and can be disputed by, "Why do you have to?" "Why do you have to make a good impression?" The person may want to make a good impression, but she doesn't *have to*.

7. In which of the following is the word *should* used rationally?
   a. He shouldn't treat me this way.
   b. If I mix white and black paint, I should have gray paint.
   c. He should take some money if he wants to buy his lunch.
   d. He should keep his promise to me.

   Answers (b) and (c) are correct. Answers (a) and (d) are examples of the irrational use of should, the should of obligation. It would be better if a person kept his promises (d) and it would be better if I were treated well (a), but it would be hard to offer evidence for why a person should do these things. Answer (b) denotes the use of should as probability and answer (c) denotes the use of should as a good idea. That is, if a person wants lunch, it would be a good idea for him to take money.

8. Write a dispute for each of the following client self-talk statements.
   a. If I do badly, people will laugh, and that would be terrible.
   b. My teacher criticized me today. I know she hates me.
   c. My child is driving me crazy.
   d. I can't do anything right! I'm hopeless.

   Suggested answers:
   a. It's only terrible if you think it is. What's so terrible about it? What is the worst thing that could happen if people laugh at you? If people laugh, does that make you stupid?
   b. How do you know she hates you? It isn't logical to say that someone hates you because of one mistake you made. Anyway, does bad performance make you a bad person?
   c. You're driving yourself crazy by your reactions to your child. No one except yourself can make you upset.
   d. You're overgeneralizing by saying that one or even two or three mistakes identify a person who fails at everything. Is there even one thing you do well? Okay, then you do some things right. And one or even several mistakes don't make you hopeless.

9. Write rational alternatives for the irrational statements in Question 8.
   a. I will feel bad if people laugh, but that won't kill me. Any-

266

way, I'll prepare and try to avoid having people laugh.
   b.   I don't like being criticized by my teacher. I won't disrupt the class tomorrow. And even though she wasn't pleased with my behavior, that doesn't mean she doesn't like me.
   c.   I'm really having difficulty with my children, and I wish they behaved better. But I'm getting myself upset by making a catastrophe out of it. I think it would help if I make some general rules for everyone and get the children to discuss these.
   d.   Boy, I messed up that situation today, but I recognize that I have in the past, do now, and will always make mistakes. I'll work to minimize the number of mistakes I make, but I'm going to accept myself anyway. My self-worth is not contingent upon my performance.

10.   Rational-emotive imagery is useful because
   a.   it helps the client imagine anxiety-provoking situations.
   b.   it enables the client to dispute irrational self-talk in imagined situations.
   c.   imagery helps reduce anxiety.
   d.   it provides an approach for preventing future emotional upsets.
   Both (b) and (d) are correct. Through imagery, the client can deal with typical real-life situations, analyzing the irrational self-talk and disputing it. Answers (a) and (c) are incorrect because imagery alone doesn't necessarily reduce anxiety.

11.   Real-life homework should not be given to a client until he has
   a.   mastered the ABCD analysis of behavior.
   b.   learned to dispute irrational self-talk.
   c.   successfully completed homework forms.
   d.   done all of the above.
   D is correct. Until the client has learned to identify irrational self-talk and dispute it successfully, real-life homework would only produce extreme anxiety. After he has learned to dispute his irrational beliefs, he can change his anxious feelings and focus more energy on changing behavior. Successfully completed homework forms (c) gives some evidence that the client has mastered the

ABCD analysis and is ready for real-life homework.

CRITERION TEST

For the following situation, (1) conduct an ABC analysis, (2) dispute the irrational beliefs, (3) substitute rational statements for the irrational self-talk, and (4) give examples of real-life homework.

The client is an 18-year-old girl who has never had a date and who vascillates between saying she never wants to go out and wishing someone would ask her to go out. In groups, she responds when someone talks to her but rarely, if ever, initiates a conversation. The specific situation she brings to the session today is her anger at Vernon. She said, "We've always been friends, but today he just ignored me. He's so stuck up and thinks he's better than anyone else. He just walked past me and talked to Martha. I give up on men!"

CHAPTER 10
CRITERION TEST ANSWERS

1. ABC analysis:

   (A) antecedent event:

   Vernon walked past me and talked to Martha. He didn't say anything to me.

   (C) consequence (feelings):

   Anger, rejection

   (B) beliefs (self-talk):

   a. He *shouldn't* ignore me.
   b. He rejected me, and that's terrible. I can't stand it.
   c. He has no right to talk with Martha instead of me.
   d. He thinks he's better than I am.
   e. I'll never make it with men!

2. (D) Dispute of irrational statements:

   a. Why shouldn't he ignore me? Who says he has to give me attention just because I demand it? Who am I to be so pompous?
   b. First of all, was I really rejected? How do I know if he wanted to avoid me? And if I were rejected, what's so terrible about being rejected? I don't like it, but I know I can stand it

because I just did. Also, being rejected once doesn't mean that I always will be.

c. Why? He can talk with anyone he feels like talking with. I have no right to dictate whom he talks with.

d. I really don't know what he thinks. I can't read his mind and am in no position to speak for him.

e. This is silly. First of all, I didn't speak to him, so I really didn't do anything myself to start a conversation. And it's ridiculous to decide I'll never be successful because I've made a mistake this time or because Vernon walked past me this time.

3. Rational alternatives:

a. I'm sorry he didn't speak to me first, but maybe next time I'll speak to him.

b. I don't like being rejected, but I'm not sure I was. In any event, I know I can *stand* it. I'll work on changing my behavior so I'm better accepted.

c. I'd be happier if he talked with me, but I'd better carry my end of the conversation too. Maybe he doesn't like doing all the "work."

d. I don't know what he's thinking.

e. I will behave differently next time. I'll speak to him and see if he responds.

4. Homework:

After the client becomes proficient with the ABCD analysis, homework such as the following may be assigned.

Sometime during the week, initiate at least three conversations with men you know.

11 Evaluating Counseling Outcomes

The counselor has the responsibility of developing an intervention to alleviate the client's problem as well as evaluating the effectiveness of it (Tharp and Wetzel, 1969). It seems, however, that more attention has typically been given to the intervention than to the evaluation. Evaluation has been an integral part of research studies. Although it is warranted in the counselor's every-day practice, it has been neglected there. Evaluation is useful for the following reasons: (1) it can show whether specific interventions produce client behavior change; (2) it can help the counselor identify which interventions are useful with which types of clients and presenting problems; and (3) it serves as a gauge for the counselor to measure her own effectiveness. Obviously, evaluation of behavior change can dictate whether the counselor should continue to use her current approach. In essence, it provides a monitoring and feedback system so that the counselor doesn't continue to operate in a way that doesn't produce change. A counselor can be more effective by checking her progress and evaluating her successes.

Since the benefit of evaluation is obvious, the remainder of this chapter will focus on how to conduct an evaluation of counseling interventions (see Figure 46).

DETERMINE IF COUNSELING OBJECTIVE HAS BEEN ACHIEVED

Check How Many Objectives Have Been Met

The evaluation of counseling is predicated upon the successful completion of its objectives. This necessitates, then, that objectives be stated in observable and measurable terms (see Chapter 5). Given operationally stated objectives, one evaluation method is simply to check out whether these objectives have been reached or how many of them have been met.

271

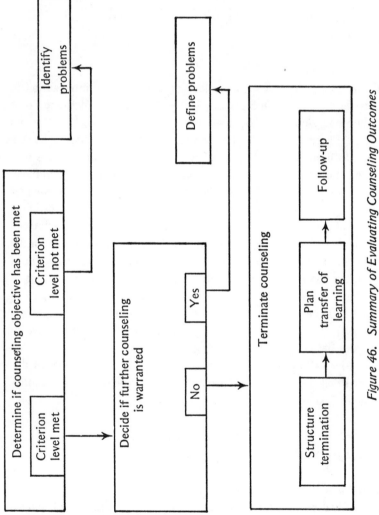

Figure 46. Summary of Evaluating Counseling Outcomes

Compare Baseline with Later Data

A second method of evaluating progress or success is to compare base-line rates of target behavior with behavior during treatment and/or at the time of termination. Graphing procedures provide a good way to illustrate this change. For example, the goal for Mike was a decrease in compulsive leg rubbing behavior, determined after the observation that Mike engaged in this behavior an average of 24 times per day over a five-day period (see Figure 47).

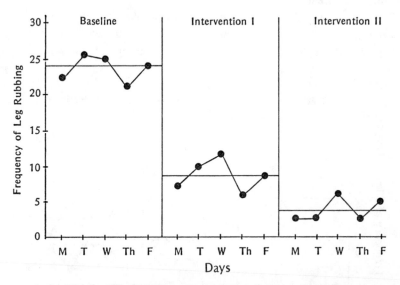

Figure 47. Mike's Compulsive Leg-Rubbing Behavior

The counselor and client initially set the goal that Mike should rub his legs no more than 10 times per day. Figure 47 shows that Mike's leg rubbing during treatment dropped from 24 to an average of 9 times per day. While the counselor and client agreed that the initial objective was met, Mike still expressed dissatisfaction with his behavior and wished to decrease it to no more than five times per day. Therefore a second intervention was begun. The graph (Figure 47) illustrates the decrease in Mike's behavior during the second intervention period. Often, the counselor and client will set initial objectives that are unrealistic (i.e., cannot be reached) or unsatisfactory (i.e., the criterion level of behavior is still undesirable). The graphing allows them to set objectives in a

273

graduated fashion and monitor the progress toward these objectives on a daily basis.

Use Multiple Baseline While a simple graphic presentation of baseline and intervention data allows the client and counselor to determine whether an objective has been reached for one client problem, other designs may be useful to measure change in more than one problem for a particular client, or a specific problem for multiple clients or across more than one situation. This design is referred to as a multiple baseline.

For example, if Mike had a fighting problem in addition to being out of his seat too much of the time, his fighting behavior can be baselined while the intervention is introduced for out-of-seat behavior.

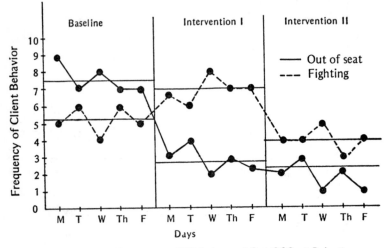

Figure 48. Frequency of Fighting and Out-Of-Seat Behavior

Figure 48 illustrates a decrease in out-of-seat behavior when exposed to an intervention, while fighting (which is not yet being treated) remains at its baseline level. When baseline stability is reached for fighting, it too is exposed to the intervention in the second period. Figure 48 illustrates that fighting doesn't decrease until that second period, when it too is under intervention. By gradually exposing each problem behavior to the intervention, one can determine if the intervention is actually responsible for changing the behavior because each client behavior should change only as it is exposed to the intervention, and not before.

274

The multiple baseline is inappropriate when target behaviors are inter-related. The effectiveness of intervention for the individual behaviors could not be judged. For example, if the counselor were targeting achievement in addition to out-of-seat behavior, achievement would likely increase as out-of-seat behavior is reduced. Mike is in his seat more, so he is more likely to study and consequently make better grades.

In some cases, the counselor may be working with two clients who have the same problem. Note the example in Figure 49.

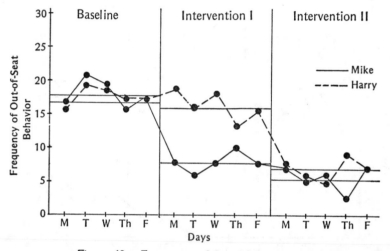

Figure 49. Frequency of Out-Of-Seat Behavior

While Mike was out of his seat an average of 18 times, Harry was out of his seat an average of 17 times. During the second week, Mike was exposed to an intervention and his out-of-seat behavior dropped to 8 times per day. At the same time, baseline conditions remained for Harry, and his behavior showed little change ($\overline{X}$ = 16). When Harry was exposed to the intervention, however, his out-of-seat behavior decreased to an average of 7 times ($\overline{X}$ = 7). This type of multiple baseline allows the counselor to determine the effectiveness of an intervention in reducing a problem behavior (out-of-seat) concurrently for two clients.

Often a problem will occur in more than one situation (e.g., home, school, job). Here, the counselor can use the multiple baseline to measure the same behavior of a client concurrently in different situations. For example, Mike may express "put downs" both at work and at home. Figure 50 shows that for the first week, the average level of "put downs" for Mike at home is 18 and 17 at work. In the second week, an intervention was introduced at home and the average level of "put downs" dropped to 5 while the baseline level at work increased to 17.6. During the third week, an intervention was introduced at work and the baseline level dropped to 7 while the level of "put downs" at home remained stable at 5.

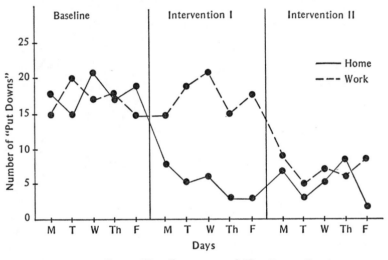

Figure 50. Frequency of "Put Downs"

Such designs are useful in determining the success of a particular technique across behaviors, individuals, and situations. In the final analysis, the counselor is able to determine if and when he is being effective or ineffective (Schmidt, 1974).

Example Exercise

Given the following graphic information (Figure 51), answer the following questions.

276

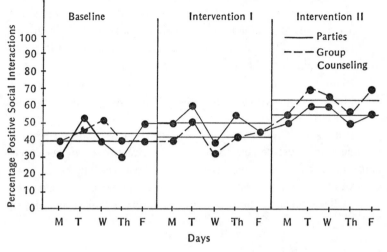

Figure 51. A Multiple Baseline Graph

1. What is being measured in the graph presented above?
   _____ across _____
2. Where/for whom is the intervention likely being introduced in the first intervention period?
3. What is likely under intervention in the second period?
4. Describe the change in percent positive social interactions from Baseline to Intervention II in
   Parties _____
   Group Counseling _____
5. In 75 words or less, describe the data presented in the graph above.

Answers

1. percent of positive social interaction *across* situations
2. parties
3. parties and group counseling
4. parties: increased by more than one-third (a factor of 1.38)
   group counseling: increased by almost one-half (a factor of 1.47)
5. The percentage of social interactions was measured for three

weeks both at parties and in group counseling. At the start of the second week, an intervention was introduced at parties and the percent social interactions increased by one-fourth (a factor of 1.25), while little change in social interaction occurred in group counseling. In the third week, the intervention was introduced in group counseling and the percent of social interaction for that situation increased by almost one-half (a factor of 1.47) from the first week of baseline.

An accurate response to the last question is important because the counselor must be able to describe the effectiveness of her procedures, both to her client and other interested persons. When clients and others can see from a graph that a procedure is bringing about a desired change, their belief in the procedure is reinforced (Sulzer and Mayer, 1972).

Compare Data from Taped Interviews The graphing procedures described earlier were applied primarily to discrete behaviors which can be easily observed and recorded. Yet, the same principle can apply to data which is more difficult to observe and quantify. For instance, the counseling goal may be to improve the client's self-confidence, as measured by the number of positive statements she makes about her ability to successfully complete things. (Self-confidence can obviously be measured in other ways; the important thing is that all counseling goals be operationalized so that there is some way of measuring progress. For instance, if the goal is stated only as increased self-confidence, this may mean different things for different people and the measure of success becomes very subjective.) Assuming that the number of positive self-statements is a reasonable measure of self-confidence, the counselor can tape interviews and record the number of positive versus negative statements in the first session or two (using this as baseline) and then chart this same behavior as intervention is implemented.

Even when objectives are operationalized, there are varying ranges of objectivity. For example, sometimes the counselor must depend on the client's self-report of behaviors, such as anxiety, marital discord, drug use, and there may be no way to verify the accuracy of such reports. Still, there is some evidence that the very act of recording one's own behavior (if this is the way the evaluation data is to be obtained) is effective in promoting the desired behavior.

278

Use Behavior Checklists To Evaluate Effectiveness

Still another approach for evaluating counselor effectiveness is the use of behavior problem checklists, filled out by the teacher and/or parents prior to and after counseling. A variety of standardized behavior checklists are available [e.g., Child Behavior Rating Scale (Cassel, 1962) and Walker Problem Behavior Identification Checklist, 1970], but some counselors devise their own, listing the common problems for which clients are referred. Table 17 illustrates how such a checklist may be devised.

Table 17. A Sample Behavior Checklist
For Evaluating Counselor Effectiveness

Name_____ Date _____

Teacher _____ (Fill out this side at termination.)

Is this behavior a problem?			Improvement	
Yes	No		None Some Much	
___	___	1. Cheating	___ ___ ___	
___	___	2. Lying	___ ___ ___	
___	___	3. Stealing	___ ___ ___	
___	___	4. Incomplete assignments	___ ___ ___	
___	___	5. Walking around the room	___ ___ ___	
___	___	6. Poor peer relationships	___ ___ ___	
___	___	7. Etc.	___ ___ ___	

Parent/Teacher
Signature _____

Date _____

Although the evaluation described in Table 17 is subjective (the teacher's judgment), it may be used in conjunction with other evaluative data, such as behavioral observation, parent report of change, achievement record (if appropriate). At any rate, it offers a good measure of whether the teacher (who may be the referring agent) is satisfied with the behavioral change which has taken place. If the teacher says little or no improvement has taken place, then the counselor and teacher can talk about alternative approaches to use with the child.

Use Tests and Other Instruments

Standardized tests, scales, and inventories also can be used to evaluate changes in counseling. For instance, standardized tests may be used to measure changes in achievement or even changes in self-esteem. For example, suppose the counseling objective is an increase in self-esteem for a group of students identified by teachers. In this case, the Coopersmith (1967) or the Piers-Harris Self-Concept measures (1964) could be given prior to and after counseling.

It is also useful to evaluate not only the ultimate outcome of counseling but also the client's progress during treatment. This can be done by setting outcome goals and by determining various objectives or subgoals related to the ultimate objectives. Consider the following example.

> Because of truancy and three instances of running away from home, Sherry was placed in a youth program which provided foster home placement. The goal of this program was to change the home situation and eventually get juveniles back into their homes. Some problems Sherry reported at her home were excessive drinking by both parents and much marital discord, resulting in physical beatings of herself and her mother.

The major goal identified was to get Sherry back into her home. The subgoals were: (1) improve parent communication, (2) decrease physical abuse, (3) decrease drinking of parents, (4) decrease Sherry's truancy and running away. Consequently, several subgoals must be reached to attain the major outcome goal. And, evaluation of counseling must be based on the subgoals which lead to the desired outcome. For instance, the first subgoal selected was improved parental communication. The counselor in this case evaluated parents' communication patterns through simulation, i.e., they were asked to role play a family situation. Following intervention (teaching and practicing new communication styles), they were given the same role-playing situation. Both the pre- and post-role-playing situation were measured by using the following criteria: (1) number of times the person responded showing she or he was listening, (2) number of times the person expressed feelings, (3) number of times he or she used put-downs or "communication stoppers," and (4) outcome of role playing (Was an agreeable solution reached? How much progress was there in that direction?).

280

DECIDE IF FURTHER COUNSELING IS WARRANTED

There are two criteria that should be used in determining whether to continue counseling. First, the client objective should be met. In some cases, the client or others (e.g., teacher, parents, friends) may feel the problem no longer exists, but the data fail to support this. In this case, counseling should continue until the objective has been met.

Secondly, the objective may have been met, but the client or others in her environment may not be satisfied with the change produced. If the client or others are no longer satisfied with the change produced, then a new objective should be established. In other cases, the client may wish to pursue another related concern (see Identify All Concerns in Chapter 3).

The termination of counseling depends upon several factors, but the process can be much easier if the counselor and client have reached their goals. If goals have been reached and no new goals have been set, then the counselor and client can focus on the maintenance and generalization of behavior change.

STRUCTURE TERMINATION

In structuring the termination, the counselor must ask three basic questions:

1. *When should termination occur?*

Counseling should generally terminate when the client has reached his goals and he and others do not wish to work on any related concerns.

2. *Who determines when counseling will end?*

Any discussion to terminate counseling should be made both by the counselor and client. In some cases, however, clients terminate by not returning. This may occur for several reasons. The client may feel that counseling is not helping or she may become angry with the counselor. Occasionally, the client may be unwilling to change some of her behavior. Unless the counselor works through these concerns early in counseling, termination may be premature.

3. *How should counseling terminate?*

The counselor should be careful not to withdraw the counseling procedure abruptly because in such cases the problem behavior generally returns to the original pre-treatment level. Prior to termination, the counselor should arrange for reinforcers to be delivered on an intermittent schedule (see Chapter 8) since they more closely approximate the reinforcement schedule in the natural environment.

PLAN TRANSFER OF LEARNING

It is important for the counselor not to assume that the client's skills will automatically generalize to new situations. Treatment effects may often be situational. For example, a client may be taught how to interact positively with others in a group, but once she leaves the group, she is unable to interact positively with others at home, on the job, etc. Thus, the counselor and client should discuss specific steps for trying out skills in extra-therapy situations. Social skills learned in a group could be tried out with specific people the client meets every day (e.g., friends, teachers, employers).

There are several things the counselor can do to facilitate generalization of learning.

1. *Treatment should approximate the conditions the client will encounter in real life.*

For example, a client may learn how to maintain a discussion with a stranger in a new situation. This hardly approximates reality, however, since on a daily basis we are often confronted with more than one new acquaintance. The counselor in this case should arrange situations in which the client must maintain conversations with groups of increasing size.

2. *If possible, treatment should occur with more than one treatment agent.*

Practicing new behaviors with friends, employers, teachers, family, and others increases the probability that behavior change will generalize.

3. *The counselor can transfer the control of behavior to reinforcing events that are most likely found in the client's everyday life.* (See Chapter 8.)

Likewise, a delay in the time in which the client receives the reinforcer (e.g., money, approval, promotion, recognition) should be built into the termination phase of the program.

4. *Finally, it is possible to increase the effectiveness of a treatment program by teaching the client how to monitor and control her own behavior.*

282

Several studies have indicated that persons can monitor and control their own performances and in turn decrease problem behaviors (Bolstad and Johnson, 1972). On the other hand, a client who cannot monitor and record his behavior probably cannot control it. Thus, self-monitoring is a prerequisite condition for successfully transferring the control of the program to the client (Kanfer and Phillips, 1970). In addition, the counselor also must train the client to self-administer reinforcers. The client must learn to reward herself according to the same standards others used to reward her.

PLAN AND EXECUTE FOLLOW-UP

Once termination has been discussed, a follow-up date should be set. Follow-up allows the counselor to find out how the client is progressing and provides a time to discuss new problems if some have developed. In addition, it often helps facilitate the client's implementation of skills. Follow-up should occur two to four weeks after the termination of treatment. If follow-up data are to be collected, the behaviors during this data collection should occur under the same conditions as they did in initial treatment.

CHECKLIST FOR EVALUATING COUNSELING OUTCOMES

	Yes	No

1. *Determine if counseling objective has been met.* _____ _____
   Evaluation criteria used: Completed?
   a. Comparison of baseline data with
      intervention behavior rates   _____
   b. Multiple baseline data   _____
   c. Self-report data   _____
   d. Behavior problem checklists
      (completed by referring agent)   _____
   e. Standardized tests, scales, and/or
      inventories   _____

2. *Determine if further counseling is warranted.* _____ _____
   (Are there additional problems to deal with?)

3. *Determine if termination is warranted.* _____ _____

a. Decide when to terminate.   ____
b. Choose someone to continue dispensing reinforcers (if needed).   ____

4. *Determine if generalization of learning is likely.*
   a. Is real life situation similar to counseling
      situation?   ____ ____
   b. Was more than one treatment agent involved?   ____ ____
   c. Are reinforcers likely to be found in
      natural environment?   ____ ____
   d. Can the client monitor his behavior?   ____ ____

5. *Has follow-up date been set?*   ____ ____

PROGRAMMED EXAMPLES

Choose one or more phrases that accurately complete the statements
and follow individual instructions for other questions.

1. In deciding whether a counseling goal has been reached, the counselor must determine
   a. whether the client has met the criterion level of performance.
   b. whether the client is satisfied.
   c. the difference between the client's average performance at
       baseline and intervention.
   d. the target behavior for intervention.
   If you answered (a) and (c), you are correct. One way to determine whether an objective has been met is to set a criterion level
   (e.g., one date a week) and meet it. The other more common
   method is to show an average increase (e.g., 30 percent in positive
   social interactions) or decrease (e.g., 30 percent in negative comments towards others) in behavior from baseline to intervention.
   Answer (b) is incorrect because the client may have reached his
   goal but is not satisfied and wishes to set a new goal. Answer (d) is
   obviously inappropriate because target behaviors should already be
   identified.

2. If Mary were experiencing difficulty in introducing herself to

people at school and at parties, the counselor might measure her behavior through a multiple baseline across

a. behaviors.
b. situations.
c. people.
d. interventions.

If you answered (b), you are correct. By introducing an intervention in one situation (party) and maintaining baseline conditions in the other (school), the counselor can measure a change in her behavior. If introductions increased at the parties and remained the same at school, the counselor then could introduce the intervention at school. If introductions increased here, we could say that introductions were under the control of the intervention. There is only one behavior (a), person (c), and intervention (d), so these choices are inappropriate.

3. Given the following data and graph (Figure 52), answer these questions.

	M	T	W	Th	F	M	T	W	Th	F	M	T	W	Th	F
Bill, %	20	25	30	30	20	50	45	70	65	75	80	75	85	80	80
Mary, %	15	20	25	25	15	30	25	30	25	20	60	65	70	58	72

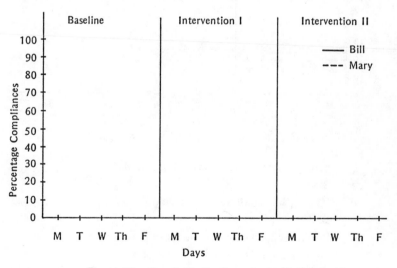

Figure 52. Graph To Be Completed (Question 3)

285

a. Label and graph the data on the axes.
b. What is being measured in this graph?

    _____ across _____

c. For whom is the intervention likely being introduced in the first intervention period?
d. For whom is the treatment likely being introduced in the second intervention?
e. Describe the change in percent compliance in social interaction from baseline to Intervention II with
    Bill _____
    Mary _____
f. In 100 words or less, describe the data presented in the graph above.

Suggested answers:

a.

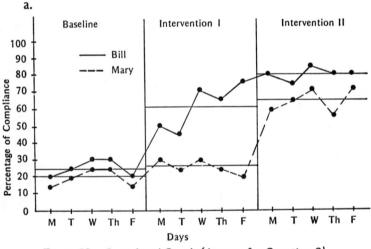

Figure 53. Completed Graph (Answer for Question 3)

b. percent of compliance *across* Bill and Mary
c. Bill
d. Mary (Bill continues to receive intervention introduced earlier.)
e. Bill: more than tripled (a factor of 3.20)
    Mary: more than tripled (a factor of 3.25)
f. The percentage of compliance was measured for three weeks

for Bill and Mary. At the start of the second week, an intervention was introduced with Bill, and his percent compliance for that week more than doubled (a factor of 2.44) the figure seen in baseline, while little change occurred for Mary. In the third week, the intervention was introduced for Mary. Her percent compliance for that week more than tripled (a factor of 3.25) that of her baseline; Bill's percent of compliance for the third week also more than tripled his baseline figure.

4. The counselor and client should terminate counseling when
   a. the original goals have been met.
   b. the client misses a counseling session.
   c. the target behaviors have been defined.
   d. the intervention has been removed.
   If you answered (a), you are correct. When the original goals have been met, the client should be terminated. If new goals keep arising, the client may be avoiding termination. Absence from one session (b), identification of target behaviors (c) or removal of intervention (d) do not warrant termination of counseling.

5. In planning transfer of learning, the counselor and client should
   a. terminate counseling.
   b. program treatment for a number of different settings and people.
   c. transfer the control of the program to the client.
   d. prepare a final report.
   If you answered (b) and (c), you are right. The counselor should ask the client to try out his new behavior in different situations with different people (b) and reward himself for his success (c). Termination of counseling (a) or preparation of the final report (d), should not occur until the counselor and client have planned for tranfer of learning.

6. Which of the following procedures are useful in evaluating counselor effectiveness?
   a. pre-post standardized tests
   b. recorded and graphed baseline and intervention behavior
   c. behavior checklists

287

d. self-report

If you answered all of the above (d), you are correct. Depending on the goals, any of the above procedures might be appropriate for evaluating change.

CRITERION TEST

Make completion choices and follow instructions for other types of questions.

1. If Jack were having problems in getting to the job on time and getting along with others on the job, the counselor might measure his behavior through a multiple baseline across:
   a. situations.
   b. interventions.
   c. behaviors.
   d. people.

2. Counseling goals have been reached when
   a. there is a sufficient difference in performance between baseline and intervention.
   b. another goal is set.
   c. the client is satisfied with his performance.
   d. the criterion level of performance has been met.

3. Given the following graphic information, answer these questions: Bill fails to comply with directions at home and school. The percentage of compliances is recorded below:

	Baseline					Intervention I					Intervention II				
	M	Г	W	Th	F	M	T	W	Th	F	M	T	W	Th	F
home:	20	10	10	15	20	40	45	50	55	50	60	50	40	50	45
school:	15	20	30	20	25	15	20	25	20	30	40	50	55	60	50

   a. Label and graph the data on the axes (Figure 54).
   b. What is being measured in the graph?
   _____ across _____
   c. Where is the treatment likely being introduced in the first intervention period?
   d. Where is the treatment likely being introduced in the second intervention?

Figure 54. Graph To Be Completed (Criterion Question 3)

    e.   Describe the change in percent compliance from Baseline to
        Intervention II in
        school _____
        home _____
    f.   In 100 words or less, describe the data presented in the graph
        above.

4. Which of the following procedures could be useful in evaluating
   counselor effectiveness?
   a.   pre-post standardized tests
   b.   recorded and graphed baseline and intervention behavior
   c.   behavior checklists
   d.   self-report

1. c
2. a and d
3. a.

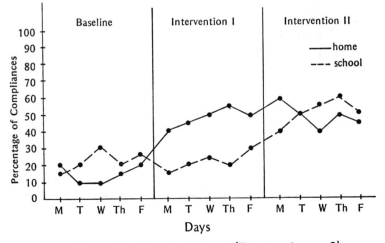

Figure 55. Completed Graph (Criterion Answer 3)

    b.   compliance *across* situations

    c.   home

    d.   school

    e.   school: more than doubled (a factor of 2.32)

          home: more than tripled (a factor of 3.27)

    f.   The percentage of compliance was measured for three weeks across school and home. At the start of the second week an intervention was introduced in the home, and the percent of compliance more than tripled (a factor of 3.20), while little change occurred at school. In the third week, the intervention was introduced at school. The percent of compliance for that week at school more than doubled (a factor of 2.32) the figure for baseline. In that third week, the percent compliance at home continued to more than triple (a factor of 3.27) the baseline figure for home.

4. a, b, c, d

References

Azrin, N. H., and Ayllon, T. Reinforcer sampling. A technique for increasing the behavior of mental patients. *Journal of Applied Behavior Analysis*, 1968, *1*, 13-20.

Bandura, A. *Principles of behavior modification*. New York: Holt, Rinehart and Winston, 1969.

Becker, W. C.; Engleman, S.; and Thomas, D. R. *Teaching: A course in applied psychology*. Chicago: Science Research Associates, 1975.

Benjamin, A. *The helping interview*. 1st ed. Boston: Houghton Mifflin, 1969.

Benjamin, A. *The helping interview*. 2nd ed. Boston: Houghton Mifflin, 1974.

Benoit, R. B., and Mayer, G. R. Extinction: Guidelines for its selection and use. *Personnel and Guidance Journal*. January, 1974, *52*, 290-295.

Bolstad, O. D., and Johnson, S. M. Self-regulation in the modification of disruptive classroom behavior. *Journal of Applied Behavior Analysis*, 1972, *5*, 443-454.

Brown, J. H. The differential effects of three monitoring procedures on achievement behavior. *Journal of Educational Research*, 1975, *8*, 318.

Carkhuff, R. F. *Helping in human relations*. New York: Holt, Rinehart and Winston, 1969.

Cassel, R. *The child behavior rating scale*. Los Angeles: Western Psychological Services, 1962.

Cautela, J. R., and Kastenbaum, R. A reinforcement survey schedule for use in therapy, training, and research. *Psychological Reports*, 1967, *20*, 1115-1130.

Coopersmith, S. *The antecedents of self-esteem.* San Francisco: W. H. Freeman and Co., 1967.

De Rath, G. W. The effects of verbal instructions on imitative aggression. *Dissertation Abstracts,* 1964, *25,* 624-625.

Edinburg, G. M.; Zinberg, N.; and Kelman, W. *Clinical interviewing and counseling.* New York: Appleton-Century-Crofts, 1975.

Egan, G. *The skilled helper: A model for systematic helping and interpersonal relating.* Monterey, CA: Brooks/Cole Publishing Co., 1975.

Ellis, A. *Reason and emotion in psychotherapy.* New York: Lyle Stuart, 1962.

Ellis, A. *Humanistic psychotherapy.* New York: Julian Press, 1973.

Eyeberg, S. M., and Johnson, S. M. Multiple assessment of behavior modification with families: Effects of contingency contracting and order of treated problems. *Journal of Consulting and Clinical Psychology,* 1974, *42,* 594-606.

Froehle, T., and Lauver, P. *Counseling techniques: Selected readings.* Bloomington: Indiana University Press, 1971.

Gagne, R. M. Curriculum research and the promotion of learning. In R. E. Stake, Ed., *AERA Curriculum Monograph Series,* No. 1. Chicago: Rand McNally, 1967.

Gelfand, D. M., and Hartmann, D. P. *Child behavior: Analysis and therapy.* Elmsford, N.Y.: Pergamon Press, 1975.

Goldfried, M. R., and Davison, G. C. *Clinical behavior therapy.* New York: Holt, Rinehart and Winston, 1976.

Goldstein, A. P. *Structured learning therapy.* New York: Academic Press, 1973.

Goldstein, A. P.; Heller, K.; and Sechrest, C. B. *Psychotherapy and the psychology of behavior change.* New York: Wiley, 1966.

Gottman, J. M., and Leiblum, S. R. *How to do psychotherapy and how to evaluate it.* New York: Holt, Rinehart and Winston, 1974.

Guthrie, C. W. Checklist for problem identification of adult clients. Southern Indiana Mental Health and Guidance Center, Jeffersonville, Indiana.

Hackney, H. Goal setting: Maximizing the reinforcing effects of progress. *The School Counselor,* January, 1973, *20,* 176-181.

Hackney, H., and Nye, S. *Counseling strategies and objectives.* Englewood Cliffs, NJ: Prentice Hall, 1973.

Hansen, J. C.; Pound, R. E.; and Warner, R. W. Use of modeling procedures. *Personnel and Guidance Journal,* January, 1976, *54*, 242-245.

Hardman, A. Behavior checklist. Southern Indiana Mental Health and Guidance Center, Jeffersonville, Indiana.

Hart, B. N.; Allen, K. E.; Buell, J. S.; Harris, F. R.; and Wolf, M. M. Effects of social reinforcement on operant crying. *Journal of Experimental Child Psychology,* 1964, *1*, 145-153.

Hendricks, C. G.; Ferguson, J. C.; and Thoresen, C. E. Toward counseling competence: The Stanford program. *Personnel and Guidance Journal,* 1973, *13*, 418-424.

Holz, W. C.; Azrin, N. H.; and Ayllon, T. Elimination of behavior of mental patients by response-produced extinction. *Journal of the Experimental Analysis of Behavior,* 1963, *6*, 407-412.

Homme, L.; Csanyi, A. P.; Gonzales, M. A.; and Rechs, J. R. *How to use contingency contracting in the classroom.* Champaign, IL: Research Press, 1970.

Hosford, R. E., and de Visser, C. A. *Behavioral counseling: An introduction.* Washington, DC: American Personnel and Guidance Press, 1974.

Institute for Advanced Study in Rational Psychotherapy. Homework Report. New York.

Ivey, A. *Micro-counseling: Innovations in interview training.* Springfield, IL: C. C. Thomas, 1971.

Ivey, A. E.; Normington, C. J.; Miller, C. D.; Morrill, W. A.; and Haase, R. F. Micro-counseling and attending behavior: An approach to pre-practicum counselor training. *Journal of Counseling Psychology,* 1968. (Monograph Suppl. 5.)

Jacobson, E. *Progressive relaxation.* Chicago: University of Chicago Press, 1938.

Kanfer, F. H., and Phillips, J. S. *Learning foundations of behavior therapy.* New York: Wiley, 1970.

Kifer, R. E.; Lewis, M. A.; Green, D. R.; and Phillips, E. C. The SOCS model: Training pre-delinquent youths and their parents in negotiation responses to conflict situations. Paper presented at the

Annual Convention of the American Psychological Association, Montreal, Quebec, Canada, August, 1973.

Kranzler, G. *You can change how you feel: A rational-emotive approach.* Eugene: University of Oregon, 1974.

Krumboltz, J. D., and Hosford, R. Behavioral counseling in the elementary school. *Elementary School Guidance and Counseling,* 1967, *1,* 27-40.

Krumboltz, J. D., and Schroeder, W. W. Promoting career planning through reinforcement of models. *Personnel and Guidance Journal,*1965, *44,* 19-26.

Krumboltz, J. D., and Thoresen, C. E. *Behavioral counseling: Cases and techniques.* New York: Holt, Rinehart and Winston, 1969.

Krumboltz, J._D.; Varenhorst, B. B.; and Thoresen, C. E. Nonverbal factors in effectiveness of models in counseling. *Journal of Counseling Psychology,* 1967, *14,* 412-418.

Lazarus, A. A. *Behavior therapy and beyond.* New York: McGraw-Hill, 1971.

Lennard, H. C., and Bernstein, A. *The anatomy of psychotherapy.* New York: Columbia University Press, 1960.

London, P. The end of ideology in behavior modification. *American Psychologist,* 1972, *27,* 913-920.

Lovitt, T. C., and Curtis, K. A. Academic response rates as a function of teacher and self-imposed contingencies. *Journal of Applied Behavior Analysis,* 1969, *2,* 913-920.

Marlett, G. A., and Perry, M. Modeling methods. In F. H. Kanfer and A. B. Goldstein, Eds., *Helping people change.* Elmsford, NY: Pergamon Press, 1975, 117-158.

Maultsby, M. C. Rational-emotive imagery. *Rational Living,* 1971, *6,* (1), 16-23.

Meichenbaum, D. H. Cognitive factors in behavior modification: Modifying what clients say to themselves. In C. M. Franks and G. T. Wilson, Eds., *Annual review of behavior therapy: Theory and practice.* New York: Brunner-Mazel, 1973.

Patterson, G. R. *Living with children.* Champaign, IL: Research Press, 1976.

Paul, G. C. Insight vs. desensitization in psychotherapy two years after termination. *Journal of Consulting Psychology*, 1967, *31*, 333-348.

Piers, E. V., and Harris, D. B. Age and other correlates of self-concept in children. *Journal of Educational Psychology*, 1964, *55*, 91-95.

Premack, P. Toward empirical behavior laws: Positive reinforcement. *Psychological Review*, 1959, *66*, 219-233.

Ryan, A. T. Model-reinforcement group counseling to modify study behavior. Paper presented at the American Personnel and Guidance Convention, Washington, DC, April, 1966.

Schmidt, J. A. Research techniques for counselors: The multiple baseline. *Personnel and Guidance Journal*, 1974, *53*, 200-206.

Shertzer, B. E., and Stone, S. C. *Fundamentals of counseling*. Boston: Houghton Mifflin, 1968.

Stuart, R. B. Operant interpersonal treatment for marital discord. *Journal of Consulting and Clinical Psychology*, 1969, *33*, 675-682.

Stuart, R. B. Behavioral contracting within the families of delinquents. *Journal of Behavior Therapy and Experimental Psychiatry*, 1971, *2*, 1-11.

Sulzer, B., and Mayer, G. R. *Behavior modification procedures for school personnel*. Hinsdale, IL: Dryden Press, 1972.

Sundel, M., and Sundel, S. S. *Behavior modification in the human services: A systematic introduction to concepts and applications.* New York: John Wiley, 1975.

Tharp, R. G., and Wetzel, R. J. *Behavior modification in the natural environment*. New York: Academic Press, 1969.

Thoresen, C. E. Behavioral humanism. Paper presented at the Colloquium sponsored by the Department of Counselor Education, Pennsylvania State University, University Park, PA. July, 1972.

Thoresen, C. E., and Hosford, R. E. Behavioral approaches to counseling. In C. E. Thoresen, Ed., *Behavior modification in education*. Seventy-second Yearbook of the National Society for Study of Education. Chicago: University of Chicago Press, 1973.

Vriend, J., and Dyer, W. W. Counseling the reluctant client. *Journal of Counseling Psychology*, 1973, *20*, 240-246.

Wahler, R. G., and Cormier, W. H. The ecological interview: A first step in out-patient child behavior therapy. *Journal of Behavior Therapy and Experimental Psychiatry*, 1970, *11*, 279-289.

Wahler, R. G., and Erikson, M. Child behavior therapy: A community program in Appalachia. *Behaviour Research and Therapy*, 1969, *7*, 71-78.

Walker, H. M. Walker problem behavior identification checklist. Los Angeles: Western Psychological Services, 1970.

Warner, R. W., and Hansen, J. C. Verbal-reinforcement and model-reinforcement group counseling with alienated students. *Journal of Counseling Psychology*, 1970, *17*, 168-172.

Warner, R. W.; Swisher, J. D.; and Horan, J. J. Drug abuse prevention: A behavioral approach. *NAASP Bulletin*, 1973, *372*, 49-54.

Winborn, B.; Hinds, W.; and Stewart, N. Instructional objectives for the professional preparation of counselors. *Counselor Education and Supervision*, 1971, *10*, 133-137.

Wolpe, J., and Lang, P. J. A fear survey schedule for use in behavior therapy. *Behaviour Research and Therapy*, 1964, 228-232.

Wolpe, J., and Lazarus, A. A. Behavior therapy techniques. Elmsford, NY: Pergamon Press, 1966.

ABOUT THE AUTHORS

Joe Brown is an Assistant Professor of Educational Psychology and Counseling at the University of Louisville. He received a Ph.D. in Counseling from Indiana University. After working in the University of Kentucky Teacher Corps, he accepted a position at Louisville where his major interests have focused on parent training, behavioral self-control, and instructional package technology for counselor and teacher trainees.

Carolyn Brown received her Ed.D. in Counseling from Indiana University. She is currently on the staff of the Southern Indiana Mental Health Center where professional duties involve conducting workshops, consulting with teachers and parents, and counseling adults and children.